Manston's

Flea Markets

Antique Fairs and Auctions

# of Germany

Including
where to find markets,
how to ship items, clear
customs, and much more.

Peter B. Manston

A Travel Key Guide
Published by Travel Keys
Sacramento, California, U.S.A.

Copyright © 1987 by Peter B. Manston

Published by Travel Keys
in association with Prima Publishing
and distributed by St. Martin's Press.

Travel Keys
P. O. Box 160691
Sacramento, California 95816 U.S.A.
Telephone (916) 452-5200

Prima Publishing
P. O. Box 1260
Rocklin, California 95677
Telephone (916) 624-5718

St. Martin's Press
175 Fifth Avenue
New York, N. Y. 10010
Telephone (212) 674-5151

Designed by Peter B. Manston
Edited and cover photo by Robert C. Bynum
Drawings and maps by Claudia R. Graham
Type Galleys by The Electric Page
Printed and bound by Arcata Graphics
Manufactured in the United States of America
First Printing January 1987

Library of Congress Cataloging in Publication Data

Manston, Peter B., 1951-
Manston's Flea Markets, Antique Fairs, and Auctions of Germany.
"A Travel Key Guide." Includes Index.
1. Flea markets—Germany (West) 2. Antiques—Germany (West)—Exhibitions. 3. Auctions—Germany (West).   I. Title. II. Title: Flea Markets, Antique Fairs, and Auctions of Germany. III. Title: Antique Shows.
HF5482.M3135 1987   381'.1   86-30908
ISBN 0-931367-08-5 (pbk.)

Contents

Acknowledgements

Many people helped provide information and support during the time while this book was written. Most of them provided help, but it isn't possible to thank them all. A few I'd like to specially thank include: Robert C. Bynum, who provided thoughtful editorial comments and strong moral support, Paula R. Mazuski for excellent help in clarifying the objective of this book, Ortrud Andelman for assistance with translations, Will Renner, and Agnes A. Manston (my mother).

Disclaimer of Responsibility

Markets move as the result of urban renewal, sometimes close during bad weather, or are rescheduled around holidays. Particularly in Germany, dates can change because the hall, plaza, or other location has already been reserved for another conflicting use. Bus lines are sometimes renumbered, parking lots turn into buildings, parking garages raise their rates, and new subways are built.

This book is as complete and accurate as possible. Facts have been exhaustively checked and rechecked. Therefore, though the information is deemed to be accurate as of press date, they may not exactly mirror your experience. Neither the author nor the publisher can be responsible if you are inconvenienced by information contained in this book.

The persons, companies, institutions, and organizations named in the book are believed to be reputable and engaged in the work they purport to be in. Any questions should be directed to them rather than the publisher or author. Inclusion or exclusion of a firm or organization is no reflection on the suitability of their service or product.

When you find differences, will you let us know? Fill out the "Will You Help?" form at the end of the book (or in a letter). What you find and suggest can make the next edition even more complete and more useful to those who follow your path.

Frankfurt am Main

Introduction

You'll find flea markets, antique fairs, and auctions just about everywhere in Germany— they burst forth in some of the most unlikely places like crocuses blooming through spring snow. Like crocuses, they are tough in spite of their apparent fragility—many have been held at the same location for decades and some for centuries, whether in large, impersonal cities or village market places surrounded by half- timbered, perfectly preserved houses giving each other mutual support.

Old porcelain pitchers, plates, and platters rest next to old books, brass doorknobs, and paintings of indefinite age, all supported by old furniture, rickety tables, permanent stands, and sometimes only by the timeworn cobblestones of the street or battered pavement of a parking lot. Sometimes a band provides background music to the babble and hubbub of hundreds of voices. The scene, full of local color, promises excitement and potential finds for the collector.

You can find anything and everything at these flea markets—sinks, scrap metal, old clothes, and cabbages. Though a lot is just plain junk, there are a few treasures lurking.

The kinds of items sold under the auctioneer's hammer are limited only by the people's imaginations and contents of their grandmother's attic.

Antique shows display long rows of exquisitely-nurtured antiques of all types and ages.

In this book, you'll find information vital to the antique dealer and collector:

- when and where to find flea markets and shows
- names, addresses, and specialties of auction houses
- basic flea market German
- how to ship your purchases home safely
- export documentation for fine arts and antiques
- how to deal with Customs

and much, much more.

This pocket-sized book provides all this information. At the back, you'll find a complete index and detailed maps to help you find what you need fast.

This book is dedicated to you, the ever-hopeful collector of exciting experience and warm memories as well as the collector of antiques, junk, and hidden treasures.

Can You
Still Make Finds?

All of us have heard about long-lost masterpieces found in a junk shop or bought for a few dollars at a flea market. We would all like to make a "great find"—a long lost Dürer, an original Jugendstil poster, a piece of original Biedermeier furniture, or a massive silver punch bowl.

These items do exist, and can occasionally be found, usually accompanied by great publicity and newspaper headlines. Finds of this type are rare.

But minor finds can more readily be made—the antique solid silver serving spoon for much less than silver plate, the finely detailed century-old religious wood carving, or a minor artist's 17th- or 18th-century painting.

The more you know about a given period or class of objects, the likelier you are to recognize and make a true find. This merely reinforces the fact that specialized knowledge has potentially great value.

Remember, you're searching for the proverbial needle in a haystack; there are thousands of German dealers and collectors in competition for the same things you are. You, however, can have the advantage of broader exposure, and you know about a radically different antique market unknown to most Europeans: the United States and Canadian market, where the selection is smaller and the prices are higher.

Since many European dealers only know about specialties of their own locality or country, you can take the broader view, surveying the products of the entire continent. Often, your best finds will be products or artwork far from their home, and, therefore, whose true value is unappreciated or unknown locally.

Trier

Why Search for Antiques in Germany?

Rich in history, opulently wealthy, with a strong tradition of quality and craftsmanship, West Germany offers some of the richest hunting grounds for the collector and flea market visitor. Markets range from piles of used overalls in the corner of a large expanse of cracked asphalt pavement surrounded by shabby warehouses to a graceful, tree-shaded, mile-long ramble along the river bank, with a double row of vendors of collectible brass, furniture, and old tools.

Antique exhibitions of great style and quality lure thousands of browsers and prospective purchasers. Some of these shows are quite exclusive: sellers can display only by invitation of the organizers. All items are certified authentic by a jury of experts. Buyers only need to pay admission to enter, but dealers—even foreign ones—are sometimes admitted free. Possession of an appropriate business card or copy of a business license is often all you need.

Flea markets are found all over Germany, and are held most often on Saturdays and Sundays. Relatively few take place during the week, though some are found on Wednesdays, weekdays before Lent, and during midsummer festivals, Oktoberfest, and the pre-Christmas season. A few old buildings are home to permanent markets, full of curio and antique dealers open five or six days a week. These permanent markets are excellent places to look for large but not easily portable items such as furniture.

Auctions usually take place during the week. Thursday and Friday seem to be popular auction days, though many are held on other weekdays and a few are held on Saturday.

Germany is organized! A number of companies put on most of the flea markets, arranging for locations, security, food concessions, publicity, and, often, parking. The rest of the markets are sponsored by cities or, in a few cases, by church or nonprofit organizations. Some markets even provide live music, ranging from rock bands to oompah bands, yodellers, and even string quartets.

Germans are very antique-conscious; millions go to the markets every weekend, rain or shine (more during shine than rain, however). In Germany, you'll rarely find fine art for a pittance—though you will often find reasonable value for your money. You'll often find small items dating from the 18th, 19th, and early 20th centuries at reasonable prices. Some century-old oil paintings are sold for only $100 to $300; others with more age, style, and better condition sell for more.

In addition to used kitchen sinks and Eurostyle faucets often seen in interior design and decoration magazines (some of the Grohe brand are chrome-plated, solid brass fixtures—adapters are available in the U.S. and Canada), German flea markets are rich in reasonably-priced porcelain, crystal and glass, and coins. Brass items—such as old door handles and window fasteners—are also common. Occasionally you'll find period clothes and old furniture. You'll also find the castoffs of a modern industrial society—used machine parts, hand tools, shop smocks, and factory overruns and seconds. Office equipment is widely found: manual typewriters, rubber stamps, signs, paper goods, and old adding machines.

Relics of the Nazi era are rare and are shown discreetly, since their public display is illegal. They are expensive and are not always genuine. To find them, look for stands where switchblades (seemingly legal and commonly sold in Germany, but illegal to import into the United States), coins, and firearms are sold.

Wood carving and folk art items are scarce, and when genuinely antique can be very expensive. Most of these types of items are found at antique shops and auctions rather than flea markets.

Silver is expensive though quality can be good. Spoons and odd pieces such as ladles and candlesticks from the 17th, 18th, and 19th centuries are common. Forks and table knives are scarce, and often are either very worn or exorbitantly priced, or both. Look for the maker's mark in combination with a city mark and the numerals 12 or 13 stating silver content as a guarantee of authenticity and silver content. (In old German measure, 16 "löthige" were pure silver; 12 löthige is 750 thousandths fine, and 13 löthige is 812.5 thousandths fine. Newer silver (since January 1888) has been hallmarked with a crown and crescent, maker's initials, and fineness of silver in thousandths (usually 800). Sterling silver, made in Britain, the United States, and Canada, is 925 thousandths fine.)

Usually only antique shops and large antique fairs (rather than outdoor flea markets) will have much furniture, probably because of the uncertainty of the weather and the difficulty of transport.

Berlin

When to Go for the Best Finds

Flea markets are held year-round in Germany, just as they are elsewhere in the world. When you go is best determined by other needs, since each season has its special charms. The types of items will not change very much, except that new clothes and fresh vegetables (in those markets that have them) will follow the seasons.

Winter has fewer markets open, somewhat fewer sellers and prospective buyers, and certainly fewer tourists. Bear in mind, however, that even in winter, you're clearly recognizable as a foreigner, often before you begin speaking. With fewer buyers, pressure to reduce prices in serious bargaining may be stronger. Weather in winter will be less pleasant, though even in northern countries there are sparkling clear, sunny, cold days.

Spring is generally more rewarding than winter; not only do people begin coming out from the cold, but more and more seasonal flea markets begin to open. Spring cleaning may not be the best known tradition in Germany, but longer, warmer, sunnier days bring out more buyers and more sellers as well. The hours of opening become earlier, as the days lengthen.

Summer is the beginning of the high season for the flea market trade, though there are far fewer major antique shows and exhibitions. Tourists swarm across the continent; while there are several million from the United States and Canada, the Germans themselves outnumber everyone else many times. Not only do Germans usually get four or five weeks paid vacations, many take vacations during the month of August. Be grateful that not all Germans are flea market visitors.

Flea markets are the most crowded during summer, and bargaining may not always yield the larger price reductions possible at other seasons of the year. On the other hand, summer is when many of the smaller, once-a-year countryside fairs and markets take place.

Fall is in many ways the most rewarding season to search the flea markets. The climate is still relatively mild, and almost every possible flea market is open. The seasonal flea markets are still operate (usually at least until the beginning of November), and most of the tourists have returned home. Fall is also when antique shows are most numerous. Also, many of the finest antique fairs are held in fall, offering museum-quality pieces at prices to match.

Learning to See What You're Looking At

Without preparation, you can find antiques, collectables, and assorted items by the thousands. You're limited only by your money, your patience, and your transportation. But discoveries of real artistic quality items will be made only from good luck, maybe aided by intuition. But for the real finds, you must know what you're looking at.

You'll be will repaid later by the effort spent now, when you are knowledgeable enough to tell a good piece from a poor or fake one later at a boisterous flea market, auction, or antique show. You'll be faced with hundreds and thousands of items, but only a few are of interest to you, and even fewer are very good value for the serious collector.

At well-known dealers and dealers' marts, such as the Antik-Center in Hamburg or the Antik-Zentrum in Frankfurt, you will often be able to obtain certificates of authenticity and provenance papers, more or less guaranteeing that you're really buying a genuine antique. Naturally such guarantees and paperwork have their (high) price.

At flea markets and junk shops, however, the motto is "let the buyer beware." The market in fakes sold to the unwary is large, and buyers' cupidity and ignorance are prime sales tools for these sellers. In Germany this is somewhat less of a problem than countries such as Spain, Portugal, and Italy.

The time to start learning about antiques and collectables is right now. Read everything you can—style guides, price guides, antique-trade and fine arts magazines, museum catalogues, and applied arts and fine arts history. Catalogues from Christie's and Sotheby's auctions are treasure-troves of knowledge, with illustrations of sale items, descriptions of the creator, the item, and characteristics of the style, and estimated sales prices. These catalogues are sometimes available at libraries, at museums, and, of course, are sold through the respective auction houses.

Study the text and illustrations carefully—what you remember will make it much easier to sort through the thousands of worthless pieces for the few excellent items at the market, show, or fair.

Your local library is an excellent place to begin your search. Search through "Books In Print" to supplement your search of library shelves. Small and medium-sized libraries can often obtain books through the "interlibrary loan" system. For details and to make a request, see the reference librarian.

Many college and university libraries have more extensive and specialized collections, particularly in the area of art and antiques. Usually the public is admitted to "open-stack" libraries and can use the books in the library at no charge. Often you can become a "friend of the library" at modest cost to obtain borrowing privileges.

Museums are another place to learn. In major museums you will be able to see actual examples of authentic works. Study the lines, the artistic qualities, and materials carefully. When you have a bit of knowledge but want more, seek out the curators in the museum.

Sometimes museums also have excellent art libraries, but rarely can their library materials be checked out.

Antique dealers in your area represent a valuable source of knowledge. How do you find a dealer knowledgeable in a particular field? Many dealers have specialties: the most knowledgeable, specialized and expensive dealers are often clustered in cities such as New York, Boston, Chicago, San Francisco, Los Angeles, and Toronto. In short, dealers congregate where there are large numbers of people with a taste for European antiques and arts, and who have money to indulge their taste. For obvious reasons, dealers won't usually share their sources of supply.

When buying, you're likely to find more interesting and beautiful items if you know what you're buying.

Let your sense of beauty and value for money guide you: learn to trust your instincts, based on a firm foundation of knowledge.

Origins of
the Flea Market

During the Middle Ages, German cities began to grow and flourish, stimulated by trade in linens and woolens, furs from Russia, herring from the Baltic, and spices from the Orient. With the passage of centuries, cities won their freedom from the rule of the Holy Roman Emperor. Special markets and fairs became more numerous.

Great markets and fairs were held in the centers that developed at trade route crossroads, such as Frankfurt, Hamburg, Munich, and Nuremberg. From these, the idea of regular scheduled markets specializing in certain products arose. In a world of slow and uncertain transport (ships pushed by sails, loaded carts drawn by animals, or packs carried by human porters), fairs offered an efficient way to exchange goods, meet new people, and hear news of and see exotic products from far-off places. Today's exquisite annual antique fairs and weekend flea markets are direct descendants of these fairs.

Though trade increased, material goods were still scarce, and used longer than they are today. Municipal garbage collection service did not exist: instead, some items were sold to roving junk dealers. The rest was thrown in the street, where rag pickers and junk men sorted through the discarded and broken goods and salvaged whatever had any value for reuse or resale. The items were sold in the neighborhoods where the rag pickers lived, or by wandering vendors, carrying their stock in trade either over their shoulders or on carts. The rest was either left in the streets or eventually carted outside the city walls.

In large third-world cities such as Calcutta and Cairo, Manila, and Mexico City, trash is still disposed of in a similar way, rather than through a municipal collection and landfill or incineration.

Types of Markets

There are a number of different kinds of German markets, each with a different name and with a different meaning and implication for the goods offered. Each name usually indicates what kinds of goods are sold. However, markets selling used and old items overlap to some degree, particularly between the Flohmarkt and Trödelmarkt. The kinds of markets include:

- Antikmarkt (antique market). The rules of the market often specify that all items must be true antiques (or at least original), and that reproductions or new items are not permitted. Sellers are sometimes restricted to bona fide dealers, which in reality means persons with business licenses and resale permits.
- Antiquitätentag, Antiktage (antique day or days). More or less equivalent to an antique fair, but with the overtone of a celebration and festival in addition to a market.
- Flohmarkt (flea market). These are classic flea markets offering used and some new items. There are usually no restrictions on the sellers, who merely have to reserve and pay for the space rental.
- Handwerkermarkt (artisans' market). This type of market is the same as the Handwerkmarkt (see below).
- Handwerkmarkt (handicraft market). These markets are expositions and sales of folk arts and crafts. Generally sellers must have made the products offered.

- Kunstmarkt (art market). These markets are fine arts markets: painting, sculpture, collage, and drawing. Many but not all of these markets have exclusively contemporary work, and the artists are in attendance with their work.
- Kunstwerkermarkt (artists and artisans' market). This is similar to a Handwerkmarkt, except that fine arts such as painting and sculpture will be more heavily represented.
- Militariamarkt (military item market). This market is limited to military items, ranging from old uniforms and medals to books and bayonets.
- Münzbörse (coin exchange). These specialized markets are held strictly for coins, medals, and other numismatic items. Coin catalogues and specialists' books will also often be offered for sale.
- Musikbörse (music exchange). These markets are restricted to sales and trades of musical instruments, sheet music, and, sometimes, recordings and stereo equipment. There are usually no restrictions on sellers beyond the requirement that items offered be musical or related to music.
- Puppenmarkt (doll and puppet market). These markets only sell dolls and puppets, which can be of any age or size.
- Schallplattenbörse (record exchange). This is a specialized gathering of phonograph records. Records of all ages are included, and often of all types of music.
- Spielzeugmarkt (toy market). The toy markets restrict sales only to toys, mostly old toys. These markets are often the province of serious, specialized collectors. Sellers can be dealers or collectors.
- Trödelmarkt (junk or secondhand market). These markets are virtually identical to flea markets, offering used and sometimes new items. The difference from a flea market is one of emphasis, in that secondhand items predominate, while flea markets offer many new items as well. Sellers can be anyone wishing to sell. Usually all that is required of a seller is payment of space rent.

The origin of the name "Trödelmarkt" (trödel =used clothes) is from the secondhand clothes dealers who pushed carts through city streets, buying and selling all the while. They congregated once or twice a week at a fixed location so that potential buyers could find them.

The end syllables (actually a complete German word) appended to the name of a market type also provide clues to the type of gathering it is. This can affect the expectation of potential visitors. The main endings are:

- —ausstellung (exhibition). The main purpose is to show items: in some exhibitions, the items are for sale as well.
- —börse (exchange). An exchange clearly implies the buying and selling of specialized items. Trading items between collectors is also fostered.
- —markt (market). A gathering where the main purpose is to sell.
- —messe (fair). A large gathering—usually only the largest events carry this title. Hundreds of vendors and thousands of browsers and collectors crowd huge convention centers. The implication of a fair is that the quality of items will be high.
- —tag(e) (day or days). A celebration of the type of goods being sold. The implication is that this is a large event.
- —treff (meeting). A small, rather informal gathering, usually for collectors of a specific specialty. The implication includes that there will be information sharing as well as buying and selling.

While you'll find almost every market in one of these categories, you may on occasion find unique markets that use other names.

Auctions

A lot of the better quality art and antiques moves through auctions rather than flea markets and antique fairs. Items to be auctioned can be usually be inspected the day before the sale and on the sale day. Often, catalogues are available by mail or at the auction house several weeks or a month prior to the auction.

Many auctions on weekdays begin at 6 p.m. or even 7 p.m. On Saturday, many auctions begin at 10 a.m. However, the starting times are variable: confirm them with the management.

Bidding procedures vary greatly: at some auctions you need merely wave your hand or catch the auctioneer's eye, and pay on the spot or before you leave, while at other auctions you must complete a formal registration to receive a bidder's paddle or number.

Mail and telephone bids may be made by arrangement with the auction house. Contact the auction house well advance for further information. The main advantage is that you need not be at the auction in person. Another is that you'll have longer to pay the bill. Most auction houses will give 10 days from the date of receipt of an invoice for payment, and won't charge for storage until two weeks after the sale.

In addition to the sales price (hammer price), a commission of between 15% and 20% will be charged. This includes Value Added Tax (Mehrwertsteur) on the auctioneer's commission (but not on the value of the purchase).

Many auctions take place away from the offices of the auction houses, and some are halfway across Germany. Some even take place in hotels and convention centers! Check exact auction locations and dates in advance.

Some of the more active auction houses are listed here; almost all have at least one auction per month. A few are seasonal and others have weekly auctions. For dates, contact auctioneers directly, check specialized German antique magazines, or the arts sections of major established newspapers, such as the "Frankfurter Allgemeine Zeitung."

Münz-Zentrum Albrecht & Hoffmann, Rubensstrasse 42, 5000 Köln, telephone (0221) 23 08 48. (Coins, medals, precious metals.)

Gebruder Berlingshof, Auktionshaus, Zwingerstrasse 18, 6900 Heidelberg, telephone (06221) 2 16 91. (Antiques in general.)

Auktionsbüro Peter Boeger, Obere Graben 13, 8900 Augsburg, telephone (0821) 51 51 60.

Bolland & Marotz, Fedelhören 19, 2800 Bremen 1, telephone (0421) 32 82 82. (Antiques in general.)

Auktionshaus Waltraud Boltz, Bahnstrasse 25, 8580 Beyreuth, telephone (0921) 2 06 16. (Antiques, religious objects, books, dolls, toys, posters, miscellaneous.)

W. Brandes oHG, Kleine Campestrasse 2, 3300 Braunschweig 1, telephone (0531) 7 50 03.

Burkhardt & Lindner, Südphila Briefmarken oHG, Tübingerstrasse 5, 7000 Stuttgart 1, telephone (0711) 2430 64. (Stamps.)

Reiner Dannenberg, Wiesbadenstrasse 82, 1000 Berlin, telephone (030) 8 21 69 79. (Miscellaneous.)

Auktionshaus F. Dörling, Neuer Wall 40, 2000 Hamburg 36, telephone (040 36 46 70. (Russian and Eastern art.)

Ebner & Duda, Karlstrasse 5, 7800 Freiburg, telephone (0761) 2 44 55. (Antiques, art, paper money, coins.)

Hermann Doepper, Kunsthandel und Auktionen, Holunderweg 2, 5064 Rösrath-Hoffnungsthal, telephone (02205) 8 20 44. (Fine arts.)

Eid-Sengle-Kraus, Auktionen, Bergheimerstrasse 101a, 6900 Heidelberg, telephone (06221) 2 27 84. (Antiques.)

Jürgen Fischel Kunstauktionshaus, Trappen-seeschlösschen, 7100 Heilbronn, telephone (07131) 7 30 64. (Glassware, crystal, beer steins, ceramics.)

Gartenich Stadtverwaltung Köln, Verkerhrsamt, Unter Fettenbrennen 19, 5000 Köln, telephone (0221) 2 21 33 43. (Postage stamps, paper money.)

Dieter Gorny, Giessener Münzhandlung GmbH, Maximiliansplatz 16, 8000 München 2, telephone (089) 22 68 76. (Coins, antique coins, medals.)

Henry's Auktionshaus GmbH, An Der Fohlen-weide 30, 6704 Mutterstadt, telephone (06234) 8 01 10. (Carpets, furniture, art, jewelry, miscel-laneous. This is an especially active auctioneer.)

Herbst-Reisen und Auktionshaus GmbH, Amsel-hang 2, 5353 Mechernich, Kommern-Süd, telephone (02443) 67 67. (Historical papers, drawings, postage stamps.)

Hermann Historica oHG, Maximilianstrasse 32, 8000 München 1, telephone (089) 29 63 91. (Military items.)

Reinhold Hess, Domäne, 6431 Neuenstein 1, telephone (06677) 4 72. (Furniture, miscel-laneous.)

Dr. Heuser & Grethe, Holzdamm 16, 2000 Ham-burg 1, telephone (040) 24 51 26. (Household ar-ticles, antiques, collectables.)

Karl & Faber, Amiraplatz 3, 8000 München 2, telephone (089) 22 18 65. (Drawings, art, anti-ques.)

Auktionshaus Karrenbauer, Obere Lauber 46, 7750 Konstanz 2, telephone (07531) 2 72 02. (Books.)

Michael Kegelman, Saalgasse 3, 6000 Frankfurt 1, telephone (069) 28 84 61. (Clocks and watches.)

Auktionshaus/Gallerie W. Ketterer, Briennerstrasse 25, 8000 München 2, telephone (089) 59 11 81. (Literature, historical papers, books.)

Auktionshaus Klefisch, Hardefustrasse 9, 5000 Köln 1, telephone (0221) 32 17 40. (Japanese, oriental art.)

Peter Klöter, Schloss Dätzingen, 7031 Grafenau 2, telephone (07033) 4 3484. (Clocks and watches.)

Dr. Krott & Schmeltzer, Pontstrasse 21, 5100 Aachen, telephone (0241) 3 69 00 (Clocks and watches, jewelry.)

Auktionshaus Alfred Krieg, Brahmsstrasse 14, 7100 Heilbronn, telephone (07131) 70 21. (Toys and games, miniature autos.)

Auktionshaus Gottfried Haas, Eglosheimerstrasse 132, 7144 Asperg, telephone (07141) 3 20 64. (Historical papers.)

Kunsthaus Carole von Ham, Drususgasse 1-5, 5000 Köln 1, Telephone (0221) 23 81 37. (Old and contemporary fine arts.)

Antiquariat Peter Kiefer GmbH, Ebersteinstrasse 14, 7530 Pforzheim, telephone (07231) 1 72 72. (Graphics, books.)

Künstlerhaus D. M. Klinger, Mülgasse 1, 8500 Nürnburg, telephone (0911) 22 76 08, telephone (089) 59 22 82. (Erotic art.)

Auktionshaus Krauth, Duisburgerstrasse 19, 4000 Düsseldorf 30, telephone (0211) 49 29 68. (Asian art.)

Helmut Labahn, Ziethenstrasse 5a, 2000 Hamburg 70, telephone (040) 6 56 28 92. (Historical postcards.)

Lankes Kunstauktionen, Klosterstrasse 22, 8670 Hof, telephone (09281) 1 82 00. (Fine arts, furniture, miscellaneous.)

Auktionshaus R. Mars, Ludwigstrasse 4, 8700 Würzburg, telephone (0931) 5 56 58. (Fine arts.)

Meerbuscher Kunstauktionshaus, H. Rosthal, Kanzlei 3, 4005 Meerbusch 1, telephone (07181) 7 65 66. (Antique furniture, fine art.)

Auktionator Karlheinz Müller, Barfüsserstrasse 4, 6250 Limburg, telephone (06431) 2 52 05. (Miscellaneous items.)

Franz Meixner, Floriansmühle 1d, 8000 München 45, telephone (089) 1 57 50 54. (Post cards.)

Auktionshaus Nusser, Nordendstrasse 42, 8000 München 40, telephone (089) 2 72 21 50. (An- tiques in general.)

Auktionshaus Peretz, Dudweilerstrasse 9, 6600 Saarbrücken 3, telephone (0681) 3 56 97. (Coins, medals.)

Auktionscontor F. Peege, Dreikönigstrasse 43, 7800 Freiburg, telephone (0761) 7 55 56. (Anti- ques, folk art.)

Auktionshaus Prinz-Dunst, Schlüterstrasse 16, 1000 Berlin, telephone (030) 3 13 59 65. (Miscel- laneous antiques and collectables.)

Theodor Prucha, Rankstrasse 3, 1000 Berlin, telephone (030) 8 81 47 21. (Jewelry, coins.)

Auktionshaus G. Ramel, Karolinenstrasse 1, 8600 Bamberg, telephone (0951) 5 55 29. (Anti- ques.)

Reimann & Monatsberger GmbH, Schlossstrasse 51, 7000 Stuttgart 1, telephone (0711) 29 4906 (Art Nouveau, Jugendstil, furniture, miscel- laneous.)

Reis & Auvermann, Zum Talblick 2, 6246 Glashütten, telephone (0647) 69 47. (Books, graphics, manuscripts, literary papers.)

Auktionshaus Rolf Richter, Brückstrasse 35, 6940 Weinheim, telephone (06201) 6 86 89. (Military items, war toys.)

Versteigerungshaus Rössler, Rothenburger-strasse 50, 8500 Nürnberg, telephone (0911) 26 88 39. (Old and antique toys.)

Auktionshaus Hugo Ruef, Gabelsbergerstrasse 28, 8000 München 2, telephone (089) 52 40 84. (Fine arts.)

Schaub & Brablec, Lüttenstrasse 5, 4000 Düssel-dorf, telephone (0211) 37 87 72. (Postage stamps.)

Kunstauktionshaus Schloss Ahlden GmbH, Schloss Ahlden, 3031 Ahlden, telephone (05164) 5 75. (Antiques, paintings.)

Auktionshaus W. Schorer, Gustav-Philipp-Strasse 26, 8858 Neuberg, telephone (08431) 72 86. (Fine arts, miscellaneous.)

Klaus Seidel, Mittelweg 3, 7632 Freisenheim, (078) 6 72 90. (Antiques. Auctions are held in Berlin.)

Auktionshaus H. Stahl, Hohe Bleichen 28, 2000 Hamburg 36, telephone (040) 34 23 25. (An-tiques.)

Auktionshaus Leo Spik, Kurfürstendamm 66, 1000 Berlin 15, telephone (030) 8 83 61 70. (Fine arts.)

Auktionshaus Steinbüchel, Sternstrasse 14, 4000 Düsseldorf, telephone (0211) 44 34 22. (General antiques.)

Auktionshaus Dr. H. Tenner KG, Sofienstrasse 5, 6900 Heidelberg, telephone (06221) 2 42 37. (Books, graphics.)

Auktionator Réné Thevis, Fischbachstrasse 86a, 5190 Stolberg-Vicht, telephone (02402) 7 35 86. (Books and graphics.)

Auktionshaus Weinel, 4047 Dormagen-Zons, telephone (02106) 4 66 91. (Antiques in general.)

Antiquitäten- und Auktionshaus J. Weiner, Rosipalhaus/Reichenbachplatz, 8000 München, telephone (089) 26 03 03 (Antiques in general.)

Auktionshaus Arno Winterburg, Blumenstrasse 15, 6900 Heidelberg 1, telephone (06221) 2 26 31. (Painting, graphics, watercolors, old prints, engravings. This auctioneer is also an art and antique dealer.)

Auktionshaus M. Zeller, Bendergasse 7, 8990 Lindau, telephone (08362) 40 27. (Fine art.)

Auktionshaus Deitrich von Zengen, Friedrich-Breuer-Strasse 105, 5300 Bonn-Beuel, telephone (0228) 46 19 55. (Art and antiques, occasionally abandoned and unclaimed items.)

Auktionshaus Friedrich Ziska und Kister, Unterer Anger 15, 8000 München 2, telephone (089) 25 38 55. (Books, graphics, paintings.)

Auktionen Zemanek-Münster, Allesgrundweg 22, 8708 Gerbrunn, telephone (0931) 70 94 00. (Antiques in general.)

Hannover

Who Are the Sellers?

You always hope to find friendly, helpful vendors
who don't know the value of what they're selling,
and therefore sell it to you for a song. While such
sellers do exist, they are only slightly more common than hens' teeth. Do not expect to find them
very often.

Sellers may vary widely in knowledge of
their chosen field. Most use reference books
and price guides to help them keep their
pricing current with the German market. The
day of the untutored and ignorant seller of
antiques has passed almost completely.

Most sellers at flea markets and antique
fairs are full-time dealers, who may close their
shops or leave an assistant to mind the main
store. Depending on the nature of the market,
they either take their best or worst—whatever
they think will sell.

Some dealers have no fixed place of business,
except their vans and trucks, and maybe a dusty
barn at their home in the country or part of an
old warehouse. They are "pickers"—that is,
picking up the best around the country, and
serving as the city dealers' source of supply. If
you can find them, they can also be a cheaper
source of supply for you as well. These
traveling dealers have the time and patience to
seek out house sales, country auctions, and
fund-raising sales of charity groups. They often
cultivate a grapevine to lead to tips and
sources of supply. Because they have no fixed

place of business, they often thrive on large turnover and take low markups.

Some vendors are junk dealers pure and simple, driving around in trucks reading (translated) "Ich Kaufe Alle (I buy everything)." They clean out basements and attics, old barns, warehouses, and garages. Some even go on early morning safaris looking for salvageable items in the trash! Even so, they may ask the same amount that the price guides suggest and consider their time as their investment.

Part-time vendors are usually found in strength only at weekend flea markets (especially on Sunday) where permanent stands aren't available. During the week, they are members of other trades and professions. While many do not have the choicest items, they may be more willing to negotiate and they are often more happy to share experiences. Many of their items may only be of garage-sale or rummage-sale quality.

Bargaining

Prices at flea markets and antique fairs are rarely fixed—you can usually obtain reductions of 10 to 50 per cent of the first asking price if you try. These reductions are often possible in the most elegant of fairs and exhibitions. Knowing the economics of the market helps.

As a rule of thumb, most dealers try to double the prices of everything they sell. They feel entitled to this for their time, trouble, skill, and luck.

The first price almost always include a "fudge factor," since most sellers (and most buyers) expect to haggle and reduce the initial price. In fact, if you fail to bargain, some vendors may be puzzled and deprived of the conversational ritual to set the final price. The conversations as well as the money constitute much of the income many part time vendors expect and enjoy.

Here are a number of tactics to try to bring the price down:

1. The seller will always make a profit: his or her initial cost is also the base price. Some sellers keep markups low to increase turnover: this will make initial prices seem more reasonable, but there maybe less price flexibility.

If the dealer just obtained the item, the price may be reduced to provide a quick profit to raise cash. The dealer may know of another more desirable object he or she may need some added money to buy. On the other hand, if the item has been a longtime dust collector, and you're the first person even casually interested, the price may be less.

2. Have enough cash to buy what you want. At flea markets, all payments are expected to be cash—in Deutsche Marks. You'll be amazed at some of the sums of cash discreetly changing hands. No checks, no credit cards, no foreign money such as dollars.

3. The price is usually on an "as is—where is" basis. If there's an imperfection, use it as a way to try to reduce the price.

4. Bargain even if you know an item is an incredibly good buy. You can still always pay the initial asking price later. Failure to bargain may make the vendor believe that either you're foolish or that the item is very valuable (and may be withdrawn from sale).

5. Treat sellers as *people* first—this will solve many of your price problems. Politeness, courtesy, and consideration will almost always make a difference.

6. Have at least a basic knowledge of German. The ability to communicate is invaluable at the market.

7. When you first see an item you want, set a price on it in your mind even before you pick it up to examine it. Don't pay more if you can help it. The "get it now" mentality used by auctioneers and high-pressure salespeople can lead you to spend far more than you planned. Conversely, there are sometimes a few items you must have, or you'll regret it forever.

8. If you find an item you know is unique, don't wait and plan to come back later. You probably won't, or it will be sold when you do come back. You may never see a similar item again, and be reminded of it every time you see the empty space on your mantel at home.

9. Don't make a beeline for the only item you want. Showing too much interest right away

may lead to a higher final price. Better to pick up five or six items of lesser interest and look at them as well as the items you want.

One maneuver that sometimes works well is to ask the price of a group of unrelated items, then ask the price of smaller groups, single items, and eventually ask the price of the item you really want.

Often, using this approach, the price of the item you want is less than its proportional share of the whole group—and a bargain besides.

Not a Tactic

Some dealers are contrary and won't reduce the price at all. It may be only with a particular item, only with foreigners, or the color of your eyes. This is rare: firm prices are almost unknown at flea markets, and uncommon in fixed antique markets, even in the very expensive Antik-Zentrum in Frankfurt.

Language

Though German at first sounds unintelligible, its structure is similar to English. The ability to speak German is very helpful, but not essential to successful purchases.

English is spoken relatively widely, but not by everyone. You're likeliest to find that people under the age of 25 speak English, since it is studied almost universally in school. People of non-German origin, such as Turks and Greeks, usually speak only their native tongue and German.

You should, however, make an effort to learn at least a few words of German. At auctions, you at least need to know numbers to keep track of bidding and the lots offered.

By making the effort to communicate in German, you'll engage the seller's sympathy, since they know you've made an effort.

Naturally, the more you can speak the more you can ask questions about any object that's interesting to you, point out defects, and haggle more forcefully about the price.

If you're a good listener, you may be able to learn about the item, its history and probable origin, and other interesting facts and opinions.

The following language key sould give you the basic phrases you need to successfully find the markets and buy there.

Language Key:

Good morning . . afternoon	Guten Tag . . . Tag
Please	Bitte
Thank you.	Danke schön.

Where is the flea market?	Wo ist der Flohmarkt?
. . . junk market?	. . . Trödelmarkt?
. . . antique market?	. . . Antiquitätenmarkt?
. . . crafts market?	. . . Handwerkmarkt?

Over there.	Da drüben.
Straight ahead.	Geradeaus.
Right. Left.	Rechts. Links.
Around the corner.	Um die Ecke.

Can you show me on the map?	Können Sie mir auf dem Stadtplan zeigen?

At the market	Auf dem Markt
How much does this cost?	Wieviel kostet es?
That is too much!	Das ist zu viel!

What is it?	Was ist es?
How old is it?	Wie alt ist es?
How is it used?	Wie benützt Mann es?
Does it work?	Wie funktioniert es?
It's broken. Look here!	Es gebrochen. Sehen Sie her!
What is it made out of?	Aus welchem Material ist es gemacht?

Will you reduce the price?	Werden Sie die Preise herabsetzen?
What is your lowest price?	Was ist Ihr niedrigste Preis?
Can you take _____ marks?	Können Sie _____ Deutsche Mark nehmen?
I don't have enough money	Ich habe nicht genug Geld.
Can I pay with dollars?	Kann ich mit Dollar bezahlen?

I would like a receipt . . .	Ich möchte eine Rechnung haben. . .
. . . for our Customs.	. . . für unsere Zoll.

Where are the toilets?	Wo sind die Toiletten?
I cannot speak German.	Ich spreche kein Deutsch.
Can you speak English?	Können Sie Englisch?
	0　Null
	1　Eins

2	Zwei
3	Drei
4	Vier
5	Fünf
6	Sechs
7	Sieben
8	Acht
9	Neun
10	Zehn
11	Elf
12	Zwolf
13	Dreizehn
14	Vierzehn
15	Fünfzehn
20	Zwanzig
30	Dreisig
40	Vierzig
50	Fünfzig
60	Sechszig
100	Ein Hundert
200	Zwei Hundert
1,000	Ein Tausend

Goodbye.	Auf Wiedersehen.

München-AuerDult

Transportation in Germany

Germany is justly renowned for an excellent public transportation system. Germany has almost legendary intercity trains: fast, on-time, and frequent (many stations' clocks even include second hands!) Cities compact by American and Canadian standards are well served by public transportation.

Where information about access via convenient public transit is available, it's included in the description of each flea market.

Public transit as the basis for a flea market tour has serious drawbacks, however. Not all markets are conveniently reached using public transit. Many are in suburbs or obscure country villages beyond the reach of subways, frequent train, or bus service.

Most markets start early; they're are at their best early Saturday and Sunday morning, soon after dawn. Busses and subways will probably be running on a weekend schedule—which means long waits or even no service. As the market opens, dealers and regulars pick over and buy the best of this week's harvest of antiques, while you still stand in the station waiting for a train or bus to come along. Or, you can easily spend two or three hours getting to a suburban market only 10 miles away: when you finally arrive, you may find the market has been cancelled, or is packing up.

When using public transit, you have to carry your purchases with you or send them along. There's a limit to how much luggage you can carry, and porters or baggage carts are often scarce. Sending your treasures to a central European point for a single shipment or shipping small parcels home every day or two can be an exercise in frustration, and cost a fortune in postal and express shipping charges.

In large cities (such as Köln and Hamburg), there are often half a dozen markets to cover on a single day. Each market has its own character and unique offerings. The markets are an hour or more from each other by public transit—but 20 minutes by car or van.

Public transit is often the fastest way to get around large cities on weekdays. During the week, a car or van in a city can be a hindrance. During the week, city driving is an exercise in fighting through the thick molasses of traffic. Cars are often best left in a parking place.

Car or Van—The Advantages

A vehicle is almost a necessity for serious flea collector or dealer.

Take a hint from the sellers: they don't usually arrive on public transit. They drive.

Drive Everywhere

Small towns and villages in the countryside or city suburbs often hold flea markets and antique fairs. Public transport is either unavailable or very inconvenient.

If you limit yourself to major cities, you eliminate at least a quarter of items for sale. You also deprive yourself of some of the most picturesque market settings, and friendly (and often lower-priced) provincial sellers. You'll may also miss country style furniture, folk art, and new but traditional artifacts.

Your Vehicle as Depository

Carrying purchases around a flea market can be exhausting—especially if you have bought heavy crystal, small bronze statues, or delicate porcelain. If you have a car, you can slip back to it to unload your purchases, reducing fatigue and worry.

If several of you travel together, you can search the market independently and find the car a convenient meeting place. Each separate marketer should have a car key. (Keys are made at a Schlüsserei.)

Probably Save Money

Renting a small car or a basic van (not a fully equipped camper!) can save you substantial, but also significant amounts of money, even after you consider the 15% Value Added Tax (Mehrwertsteur) and the high price of gasoline.

The price of renting or leasing a very small car in Germany is little more than the price of a Eurailpass or West German Railways Touristenkarte or Bundesnetzkarte discount tickets for the same period of time. It is rarely more than one and a half times the price of a Eurailpass. Therefore, with two or more people, it is cheaper to rent a car than to take the train.

City center hotels cost more than those in the outskirts and in the countryside. With a car, you'll have a wider selection of hotels to choose from. You'll also be able to stay in country inns unserved by any public transportation at all.

Parking: A Potential Problem

One drawback of driving is parking. European cities were not designed for motor vehicles, or for parking. If you arrive at the market early, you'll probably get a parking place within a few blocks of the market's center—impossible later in the day. Street parking places may be free, especially on Sunday. Watch, however, for no-parking signs. Sometimes the police will tow illegally parked cars away Tow-away zones are usually signed, with a picture of a car being towed. To redeem a towed car may cost several hundred Deutsche Marks..

You may find signs directing you to pay car parks, where for a dollar or two you'll have a legal parking place.

German pay· parking garages almost all operate on the same system. Take a ticket as you enter, and keep it with you. After you're done with your marketing, before you return to your car, go to the cashiers (Kassa), usually near the main pedestrian entrance to the garage. Pay there, and then you usually have 10 minutes to return to the car and get past the exit gates. The Kassa is rarely near the auto exit, and an unpaid (and unvalidated) ticket won't open the exit gate.

Carrying Your Finds at Market

Sellers' Packing Materials

Few sellers have adequate, secure, convenient packing materials. Most will hand you the item, possibly wrapped in an old newspaper or a flimsy shopping bag. These bags, though better than nothing or a newspaper, are lightweight, and stretch and tear if filled with heavy or sharp-pointed objects. Bring your own bag.

One exception to the general rule of "carry and ship it yourself" is when you buy a large quantity of merchandise from one seller. Often the seller can crate it and arrange for its shipment. In that case, you can generally rely on the seller's packing materials and procedures. Try to watch the crating or container-packing operations. It be interesting, and you'll also ensure that the correct items are packed. Buy adequate insurance for the shipment.

Selecting a Market Bag

There are a large variety of carry bags available. Take a day pack or gym bag. Nylon bags are best: they are strong, light, fold into small places, and shield the contents from the prying eyes of potential thieves. Shoulder straps leave your hands free to inspect items. In general, bags of this type are cheaper and more strongly constructed when bought in the United States and Canada.

Carefully check a bag before you buy it. Look for durability and convenience, not style. A good bag has these qualities:

1. The material is strong. Rip-stop nylon is the most durable lightweight fabric. Canvas is heavier (in weight, not strength) and can rot if left in the damp for extended periods.

2. The stitching is strong and seams are secure.

3. The zippers are strong and substantial, and open and close easily.

4. All metal parts are thick and strong: solid brass is best.

If you plan on extensive purchases of small items, take an extra bag with you.

Luggage Carriers

Tourists at very large markets sometimes bring wheeled luggage carriers. They have a number of limitations that make them less useful there than at airports and train stations. Many flea markets have a lot of barriers to the small wheels of these devices. Flea markets are often held on dirt, gravel, or uneven cobblestone surfaces. Curbs may interfere with smooth rolling. Many indoor flea markets have stairs, which further reduce the utility of these carriers.

Flea markets and antique fairs by their very nature are very crowded, full of jostling people intent on their business. They don't expect to find luggage carriers in their way, and may trip over them.

If you do use a luggage carrier or dolly, be sure it is strong and will take a lot of punishing use without breaking. And be sure that boxes or suitcases can be securely fastened to the carrier.

München

Amenities at the Flea Market

Food at the Fair

Most flea markets have food and drink for sale at concession stands. Such convenience food, not noted for offering quality or good value, can range from cans of soda pop to walk-up stands selling small pizzas, shishkabob, bratwurst and other sausages on a roll, and fried potatoes.

Snack food sold at flea markets is usually as safe as any food elsewhere in Germany. Use the same precautions you would use anywhere.

If the market is also a general market with vegetable vendors as well as a antiques and junk, you may find lower prices, better variety and more quality for your money.

Toilets

There are toilets at most flea markets or close by. These may be the most primitive, smelly, and ill-maintained in Germany. There may not be any toilet paper—or it may have been scattered all over the floor. Some of the worst ones have an attendant to collect money, usually 30, 40 or even 50 pfennigs per use.

Often facilities for women are unequal to the demand—plan to wait.

In a number of markets held in open spaces or fields, toilets may be placed in portable trailers. Look for the trailers looming up above the stands. They are often but not always marked.

In major weekend flea markets with permanent, open-air locations, public toilets may be totally absent. In this case, there may be bars or restaurants where you can find relief. You needn't be a patron—unless you see a sign in the local language that translates to "restrooms for patrons only."

If there are toilets in the area, look for these signs: Toiletten, W.C., 00, Herren (Men), Damen (Women).

Export Laws and Regulations

"Protection of Cultural Assets of National Importance"

The law regulating the export of arts and the cultural assets of national importance is the "Law for Protection of German Cultural Property Against Exportation," which was filed in the Bundesanzeiger (Federal Register) on August 6, 1955, Part 1, Page 501.

This law covers items so important that their export would be considered a serious loss to the German cultural heritage.

Each German state (Land) must keep a register of listed items; the federal government Interior Ministry (Bundesministerium des Innern) in Bonn keeps a compilation of all state lists in the "(Verzeichnis national wertvollen Kulturgutes (Inventory of Cultural Assets of National Importance)." Export of listed items without a permit is prohibited.

Strict penalties exist for the attempted export of a registered item without a permit: 300,000 Deutsche Marks (over $150,000) fine, imprisonment, and confiscation of the item. An owner of a registered item wishing to export it may apply for an export permit. The government may grant or deny the permit. If the permit is denied, the owner may decide to keep the work in Germany, or sell it to the government at a price determined by arbitration, or sell the item privately in Germany.

Generally, works and items found in flea markets, shows, and antique shops are not on the list of registered items, and there is no prohibition or restriction of the export of unlisted items.

For further information, contact:

Bundesministerium des Innern
Referat V + K II 1
Dietkirchenstrasse 30
Postfach 170290
5300 Bonn 1
Telephone (0228) 69 40 21 through 69 40 26

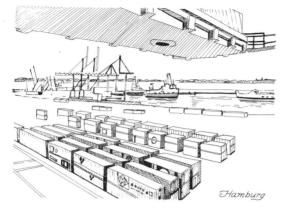

Hamburg

Getting Your Purchases Home

Once you have your antiques and other items, you need to be able to get them home. How you do this depends on many factors: how much material there is, its weight and volume, and how soon you need or want it. You have several options: you can take your purchases with you as baggage, ship them by mail, package express, air freight, or for large items, in a shipping crate. If of great volume, it can be shipped in a 20-foot, 40- foot, or 45-foot (jumbo) shipping container.

Bringing Purchases Home with You

Packing Your Bags

When ready to return home laden with your purchases, you can carry them on the plane as hand luggage or check them as baggage. Remember that your baggage is not insured against loss or damage to precious metals, glass and crystal, money, and jewelry. Therefore, you may wish to consider carrying those items onto the plane.

If you decide to check your valuables as baggage, surround breakables with clothes, and, if available, plastic bubble-pack or Styrofoam packing peanuts and shells. These materials are available from shipping supply merchants and moving companies (check "Speditionsgeschäfte" or "Transporte" in the Yellow Pages). Sometimes you can find these materials in the early morning along sidewalks in retail shopping areas or wholesale markets.

Sturdy cardboard boxes provide excellent protection. Cartons made for shipping household goods (available from moving companies) and those made in China for shipping food (available in early morning before trash pickup in front of Chinese restaurants and grocery stores) provide the most protection. Almost as durable are cardboard fruit shipping boxes made in France and Italy (available at open air markets and food stores). Those used for apples are very good in size and durability.

Avoid boxes made of a soft grade of cardboard. If you try to fold a corner of a box flap and it bends easily, cracks, or tears, don't use that box.

Reinforce every cardboard box, especially at seams and corners, with filament tape. Since this tape is not widely available in Germany, you may want to take a roll with you. Have a sharp knife to cut it—the tape is extremely strong. A flimsy shipping tape is available in some German stationery stores as well as shipping supply companies.

Baggage Allowances Between Germany and North America

Checked baggage on air flights between Germany and North America is counted on the piece system, rather than strictly by weight. If you return from Europe by air, you are entitled to check two pieces of luggage free and take a carry-on with you onto the plane. Each checked package must have a combined length, width, and height less than 62 inches (1.60 meters) and weigh no more than 70 pounds (32 kilograms). Some airlines limit the second piece of checked luggage to 55 inches (1.50 meters) and 70 pounds (32 kilograms). The limits are enforced sporadically, depending on the airline and the airline counter agent.

Carry-on luggage can weigh up to 70 pounds (32 kilograms), but sometimes some airlines will, on some airplanes, limit the luggage to 22 pounds (10 kilograms). In addition to your carry-on, you can often take your camera, purse, day pack and duty-free shopping bag.

Generally, if your purchases are small items and you travel light, the transatlantic baggage allowance will prove sufficient. However, if you have excess baggage, charges can vary wildly between airlines. If you believe (before you make your reservation) that you'll have excess baggage, find out the charges. If they seem excessive, consider changing to an airline with lower excess baggage charges.

If you are not flying directly from Europe to North America, you can expect to have baggage treated on the European weight-based system (see next section).

Baggage Allowances Within Europe

Airlines in Europe (and, most of the rest of the world) accept baggage strictly on weight. Each first-class passenger is entitled to 66 pounds (30 kilograms) of checked luggage and one carry-on. Each business and coach passenger is entitled to 44 pounds (20 kilograms) of checked luggage and one carry-on.

The strictness with which the rules are applied will vary between different airlines at the same airport, the same airline at different airports, and even between one airline counter agent and the next.

Excess baggage charges are often steep! The rule of thumb is to charge one per cent of the first-class fare to every kilogram (or fraction), even if you're not in a first-class seat.

Shipment by Mail (Parcel Post)

There is usually a limit of 11 pounds (5 kilograms) per package, and costs are relatively high.

You pack the items yourself, either with your own box or an approved carton sold at the post office.

At the post office, go to the window marked "Paketen" (packages). You'll have to complete a small green customs declaration, which is in French as well as German, which the clerk will give you. On the declaration, you have to state the contents and the value. In addition, you'll have to pay postage, which varies with the type of contents. (Books and papers have a special reduced rate.)

Expect packages to take one to two months to arrive at their destination.

Parcels for delivery in the United States are inspected by the United States Customs Service at the port of entry and then forwarded to you. If any duty is payable, the post office will bill you the amount of duty, a $5 Customs fee, and a collection surcharge. If the shipment is entirely duty free, there is no charge.

If the package contains a gift, it can be admitted duty free if you write "Unsolicited Gift—Value Under $50." You cannot mail gifts to yourself; and only one will be admitted duty free if addressed to the same party and passes Customs on the same day.

Canadian Customs and Excise inspects parcels at the port of entry, and assesses duty. You pay any duty when the parcel is delivered.

Gifts can be sent duty free if they are marked "Unsolicited Gift—Price Under $40 Canadian."

Package (Railway) Express

If the package weighs over 11 pounds (5 kilograms), you may ship it by rail to a port, by sea passage, and, in North America, accept delivery from the post office.

Take the package to the "Gepäck" (Baggage) at any main railway station. You will have to fill out a customs declaration, as described above. Often, smaller stations don't have these forms: get one from a post office.

Delivery takes approximately four to eight weeks. United States or Canadian Customs inspection is the same as detailed above in the "Shipment by Mail" section.

Air Freight

When you need quick delivery, you can send packages by air freight. When shipping by air freight, your parcel is best packed in a wooden shipping carton.

You can take the parcel to the city check-in terminal in major cities such as Frankfurt, Hamburg, or Munich, or directly to the air-freight terminal at the airport. You can also call air- freight shippers, who include pickup and delivery. (See "Luftverkehr" and look for "Cargo" in the Yellow Pages.)

Costs are higher than surface transport, but delivery is between three days and one week, including Customs clearances.

While air freight is charged by weight, in general the larger and heavier the item, the less the charge per pound will be. The exact cost will vary, often with the category of merchandise the package contains.

If you ship through an air express company (many familiar names also operate out of Germany), the company will handle United States or Canadian Customs clearance. If you ship with an airline, you can either clear the package yourself or hire a customs broker to perform these formalities.

Shipping Through Packers/Shippers

If your purchases are too bulky to take with you or ship by parcel post or express, or because of their age or importance to the German national heritage require permits for export, you'll probably become involved with a packing and shipping company. If you choose to work through a packer/shipper, most of the small but important details will be taken care of.

For large shipments, the packer's and shippers's costs are more than justified by the time and energy saved. There are several types of shipment, but the packer's and shipper's involvement and most of the paperwork will be the same.

Many shippers' services include:

- picking up of merchandise within a metropolitan area (such as Munich or Frankfurt)
- packing the merchandise in a shipping crate or container
- preparing care of all export documentation, such as customs forms and a bill of lading)
- carrying freight to a German port (or, sometimes to Rotterdam in the Netherlands), and airport, any North American port of entry you designate, or even to the final delivery location.

While to some extent the costs will vary with the shipper, you can expect to pay in the neighborhood of 5,000 to 10,000 Deutsche Marks for a 20-foot container and 7,500 to 15,000 Deutsche Marks for a 40-foot container for pick up in a single metropolitan region, packing, export documentation, and delivery to the port. The differences in costs are often reflected in the pickup radius, and care taken to cushion the items and to tightly fit them in for minimum shifting during the shipment.

Note: If you have the shipper perform the pickup, you'll need to provide the shipper with the name and address of every vendor, as well as the invoice for every item. This will ensure that all of the pickups can be scheduled and all items can be accounted for. Pickup usually can be accomplished within a week to ten days.

Choosing a Shipper

Shippers can be found in several ways: by discussion with antique dealers, through shippers' and packers' advertisements in the antiques trade press, and at shipping offices at major antique shows and fairs. Many shippers have specialties or limitations. Ask carefully and listen to the answers, and obtain competitive bids for the exact same services.

Most reputable shippers will be pleased to quote a price and specify exactly what the price includes.

You should ask to see the premises where from which the packer operates: some resemble laboratories and specialize in the shipment of fine arts and rare paintings, while others are in run-down warehouses and fit huge loads of miscellaneous furniture and bric-a-brac into large shipping containers at a lower price.

Ask for references from the shipper before entering a contract: any reputable shipper will have a number of references.

Crate or Container?

Generally, smaller loads are packed into wood shipping crates. Some are standard size, while others are custom made for particular items. Larger loads are packed into metal shipping containers eight feet high, eight feet wide, with lengths of 20-feet, 40-feet, or 45-feet (jumbo). Since the price between a crate and a container may be small, it may be worth buying cheap items just to fill up a container. Containers are strong and are sealed at the packer's and are generally opened only by customs officials. Crates are more easily damaged and a bit easier to pilfer.

Delivery times are approximately the same for containers of any size. Sometimes crates take longer than containers.

Air Freight

Smaller, lightweight items of great value are usually sent by air freight. Some shippers, often those specializing in shipping paintings for museum exhibitions, are specialists in this type of shipment.

Air freight, though not cheap, takes only a few days. In addition, air freight insurance is much less that marine insurance. Generally it costs between one and two per cent of the value declared on the invoice, air bill, and customs declaration.

Shipping By Sea

All international sea shipping companies quote prices in U. S. dollars.

When considering sea shipment, be sure to consider several factors.

Shipping companies are divided into "Conference" lines and "non-Conference" lines. The "Conference" is a price-fixing group of shipping lines. In general, Conference lines charge several hundred dollars more per container, and consist of many of the largest shipping lines with the most frequent schedules.

Non-Conference lines are independents, often working with agents to line up complete cargoes for shipment. Non-Conference lines are more numerous, and service appears to be as reliable as with the Conference lines. The costs are approximately 10 to 20 per cent cheaper than the Conference lines.

Shipping rates (known as "tariffs" vary by the type of goods you ship—often widely. The approximate cost to ship used furniture and bric-a-brac to an East Coast port (such as Montréal, Boston, New York, or Baltimore) is: 20-foot container: Conference $2000, non-Conference $1900; 40-foot container: Conference $2400, non-Conference $2200.

The approximate cost to ship to a Gulf port (such as Miami, New Orleans, or Houston) is: 20-foot container: Conference $2100, non-Conference $1900; 40-foot container: Conference $2400, non-Conference $2250. The approximate cost to ship to to a West Coast port (such as Los Angeles, San Francisco/Oakland, Seattle, or Vancouver, B.C.) is: 20-foot container: Conference $1925, non-Conference $1800; 40-foot container: Conference $3190, non-Conference $3050.

If shipping to the West Coast, be sure to specify shipment through the Panama Canal; some shipments have been routed on a "land bridge" via Houston and truck or rail from there, with delays and damage en route.

When deciding whether to make your own sea shipment arrangements leave or it to your packer, remember that most packers and some shipping companies add a premium (often around 11 per cent) of the estimated shipping charge to ensure that they don't lose money on currency fluctuations. (This is because the Deutsche Mark-to-dollar rate is calculated at the time it passes midpoint in the ocean rather than at delivery on board the ship.) If you deal directly with the shipping and pay in U.S. dollars, you can sometimes avoid this premium.

Marine Insurance

You can purchase two basic types of marine insurance: all-risk, or total-loss. Many importers of less valuable antiques and used items purchase only total-loss insurance, since proving when or how breakage occurred can be difficult if not impossible. However, when shipments of great value are made, the additional cost of all-risk insurance is worth paying. Generally, total-loss insurance costs from one to three per cent of value declared on the bill of lading and customs declaration. All-risk insurance (which covers water damage and damage during port operations, but not damage due to strikes, war, acts of violence, nuclear disaster, or certain other exclusions) costs about twice as much as total loss insurance.

If you choose all-risk insurance, be sure to document the condition of goods shipped before they are packed. Invoices and a photograph of every item are the best proof of condition and value.

Delivery to the Port of Your Choice

Be sure to specify which port you wish to have as the port of entry in the United States or Canada. Avoid entering the shipment through a distant port: although customs brokers at any port of entry can solve many problems, the farther away the port of entry is from the ultimate destination, the more you'll have to pay for truck or rail shipment inside the United States or Canada.

Clearing United States Customs

Customs inspection! The very words can strike terror or great amounts of irritation into many travelers: visions of weary inspectors pawing through your luggage in search of contraband are not pleasant, particularly when you have a tight connection to your final destination.

Constitutional protections, such as freedom from arbitrary search or the right to be warned if you're suspected of a crime, don't apply when dealing with any Customs officer at the border. The Customs Service is virtually unique in American government in this regard. The laws relating to the search of vehicles and persons are found in the United States Code at 19 U.S.C. Section 482. Case law interpreting this section gives the Customs Service the "broadest possible authority for search." Border searches may be conducted with or without cause.

However, bringing in antiques and collectables can require anything from a simple oral statement of what you bought to what seems to be an almost endless round of paper shuffling and frustration.

If you completely and fully declare every item at the correct price, and make it available for inspection, you shouldn't have to worry.

What Customs Can Inspect

Every item brought into the United States from any other country must be presented to United States Customs for inspection. The customs inspector, at his discretion, can decide to accept your word and inspect nothing, whether a simple suitcase or an entire shipping container. The inspector can decide for any reason, or no reason, to pull every item out of every package and inspect every item.

The reasons for customs inspection include not only the collection of customs duty but also to ensure that all imports are safe, don't violate copyright or trademark laws, meet varying federal regulations, and are not prohibited (such as narcotics or items made from endangered species).

In general, the procedures fall into two categories: "informal entry" for all shipments whose purchase price or value is less than $1,000, or "formal entry" for all shipments valued over $1,000.

Informal Entries

Informal entry is the easiest and least time-consuming way to ensure that your purchases quickly pass through customs.

In general, all shipments (whether commercial or for your own use) whose purchase price (including packing but not transportation) is less than $1,000 qualify for informal entry whether with your baggage or sent by mail.

When your purchases accompany you, you can usually use an informal entry. When they are over $400, fill out the simplified declaration form handed out on most planes, ships, and busses. If you're in a car (for example from Canada or Mexico), you can make an oral declaration.

In addition, if the importation is for your own use and is with you as baggage, you can also usually use the informal entry procedure, even when the value of your purchases is over $1,000. An oral declaration to the inspector is often sufficient.

In all cases, you should have every bill of sale and receipt readily available to show the customs inspector upon request.

If you have packed goods in boxes, you should have shipping tape, twine, or other materials to reseal the containers when the inspector has finished. While some officers have some tape or other materials available, you can't count on it.

Remember that true antiques are duty free, but the inspector may demand proof. Paintings (but not frames) and many products from underdeveloped nations are also duty free.

Duty-Free Allowance

If your purchases cost under $400 and you have been outside of the United States for at least 72 hours, you can bring in your purchases duty free as part of your baggage once every 30 days. Duty is assessed at 10% on the next $1,000 of goods. After that, the agent will assess duty as prescribed by regulations: the amount will vary depending on the exact classification of the merchandise. (This exemption is valid only when the items are part of your baggage and you present them in person for inspection.)

Unsolicited Gifts

You're permitted to send unsolicited gifts duty-free if no more than one package to one individual clears Customs on the same day. The gifts must be worth less than $50. The outside must be clearly marked "Unsolicited Gift—Value under $50." You're not permitted to send these packages to yourself or residents of your house.

Informal Mail Entries

If you mailed antiques home, obtain a customs declaration form from the German post office, complete it, and glue it to the package when you mail it.

Enclose a copy of the invoice inside the package. Customs will inspect the parcel at the port of entry. If duty is payable, the post office will collect the duty and a $5 inspection fee from you when the parcel is delivered to you. (There is no fee for completely duty-free items.)

Formal Entries

For all commercial shipments entering the United States with a purchase price or value over $1,000, you have to make a formal entry.

Inspectors in some airports may sometimes treat amounts over $1,000 as informal entries when the purchases are part of your baggage. When you're not actually there with the shipment, the formal entry procedure is invariably followed by the Customs Service.

Here are the steps that must take place when your purchases arrive at the port of entry:

1. Provide Customs with an acceptable commercial invoice (as defined in the section on steps to clear Customs), or "pro forma invoice" (an invoice you make up reflecting the actual conditions of the sale; later you will have to provide a commercial invoice).

2. File an Entry Manifest (Customs Form 7533) or other equivalent form (usually taken care of by the shipping company).

3. Complete the Entry Summary (Customs Form 7501).

4. Provide a bond or deposit with the Entry Summary to ensure the payment of duty.

5. Make the goods available for inspection.

6. Pay any estimated payment of duty.

7. Arrange for local delivery of the goods.

If you live near the port of entry and want to oversee each step of the process, you can do it yourself. However, you can also hire a customs broker to handle this process for you.

Why Hire a Customs Broker?

Customs brokers are licensed and bonded and can handle all of the details of clearing customs if you can't or don't wish to. Naturally they charge a fee for service.

When using a broker, you must still play a part by providing a complete commercial or pro forma invoice and ensure that a complete bill of lading (or air bill) accompanies the shipment. The bill of lading should (if possible) specify the broker who will be clearing the shipment.

Customs brokers cluster around all major ports of entry; they're listed in the Yellow Pages. The local Customs office often has lists of brokers in the area. However, the Customs staff will not recommend brokers.

How to Select a Broker

Since there may be at least several dozen brokers near most major ports of entry, you need to carefully select the one that will work best for you. Sometimes antique dealers specializing in imported items will tell you which brokers they use, if any (some dealers take care of this themselves).

Ask these questions of any broker you're considering:

1. What experience do you have with antiques and collectables (or type of merchandise you're importing)? How many shipments of such items have you recently cleared?

2. Can you refer me to several recent customers for whom you have cleared this type of merchandise?

3. How much do you charge? Get a breakdown and ask:
• is this fee all inclusive?

• if not, what extra charges can be added?

Some brokers provide all services for a set price, plus the exact amount of any customs duty payable. Others may have a reasonable base price, plus a charge for every single entry they type on forms and every phone call they make or every paper they handle. There is often no relationship between charges and quality of service.

Brokers will commonly charge between $75 and $300 to clear a single shipment, and the value of the shipment often does not have a bearing on the fee.

A knowledgeable broker should be able to clear your shipment in just a few days.

Steps in Clearing Customs (if you do it yourself)

1. Provide   Customs   with   an   acceptable commercial or pro forma invoice.

Every formal entry must be accompanied by a commercial invoice. While most of the things that must appear on the invoice are commonplace, the requirements for a complete invoice are spelled out in Federal regulations (1 CFR Title 19, Sections 141.83 (c) and 141.86 through 141.89).

In general, the invoice must state the exact type and quantity of each item, what each type of item is made of, and the price paid (including and specifying whether containers and packing were included). It must also include the name and address of both buyer and seller, and specify the U.S. port of entry. The invoice should be signed or sealed by the exporter. If you have a number of invoices from different sellers, you can combine the items in one shipment. In this case, you can make out a combined invoice, but all of the original invoices should be attached to the combined invoice.

Pro forma invoices can be used to clear Customs but a true invoice must be provided within six months of entry. Otherwise a penalty will usually be assessed out of the customs bond (see below in Section 4).

A special U. S. Customs invoice can be used in place of a regular commercial invoice; contact Customs for more detailed information.

2. File an Entry Manifest, Customs Form 7533 or other equivalent.

(This is usually taken care of by the shipping company.)

3. Complete the Entry Summary (Customs Form 7501).

The Entry Summary form provides, together with the invoice, the basis upon which duty will be determined and assessed.

When filed, it must be accompanied by the invoice, the bill of lading, and bond (or acceptable alternative).

You or your customs broker must complete the form and present it with the rest of the entry documents at the Customs office within five days the shipment's unloading. (While Customs officers may provide information, you or your agent must complete the form, and propose the correct classification for entry.) For exact information to complete the Entry Number, Entry Type Code, Port Code, and similar codes, you will have to contact the regional Customs office.

You must also complete the Description of Merchandise (Items 29-32). This includes not only the description (quantity, value, duty rate, amount of duty payable), but also the tariff classification, which is found in the Tariff Schedule of the United States of America (T.S.U.S.A., usually pronounced "Tsoosuh").

The Entry Summary form must then be signed (press hard—this is a five-part form) and submit these with your Customs bond or equivalent and the invoice.

Using T.S.U.S.A.

This document, usually in the form of a large binder, contains tens of thousands of tariff classifications and rates. What you must do yourself is to determine both the correct classification for the merchandise and the correct rate of duty. Customs officers will not usually tell you what the exact classifications your items fit.

The tariffs are broken down into seven major categories, and then further subdivided. T.S.U.S.A. is available for reference at all Customs offices, major "depository libraries" (usually public or university libraries), or found in bound form in the United States Code Annotated (19 U.S.C. Section 1202 and following sections. Related provisions are found in 19 CFR Chapter 1. Both of these are available in large law libraries, or you can buy a copy from the:

United States Government Printing Office
Washington, D. C. 20402

4. Provide a bond or deposit with the Entry Summary to ensure the payment of duty.

This must be submitted even if you believe the goods are duty free. The purpose of the bond is to ensure the correct payment of duty.

Customs bonds must be issued by an approved customs bonding company. The local customs office will have a list of local bonding companies. (Most customs brokers include the bonding with their other services.)

The amount of a single entry bond varies, but is generally the value of the shipment and the estimated amount of duty.

A customs bond can be issued either on a permanent basis for importers on a regular basis, or as a single entry bond for a single shipment.

Alternatives to a Customs Bond

There are several alternatives to a customs bond, but they are less convenient. They include:

- A cash deposit equal to the value of shipment (no interest is paid and the cash is held for two years).
- Personal surety (requiring two signatories with real assets in the state in which the port of entry is located).
- Treasury bills, notes or bonds (but not U. S. Savings Bonds) which will also be held for two years, but you eventually receive the interest.

The bond or its alternative must be presented to Customs when you present the invoice and Entry Summary (Customs Form 7501).

5. Make the goods available for inspection.

Usually shipments are held in a customs warehouse at the port of entry for up to 10 days. During this time, the inspection should take place. Under certain circumstances, the shipment can also be shipped in bond to a more convenient place (usually a bonded warehouse), or opened in the presence of a Customs officer.

6. Pay the estimated payment of duty.

You already have estimated the amount of duty (at the rate found in T.S.U.S.A.) and included it on the Summary Entry form. Make payment of any amount needed; the goods won't be released until the estimated duty is paid.

Rates of Duty

From the thousands of rates found in T.S.U.S.A., most of the ones needed by antique dealers and collectors are here:

All antiques (defined as certifiably at least 100 years old) enter the United States duty free.

All paintings made entirely by hand are duty free, regardless of age (but you may have to pay duty on the frame and packing).

All sculptures made and signed by a "recognized" artist in an edition of 10 or fewer (usually a photocopy of an entry in a bibliography of art and artists will suffice).

Items that are old but do not qualify as antiques are assessed duty as found in T.S.U.S.A.; duties on most items are much lower than you might expect, in the neighborhood of free to about 8 per cent. Naturally exceptions exist, and depend not only on the item but also where it was made or acquired. Duty is imposed based on the classification of the merchandise and its country of origin. In general, imports from West Germany (but not East Germany) receive the "most favored nation" rate.

7. Arrange for local delivery of the goods.

When you have paid the estimated duty, you are able to pick up or have your goods shipped to their final destination.

While for most purposes, the procedure is finished when you pay the duty, Customs has 90 days to review the paperwork and finalize the transaction. The entry (shipment of merchandise) is completed in 90 days; at that time the entry is "liquidated" (the paperwork is considered final by Customs).

Clearing Canadian Customs

Customs inspection! These words make many people a bit nervous, and can strike terror in some people. However, when entering Canada, a full and truthful declaration of merchandise will speed re-entry of both you and your purchases. If your purchases are shipped, you'll have to clear them through Customs and Excise yourself or hire a customs broker. Depending on where the merchandise enters Canada and how much there is, clearing customs can require anything from a simple declaration to the customs officer to a formal entry, with all of the paperwork that that may entail.

What Customs Can Inspect

Every item brought into Canada from any other country must be presented to Customs and Excise for inspection. The customs officer can, at his discretion, accept your declaration or open and inspect any and all portions of the shipment. In general, procedures fall into two categories: informal clearance of items included in personal baggage that you have with you, or formal clearance for shipments of high value, whether with you or sent separately.

Customs inspections are carried out for the purposes of collection of duty, federal sales tax, excise taxes, and to ensure that imports are safe, don't violate copyright, trademark, or drug laws, and that no items made from endangered species are imported.

Informal Entries

Once a year, travelers returning to Canada after an absence of at least seven days may import items for personal use without paying duty or federal sales tax to the value of $300. After the first trip abroad, Canadian residents can bring up to $100 duty free with them once every calendar quarter after an absence of at least seven days.

All goods exceeding that amount or for resale are subject to duty and federal sales tax (12 per cent), though some items are exempt from sales tax. Excise tax (usually 10 per cent) is added to some categories of imports as well.

Mail Entries

If you send a package by mail or package express, it will be inspected by Customs and Excise at the port of entry. The assessment will, in large part, be based on the customs declaration you attached in Germany. Any duty, federal sales tax, and excise tax payable will be collected upon delivery.

Formal and Commercial Entries

If your goods are for resale, you (or your customs broker) must complete the "Canada Customs Import Entry Coding Form (B3)" or the "Commercial Short Import Entry Coding Form (B8)." These forms are available from any Customs and Excise office at any major port of entry (seaports, land crossings, or international airports). Information is also available from:

Customs and Excise
Revenue Canada
260 Coventry Road
Ottawa, Ontario K1K 2C6
Telephone (613) 993-0534

To make a formal entry, you must fill out every box in the form except those reserved for the duty stamp. The most difficult part to complete is the classification of goods. You must make the declaration based on the classifications in the Tariff Schedules. The Tariff Schedules consist of a large looseleaf notebook containing thousands of different Tariff Items. The Tariff Schedules can be reviewed at any Customs and Excise office.

You must decide the exact classification under which each item falls (there are thousands). To find the correct classification, you must determine which the correct tariff classification. Some common classifications for antiques and collectables include:

- 69315-1: Articles (other than spirits or wines) produced more than 50 years prior to the date of importation. Antiques are admitted duty free but those less than 100 years old must pay 12 per cent federal sales tax. Antiques over 100 years old are exempt from both duty and federal sales tax. Proof of age is usually required.

- 51900 series: Furniture. There are about seven relevant categories, with duty from 10 per cent to 45 per cent, depending on the exact classification and country of origin. In addition to the tariff, a 12 per cent federal sales tax must be paid.

- 32600 series: Glass. There are several dozen separate tariff categories, with duty rates ranging from free (glass eyes) to 32.5 per cent (carbouys and demijohn jugs), plus 12 per cent federal sales tax.

- 36200-1: Sterling or other silverware (except silver plate) and gold, with duty ranging from 7 per cent to 45 percent plus 12 per cent federal sales tax plus 10 per cent excise tax on some items.

- 28700-1: All tableware of china, porcelain, semi-porcelain (such as faience), or white granite, but not including earthenware, with duty rates ranging from free to 35 per cent, plus 12 per cent federal sales tax.

- 28600-1: Earthenware and stoneware, with duty rates ranging from 11.3 per cent to 35 per cent, plus 12 per cent federal sales tax.

Determining Duty Rates Within a Tariff Classification

The duty charged depends to a great extent on the country of origin. The Tariff Schedules include five categories: British Preferential Tariff, Most Favoured Nation Tariff, General Tariff, General Preferential Tariff, and U. K. and Ireland Tariff. In general, imports from West Germany (but not East Germany) are entered under the Most Favoured Nation Tariff.

Release of Goods

Goods will not be released from Customs and Excise until all duty, and, when imposed, federal sales tax and excise taxes have been paid.

Customs Brokers

Customs brokers are licensed and bonded and can handle all of the details of customs clearance if you can't or don't wish to. They charge fees for all services they perform.

Customs brokers are found in all major ports of entry, particularly seaports. They are listed in the Yellow Pages under "Customs Brokers."

How to Select a Broker

Since most ports have at least several brokers, and charges for customs entries are not uniform between one and another, consider several factors before choosing a broker.

Ask these questions of any broker you're considering:

1. What experience do you have with antiques and collectables (or type of merchandise)? How many shipments of similar items have you recently cleared?

2. Can you provide references of recent customers for whom you have cleared this type of merchandise?

3. How much do you charge? Request a breakdown of fees and ask:
- is this fee all-inclusive?
- if not, what extra services will be incur a charge? And how much are the extra charges likely to be?

Carefully compare brokers' charges and services: some specialize in certain types of imports, and some have fee schedules better suited to certain types of shipments.

Antiques in East Germany

East Germany, formally known as the German Democratic Republic (GDR), has large quantities of antiques. Unfortunately for collectors outside of the country, they are difficult to find and virtually impossible to export. (Prior to the Berlin Wall, many antiques drifted into West Germany through West Berlin.)

There are few if any flea markets or antique markets in East Germany. A few antique and used goods shops are found in major cities such as East Berlin, Leipzig, and Dresden. However, the regulations regarding the export of almost anything from the country are difficult: you can export up to 20 Marks per day of East German goods (maximum 100 Marks) free of export duty. For quantities above that, many items are subject to almost confiscatory export duties, which must be paid in Western currency, such as West German Deutsche Marks or dollars. Many categories of items (including many foods!) cannot be exported at all.

There are no export restrictions on items purchased with Western currency at the Intershop chain. Unfortunately, antiques are rarely if ever offered at Intershops.

Export of Antiques Laws

The laws regarding the export of antiques from the GDR are found in the Decree of 2 April 1953 regarding the protection of the German heritage of works of art, scientific documents and materials. and in the Law of 19 June 1975 regarding the preservation of monuments (which includes paintings, sculpture, and any other artwork the State determines is part of the German heritage).

No works of art or materials of cultural value may be exported without a permit (regardless of age!). The permits are rarely if ever granted. Further information can be obtained from the Ministry of Culture in Berlin:

Ministerium für Kultur
Karl-Liebknecht-Strasse 34
DDR-1020 Berlin
Central information telephone: (02) 2 30.

The attempt to export an item without a permit is punishable by confiscation of the item, a fine of 1,000 Marks, and imprisonment for up to one year, though other acts committed at the same time which are punishable under the East German law can substantially to increase these penalties.

Bear in mind that East German border inspections can be incredibly thorough, and that, for the purposes of the law, West Germany is considered a foreign country.

Düsseldorf

Writing and Calling

Cities with markets are listed in alphabetical order; the number just after the place name is the postal code. In many indexes, German cities are listed in the numerical postal code order instead of alphabetically.

The postal codes are geographical: West Germany has been divided into eight regions. The code for the largest city in each region ends in 000 (example: 3000 Hannover), other large cities' codes end in 00 (example: 5100 Aachen), smaller cities' codes end in a single 0 (example: 6650 Homburg am Saar), and small towns and villages have four numbers but never 0 as the last digit (example: 4132 Kamp-Linfort).

The key map to the detailed map of Germany shows the major largest city in each postal region and its postal code. Other locations starting with the same digit will always be in the same region.

Regularly scheduled markets have been going for centuries on the same days and often at the same places. However, some are held irregularly, or once or twice a year. In that case, it's a good idea to contact the organizer to ensure that the market is actually being held. The name and phone number of the organizer is found at the end of each listing.

Writing to a German Address

When writing to any address in Germany (such as an auction house or market organizer), the postal code is always written before the city name. Often, a capital "D" is written in front of the postal code. This letter insures that the letter is being mailed to West Germany. In addition, in many cities there are postal zone codes, written after the city name (for example, many dealers are found in Munich in zone 2; write to them at D-8000 München 2). Always include all codes to insure prompt delivery.

Using German Telephones

German phone numbers have city codes in parentheses in front the local numbers. When making a phone call inside the same city, only the local number is dialed. If calling from elsewhere in Germany, dial the proper city code and then the local number. If calling from another country, dial the West German country code, 49, the city code (without the initial "0"), and the local number. For complete details, read the section on German telephones in "Manston's Travel Key Europe."

Note that there will be varying numbers in a phone number (from three to seven) and in the city code (from four to seven). There are even different numbers of digits to telephone numbers in a single town or city.

You can't always expect that anyone at the organizer's office will speak English.

Cities A to Z

Aachen 5100

(Please also see Wurselen.)

Flohmarkt in der Altstadt (flea market in Old Town), third Sunday of every month from March through December, and the second Saturday of May, which is Mothers' Day in Germany. The market, in a picturesque setting straight out of the Middle Ages, takes place on five squares around the Carolingian cathedral (about 800 A.D.), and the city hall dating from the Middle Ages in the old city. Not many of the items for sale are quite that old. There is a wide variety of merchandise, mainly collectables and some 19th-century items. This is by far the largest market in the area and is one of the oldest flea markets in Germany. A day here can be combined with a visit to the La Batte market in nearby Liége, Belgium. Parking can be difficult, though there are several garages at and near Katschhof. Organized by Harry Owens Flohmarkt GmbH, Blaubach 30, 5000 Köln, telephone (0221) 23 53 65.

Flohmarkt (flea market) on the first and fourth Sunday of most months from April through December at the Allkauf Parkplatz Plaza (Allkauf shopping center parking lot). This large market has all kinds of items: new, used, and antique. Lots of food and even a few games to amuse the young at heart. Parking is available at the site. Information from Hermann & Lampert, Hasselholzerweg 9, 5100 Aachen, telephone (0241) 7 20 21.

Trödelmarkt (junk market) first and third Sunday from April through November. This market is a twin of the market in the previous listing, and is held at the Globus shopping center in the suburb of Aachen-Verlautenheide. Parking is available at the site. Organized by Hermann & Lampert, Hasselholzerweg 9, 5100 Aachen, telephone (0241) 7 20 21.

Antik- und Trödelmarkt (antique and junk market) third Sunday in January at the Mehrzweckhalle in the suburb of Aachen-Haaren (7 kilometers northeast of the city center on route 264). Organized by Hermann & Lampert, Hasselholzerweg 9, 5100 Aachen, telephone (0241) 7 20 21.

Trödelmarkt (junk market) last Sunday of October at the Plus- Einkaufzentrum (Plus shopping center) in the suburb of Aachen-Richterich. Organized by Norbert Junge, Obersteinstrasse 51, 5190 Stolberg, telephone (02402) 2 30 07.

Musikbörse (music exchange) first Sunday of October at the Mensa. Only sheet music and musical instruments are exchanged. Information from Kogel & Lauber, Kornmarkt 10-12, 6900 Siegen, telephone (0271) 5 15 01.

Aalen 7080

Trödelmarkt (junk market) second Sunday in October at the Gentner-Center. Information from Agentur Zelinka, Gmünderstrasse 18, 7070 Schwäbisch-Gmünd, telephone (07171) 8 52 32.

Ahlen 4730

Antikmarkt (antique market) first, second and sometimes third Sunday of every month year round at the Stadthalle. Organizers vary; ask for information at the Stadthalle.

Aichach 8890

Antikmarkt und Flohmarkt (antique market and flea market) first Saturday of every month at the Volksfestplatz (festival grounds). Thomas Seitzmeier, Enthofstrasse 35, 8068 Pfaffenhofen an der Ilm 2, telephone (08443) 4 53.

Ahrweiler 5483

Antik- und Trödelmarkt (antique and junk market) first weekend in June and last weekend in September in the Marktplatz and Fussgängerzone (market place and pedestrian zone) in the village center. Organized by Agentur W. Demandt, Domackerstrasse 29, 5010 Bergheim 3, telephone (02271) 9 54 94.

Altwarmbüchen

Antik- und Trödelmarkt (antique fair and junk market) third Saturday of October at the Einkaufzentrum Adler (Eagle shopping center). Information from Novema Hannover, Hahnensteg 22, 3000 Hannover 91, telephone (0511) 41 41 14.

Altenkirchen im Westerwald 5230

Kunsthandwerkermarkt (art and artisans' market), the last Sunday of October and the first Sunday of November at the Stadthalle, or Marktplatz in the town center (location alternates from year to year). Information from Kogel & Lauber, Kornmarkt 10-12, 6900 Siegen, telephone (0271) 5 15 01.

Alzey 6508

Trödelmarkt (junk market) last Saturday of October in the Fussgängerzone (pedestrian zone in the town center. Organized by Horst Zehnpfennig, Pestalozzistrasse 54, 6504 Neirstein, telephone (06133) 5 85 11.

Andernach 5470

Trödelmarkt (junk market), last Sunday of October in the Innenstadt (old inner town). Organized by Junge und Schönenbrücher, Talbahnstrasse 4, 5190 Stolberg, telephone (02402) 8 27 67.

Appenweier 7607

Antikmarkt (antique market) last Sunday of October in the Schwartzwaldhalle (Black Forest Hall). Organized by Antiquitariat Peter Kiefer GmbH, Kirchstrasse 4, 7537 Remchingen-Wilferdingen, telephone (07231) 1 72 72.

Ascha/Geschwendt 8441

Flohmarkt (flea market) first Saturday of every month at the parking lot of the Gasthäus Zum Freischütz. Organized by Margot Achatz, Gasthäus zum Freischütz, 8441 Geschwendt/ Straubing, telephone (09961) 66 90.

Aschaffenberg 8750

Antik- und Trödelmarkt (antique and junk market) first Sunday of every month year round at the Basar Einkaufzentrum on Hanauerstrasse. Organized by Nicholas Dollmann, Teichstrasse 16, 5000 Köln 30, telephone (0221) 53 17 44.

Attendorn 5952

Antikmarkt (antique fair) second weekend of October in the Stadthalle (City Central Hall). Organized by Franz Stefan, An der Mühle 32, 4052 Korsenbroich 4, telephone (02166) 8 35 09.

Auggen 7841

Antik- und Trödelmarkt (antique and junk market) third Saturday of February and second weekend of November at the Winzerhalle. Organized by Media Messegesellschaft GmbH & Co., Ausstellungs-KG, Bahnhofstrasse 1, 7030 Böblingen, telephone (07031) 2 30 48.

Augsburg 8900

Flohmarkt (flea market) every Saturday year round near the Möbel-Jakob building. Organized by Marktamt (City Market office), Rathaus, 8900 Augsburg, telephone (0821) 3 24 48 66.

Antikmarkt (antique market) second weekend of October in the Augustanahaus. No reproductions or new items may be offered at this sale. Organized by Max Koch, Jacob-Hagenbucher-Strasse 16, 8000 München 50, telephone (089) 29 53 06.

Aurich (Ostfriesland) 2960

Antikmarkt (antique market) second Sunday of every month year round in the Stadthalle (city convention hall). Information from Inter Antik, Mommsenstrasse 10, 4006 Ekrath, telephone (02104) 4 61 52.

Backnang 7150

Trödelmarkt (junk market) second Sunday of October, or third (alternates each year), at the Handelshof. Organized by Firma Syntis, Jacobsgasse 29, 7400 Tübigen, telephone (07071) 2 70 22

Bad Bentheim 4444

Trödelmakrt (junk market) last weekend in August on Schlossstrasse. This annual affair is a very large amateur radio operators' market, though there are normal flea market items including antiques and collectables, some mass-produced items, and reproductions. Organized by Friedrich Begemann, Dessauer Strasse 10, 4460 Nordhorn, telephone (05921) 42 29.

Bad Berleburg 5920

Trödelmarkt (junk market) first Saturday of every month at the Brotmarkt or at the Einkaufzentrum am Sähling. This market also takes place with special emphasis and much larger size on the first Thursday of October as part of the Oktoberfest celebration and the second Saturday of December as part of the Weinachtenfest (Christmas festival). Information from Stadtverwaltung Verkehrsbüro (Visitors Bureau), Postfach 1624, 5920 Bad Berleburg, telephone (02751) 70 77 or Kogel & Lauber, Kornmarkt 10-12, 6900 Siegen, telephone (0271) 5 15 01.

Bad Breisig 5484

Flohmarkt (flea market) first Saturday of October and November in the Goldene Meile Einkaufzentrum. Organized by Helene Schmidt, Karl-Marx-Strasse 35, 5450 Neuweid 12, telephone (02631) 7 66 44.

Bad Driburg 3490

Trödelmarkt (junk market) second Saturday of October in the pedestrian zone of the town center. Organized by Galerie G. Krencky, Heidestrasse 9a, 4900 Herford, telephone (05221) 5 67 41.

Bad Dürkheim 6702

Flohmarkt (flea market) first Saturday of October in the parking lot in the Silz. Organized by Person-Werbung, Weinstrasse Süd 20, 6702 Bad Dürkheim, telephone (06322) 6 66 00.

Bad Dürrheim 7737

Flohmarkt (flea market) first Saturday of October at the Marktplatz in the center of the village. Information from Marktorganisation-zentrum Michaela März, Gerwingstrasse 2, 7742 St. Georgen, telephone (07724) 35 05.

Bad Ems 5427

Antikmarkt (antique market) third weekend of October at the Kursaal in this cure resort. Only antiques may be offered. Information from telephone (02602) 1 22 88.

Flohmarkt (flea market) last weekend of October at the Tengelmann Selbst-Bedienung Markt. Organized by Rolf à Brassard, Rheinstrasse 4, 5434 Dernbach, telephone (02602) 70839.

Baden-Baden 7570

Antiktage (antique days) third weekend of October at the Alten Bahnhof, a parking lot and plaza at the north end of town. Organized by Peter Fuchs, Bahnhofstrasse 5, 6940 Wein-heim, telephone (06201) 1 22 32.

Antik- und Trödelmarkt (antique and junk market) last Sunday of October in the Ooser Festhalle in the center of this gracious resort town. Organized by Hans W. Nippen, Im Ferning 4, 7505 Ettlingen, telephone (07243) 1 21 06.

Bad Friedrichshall 7107

Antikmarkt (antique market) first Sunday of November in the Lindenberghalle. Organized by Antiquariat Peter Kiefer GmbH, Eberstein-strasse 14, 7530 Pforzheim, telephone (07231) 1 72 72.

Bad Godesberg (Bonn) 5320

Antikmarkt (antique market) second week in March from Wednesday through Sunday at the Stadthalle. Organized by EXPO Management

GmbH, Eichenwg 59, 2300 Kiel 17, telephone
(0431) 32 46 60, or the flea market office,
telephone (0228) 77 26 36.

Trödelmarkt (junk market) second Saturday and
third weekend of October in the Altstadt
Center (old city center). Organized by Junge &
Schönenbrücher, Talbahnstrasse 4, 5190 Stolberg, telephone (02402) 8 27 67.

Bad Homburg 6380

Antikmarkt (antique market) second Sunday of
every month in the Alter Bahnhof (old railway
station). Organized by R. Blank, Friedrich-
Ebert-Strassse 2, 6368 Bad Vilbel, telephone
(06101) 82 12.

Bad Kreutznach 6550

Antik- und Handwerkmarkt (antique and
handcrafts market) first Saturday in October
in the Römerpassage. Information from WEWO
Antikmärkte, Rudi-Stefan-Allee 14, 6520
Worms, telephone (06241) 7 58 71.

Antikmarkt (antique market) first day of
November in the Kurhaus. Information from
WEWO Antikmärkte, Rudi-Stefan-Allee 14, 6520
Worms, telephone (06241) 7 58 71.

Bad Nenndorf 3052

Antikmarkt (antique market) second Sunday of
November in the Parkplatz R-Kauf. Organized
by Galerie G. Krencky, Heidestrasse 9a, 4900
Herford, telephone (05221) 5 67 41.

Bad Rappenau 6927

Flohmarkt (flea market) first Saturday in the
Rathausplatz, facing City Hall in the center of
town. Information from Klaus Sheppe,

KS-Management, Fidel Fischer Strasse 1, 7580 Bühl, (07223) 48 95.

Bad Salzuflen 4902

Antikmarkt (antique market) second Sunday of every month in the Festhalle (Festival Hall). Information from Theodor Wessling, Königstrase 68, 4690 Herme 2, telephone (02325) 4 40 79.

Bad Segeberg 2360

Flohmarkt (flea market) third Sunday of October in the parking lot of the Handelshof. Organized by Wolfgang Mayer, Max-Planck-Strasse, 2085 Quickborn, telephone (04106) 6 91 80.

Bad Schwartau 2407

Trödelmarkt (junk market) first Saturday of May and June, first weekend in September (as part of the annual Sonnenblumfest celebration) and first Sunday and Monday of October (as part of the Oktoberfest). Organized by Aktivgruppe für Handel und Gewerbe (business and trade group), 2407 Bad Schwartau, telephone (0452) 2 10 08.

Bad Soden 6232

(Please also see Frankfurt and Offenbach.)

Antiquitätentage (antique days) second weekend of October at the Kur- und Kongresszentrum. Only true antiques may be sold; no reproductions are permitted. Organized by Firma Blank, Friedrich-Ebert-Strasse 2, 6368 Bad Vilbel, telephone (06101) 82 12.

Balingen 7460

Floh- und Trödelmarkt (flea and junk market) first and second Saturday of October and second

Saturday of November at the Einkaufzentrum
shopping center. Organized by Agentur Floma,
Industriestrasse 15, 7340 Geislingen, telephone
(07331) 4 04 51, or by Marktorganization-
zentrum. Michael Mürz, Gerwingstrasse 1,
7742 St. Georgen, telephone (07724) 34 05.

Bamberg 8600

Antikmarkt (antique market) last Sunday of
October or first weekend of November at the
Harmoniesäle (music halls). Organized by Firma
Weber, Semmelstrasse 42, 8700 Würzburg,
telephone (0931) 1 37 03.

Barsighausen 3013

Antikmarkt (antique market) third weekend of
October in the Schulzentrum (schools center).
Organized by Clivia Müller, Körnerstrasse 18,
3000 Hannover 1, telephone (0511) 32 86 31.

Beckum 4720

Trödelmarkt (junk market) first weekend in
September in the town center in the square in
front of the Altes Rathaus (old city hall). This
market is part of the annual "Pütt-Tage"
celebration. Another market takes place from
the end of November until December 7; however,
this Christmas market is still new and small.
Organized by Herr Schiller, Gewerbeverein
(Retail Merchants' Association), 4720 Beckum,
telephone (02521) 70 66 or 2 91 31.

Beilstein 7141

(Please also see Heilbronn.)

Antik- und Trödelmarkt (antique fair and junk
market) last Sunday of October at the Stadthalle
(city auditorium). Information from Agentur
Floma, Industriestrasse 15, 7340 Geislingen,
telephone (07331) 4 04 51.

Antik- und Trödelmarkt (antique and junk market) second Saturday of November in the Stadthalle. This is a small market in a small town. Information from H. & H. K. Fischer, Uhlandstrasse 18, 7255 Rutesheim, (07152) 5 43 77.

Belm (Osnabrück) 4513

Trödelmarkt (junk market) first and third Sunday every month year round at the Marktplatz Parkgarage. Information from M. Nordmann, Leconskamp 18, 4513 Belm, telephone (05406) 40 40.

Bensburg 5060

(Please also see Köln and Bergisch Gladbach.)

Flohmarkt (flea market) second Saturday of October at Rathausplatz (the square in front of City Hall). Access by public transit from Köln on tram line 1 to the end of the line or the Bahnhof. Organized by Rita Schneider, Wipperfürther Strasse 45, 5060 Bergisch-Gladbach 1, telephone (02204) 5 24 00.

Bergheim 5010

Flohmarkt (flea market) first Ssunday of October in the Fussgängerzone (pedestrian zone) in the town center. Organized by W & R Titz, Heerstrasse 44, 5010 Bergheim, telephone (02271) 5 24 00.

Bergisch Gladbach 5060

(Please also see Köln and Bensburg.)

This town is only about 15 kilometers from Köln, and is accessible by S-Bahn.)

Antikmarkt (antique market) second Saturday
and Sunday of March and October at the
Bürgerhaus Bergische Löwe. This is one of the
largest markets in the area. Only authentic old
items can be sold here—no new items or
reproductions. Likewise, true junk of small or no
value is banned from this show. The building is
full of steps and different levels. Potential buyers
must pay a small admission charge. Street
parking is usually available in the vicinity.
Access by public transit from Köln on the train
to the Bahnhof and walk. Organized by
Komischke & Lange, Heiderweg 53, 4000
Düsseldorf 31, telephone (0203) 7 43 01.

Antik- und Trödelmarkt (antique and flea
market) fourth Saturday and Sunday of
October throughout the pedestrian zone in the
city center. This is part of the city's annual
Stadtfest. Access by public transit on the train
from Kö to the Bahnhof and walk. Information
from Richard Altmann, Mediascher Gasse 13,
5276 Siel 3, telephone (02262) 18 66, or from
Norbert Junge, Talbahnstrasse 4, 5190 Stolberg,
telephone (02402) 2 30 07.

Antikmarkt (antique market) on the second
weekend of November throughout the center of
the town, centered on the Bügerzentrum. Access
by public transit on the train to the Bahnhof and
walk. A puppet and antique toy market also
takes place on this weekend in the same vicinity.
Information from Alida Schleusener, Waldfriedstrasse 1, 5000 Köln 60, telephone (0221) 72
34 14.

Berlin 1000

This lively island of capitalism in a Socialist
sea has several markets, including one that is in
old subway cars in a former subway station.
There are not flea markets or antique markets in
East Berlin. A few antique stores do exist in East
Berlin, but export of antiques from East
Germany (including East Berlin) is almost
impossible.

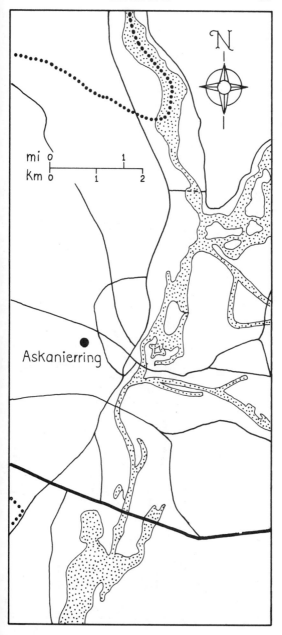

Askanierring

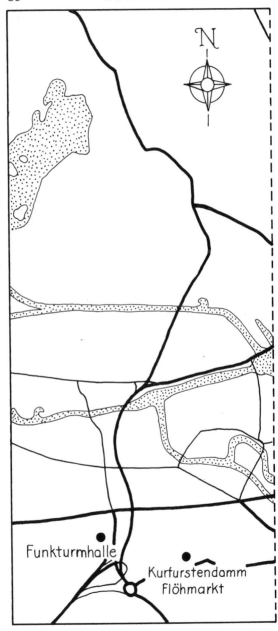

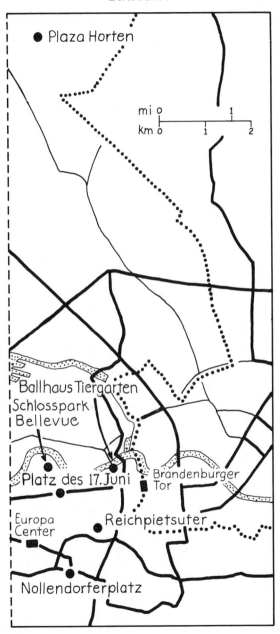

● Plaza Horten

mi 0   1
km 0   1   2

Ballhaus Tiergarten
Schlosspark
Bellevue

Platz des 17. Juni

Brandenburger
Tor

Europa
Center

Reichpietsufer

Nollendorferplatz

The market locations in parenthesis are found on the map.

Flohmarkt (flea market) (Strasse des 17. Juni, and Reichpietsufer) every Saturday and Sunday, year round at the Platz am 17. Juni and the nearby Krempelmarkt on the Reichspeitsufer. Access by public transit on U-bahn Nollendorferplatz and walk south to the canal. The market is on the north bank. Information from M. Wewerka, Kaminastrasse 9, 1000 Berlin 10, telephone (030) 3 44 99 09.

Flohmarkt (flea market) (Plaza Horten) every Sunday year round at the Plaza Horten on Senftenberg Ring in the northern Märkishes Viertel district. Access by public transit on the S-Bahn to Göschenplatz-Wittenau, then walk east along Wilhelmaruher Damm (to the east) to Senftenberg Ring (on your left). Information from Brigitte Vodrazka, Burgfrauenstrasse 28, 1000 Berlin 28, telephone (030) 4 04 30 72.

Trödelmarkt (junk market) (Askanierring) every Saturday and Sunday at the Askanier-ring in the Berlin-Spandau district. Access by public transit on U-bahn line 7 to the end. Follow Munsingerstrasse to the station's north, which turns into Askanierring after one block. Organized by Agentur Thurmann, telephone (030) 3 36 37 50.

Flohmarkt (flea market) (Nollendorferplatz) almost every day in the former Nollendorferplatz U-bahn (subway) station. The shops are actually in old subway cars. Dozens of vendors sell all types of junk and minor antiques, including old clothes, bric-a-brac, and clocks. Access by public transit on the S-bahn to the Zoologischer Garten station, then walk along the south side of the Europa-Center, continue on Tauentzein-strasse, for about 600 meters. (The street name will change to Kleiststrasse.)

Flohmarkt (flea market) (Kurfürstendamm Flohmarkt) Wednesday through Friday from 3 p. m. to 10 p. m. and Saturday and Sunday from noon to 10 p.m. year round at the

Kurfürstendamm Karree on Kurfürstendamm between Uhlandstrasse and Knesebeckstrasse. This permanent market has about 40 dealers, including specialists in old clothes, clocks, stamps, postcards, and dozens of old record players and thousands of old 78 records. Information from Ku-Damm-Karree GmbH & Co., Kurfürstendamm 206-208, 1000 Berlin, telephone (030) 8 81 41 71.

Foto, Hi-Fi, und Tecknik Markt (photography, hi-fi, and technical equipment market) (Ballhaus Tiergarten) first Sunday and fourth Thursday of every month at the Ballhaus Tiergarten (in the zoo, district 21). Organized by Kreutzbergmarkt, 1000 Berlin, telephone (030) 7 86 10 09.

Sammler- und Münzbörse (coin collector's exchange) (Funkturmhalle) third weekend of October at the Funkturmhalle 146 (television tower center). Organized by ICC, Konrad Schuster, Nassauischestrasse 32, 1000 Berlin 31, telephone (030) 8 61 34 23.

Antikmarkt (antique market) about April 10 through 15 at the Logenhaus, and in the fall from November 5 through 11. This is a major antiques fair with dealers selling quality items at prices to match. Organized by EXPO Management GmbH, Eichenweg 59, 2300 Kiel 17, telephone (0431) 32 46 60 or 80 44 10.

Berliner Antikmesse (Berlin antique fair) (Schlosspark Bellevue) the first two weeks of December at the Schlosspark Bellevue (Bellevue Exhibition Hall). This is one of the major antique shows in Europe, drawing several hundred dealers from Germany and a few other countries. Only dealers may sell; only true antiques may be sold. Access by public transit on the S-Bahn to the Tiergarten stop, then walk along the riverbank road about two hundred meters. Organized by the Freier Verband Berlines Antiquitätenhändler e. V., Kurfürstendamm 85, 1000 Berlin 15, telephone (030) 7 81 76 44.

Bermatingen 7775

Antik- und Trödelmarkt (antique and junk market) second weekend of October in the Festhalle. Organized by Antik Horst Keller, Bahnhofstrasse 9a, 7778 Marktdorf, telephone (07544) 28 78.

Bernkastel-Kues 5550

(Please also see Krov and Zeltingen.)

Antik-Expo (antique exposition), a five-day sale in mid-February and one around the first weekend in April at the Logenhaus. Organized by EXPO Management GmbH, Eichenweg 59, 2300 Kiel 17, telephone (0431) 32 46 60.

Betzdorf 5240

Antik und Trödelmarkt (antique and junk market) first Saturday of every month in the Stadthalle. This show has normal flea market items. Information from the Rathaus (city hall), Betzdorf 5240, telephone (0271) 4 61 69.

Trödelmarkt (junk market) first Sunday of October at the minimal-markt. Organized by Kogel & Lauber, Kornmarkt 10-12, 6900 Siegen, telephone (0271) 5 15 01.

Flohmarkt (flea market) third Saturday of October in the Innenstadt (inner town). Information from Dieter Endress, Sonnenhang 6, 5242 Kirchen, telephone (02791) 6 16 11.

Biberach 7950

Antikmarkt (antique market) first weekend of November at the Stadthalle. Organized by Mezger Organization Märkte-messen, Zeppelinstrasse 4, 7210 Donaueschingen, telephone 0771) 1 39 99.

Bielefeld 4800

(Please also see Bad Salzuflen, Gütersloh, and Schloss Holte.)

The city-run antique and flea markets are held all over this Ruhr valley city, especially from May through October. While the days are constant, the places change from week to week and month to month. At these city-run markets, merchants are prohibited: only private parties may sell. The best way to find out the location is to contact the Ordnungsamt der Stadt Bielefeld, Kavallierenstrasse 26, 4800 Bielefeld, telephone (0521) 5 15 22 23.

In addition, there are private markets, which admit dealers as well as private sellers.

Flohmarkt (flea market), second weekend of most months but occasionally the third or fourth weekend in the Johannisberg district at the Redrennbahn (race track) at the Festplatz; in the winter, it is sometimes held in the Festhalle Asemissen at the same site. Organized by A.M.V.V. Jörn Werber, Am Grossen Holz 9, 4817 Leopoldshöhe, telephone (05208) 14 23.

Antik- Trödel- und Handwerkermarkt (antique, junk, and artisans' market) last Sunday in June at the WISA-Gelände Messeplatz (WISA fairgrounds). Organized by A.M.V.V. Jörn Werber, Am Grossen Holz 9, 4817 Leopoldshöhe, telephone (05208) 14 23.

Flohmarkt (flea market) third Saturday of the month from May through October at the Klosterplatz in the Stadtmitte/Altstadt (city center). Organized by the Stadt Bielefeld.

Trödelmarkt (junk market) first Saturday of the month: locations vary, for example in May at Reichowplatz in the Sennestadt district, June on Treppenstrasse in the Brackweide district, in July at the Schulhof Tiplatz in the Heepen district, and so on. Organized by the Stadt Bielefeld; check for exact location of the month's market.

Antik-und Trödelmarkt (antique and junk market) third weekend in April, and August, second weekend in July, and last weekend of October, at the Gleisdrieck Festplatz/Schweinmarkt in the Brackwede district. Organized by A.M.V.V. Jörn Werber, Am Grossen Holz 9, 4817 Leopoldshöhe, telephone (05208) 14 23.

Trödelmarkt (junk market) third Sunday of the month at the Parkplatz Dixi Discount. Organized by Galerie G. Krencky, Heidestrasse 9a, 4900 Herford, telephone (05221) 5 67 41.

Puppen- und Spielzeugmarkt (puppet and toy market) first Wednesday through Friday of October and November, beginning at 2 p.m. at "Am Kesselbrink." This market sometimes changes dates shortly before the market dates: check exact dates first. This market only offers toys and puppets, some of which are antiques. Information from Karin Schimanzik, Puppenund Spielzeugbörse, Werner-Bock Strasse 3, 4800 Bielefeld 1, telephone (0521) 6 06 88.

Bietigheim-Bissingen 7120

Antik- und Trödelmarkt (antique and junk market) first Sunday of October at the Kunsteisbahn. Organized by Dieter Krauss, Pfarrweg 32, 7064 Remshaden, telephone (07181) 47 08

Flohmarkt (flea market) second Sunday of October at the Grosso- markt in the Bissingen district. Organized by Agentur Hoffman und Stapf, Talstrasse 134, 7024 Filderstadt, telephone (0711) 70 68 28.

Bleiskastel 6653

Flohmarkt (flea market) fourth Saturday of October at the town center. Organized by Heinz F. Braun, Rohrbacherstrasse 11, 6683 Speisen, telephone (06821) 7 76 82.

Blaubeuren 7902

Antik- und Trödelmarkt (antique fair and junk market) last Sunday of October in the Stadthalle (city auditorium). Organized by Dieter Krauss, Pfarrweg 32, 7064 Remshalden, telephone (07181) 47 08.

Böblingen 7030

(Please also see Gerlingen, Sinfeldingen, and Stuttgart.)

Flohmarkt (flea market) first Saturday of October at the Oberer See. Organized by Veranstaltungen Gertrun Birkenbach, Blücherstrasse 11, 7031 Gärtringen, telephone (0734) 2 16 43.

Antik- und Trödelmarkt (antique and junk market) the first Sunday in February, June, and October, Palm Sunday in March, and Advent Sunday in December at the Sporthalle. Information from Media Messegesellschaft mbH & Co. Ausstellungs KG, Bahnhofstrasse 1, 7030 Böblingen, telephone (07031) 6 40 40.

Trödelmarkt (junk market) first weekend in June at the Marktplatz in the town center. This event is part of the annual Jahrmarkt festival. Information from Herr Henne, Presseamt (Press and Information Office), Rathaus, 7030 Böblingen, telephone (07031) 66 92 35.

Bocholt 4920

Antiquitätenmarkt (antique market) first Saturday of October in the Parkhaus (city parking garage) near the center of town. Information from Franz Stefan, Mittelstrasse 5, 5820 Gevelsberg, telephone (02332) 21 87.

Bochum 4630

(Please also see Essen, Gelsenkirchen, Hattingen, and Witten.)

Trödelmarkt (junk market) Monday through Saturday year round at the Hannibal Selbst Bedienung Möbel store. This is an indoor market of full-time dealers' shops and stalls. Information from Veranstaltungen Beck, Postfach 266, 4630 Bochum, telephone (0234) 53 41 19.

Trödelmarkt (junk market) first and third Sunday year round in the suburb of Bochum-Wattenscheid at the Stadhalle, also called the Agros after the Agora (city square) in ancient Greece. Information from L. Rau, Luitpoldstrasse 38, 4650 Gelsenkirchen, telephone (0209) 20 49 46.

Theater-Flohmarkt (flea market emphasizing theatrical items and props) third Saturday of every month in the central city Rathaus (city hall). All kind of items show up at this market, since many private sellers try to sell all kind of things. Street parking is virtually impossible, but there is an underground parking garage. Information from Amt für Verkehrs- und Wirtschaft, Stadt Bochum, Hans-Böcklserstrasse 19, 4630 Bochum, telephone (0234) 1 30 31 or 3 70 61.

Flohmarkt (flea market) third Sunday and Monday of May (Pfingst) and first Saturday of October at the Ruhrpark Einkaufzentrum (shopping center). Organized by Hermann & Lampert, Hasselholzerweg 9, 5100 Aachen, telephone (0241) 7 20 21.

Musikbörse (music and old record exchange and sale) middle of October at the Ruhrlandhalle. Organized by Norbert Junge, Obersteinstrasse 51, 5190 Stolberg, telephone (02402) 2 30 07. Other shows including paper and coin shows also take place in this hall during the year.

Musik- und Plattenbörse (music and record exchange) first Sunday of November on Prinz-Regentstrasse. Only music-related items are offered. Organized by Kogel & Lauber, Kornmarkt 10-12, 6900 Seigen, telephone (0271) 5 15 01.

Bonn 5300

(Please also see Bornheim, Bad Godesberg,and Saint Augustin.)

Antik- und Trödelmarkt (antique and junk market) last Sunday of every month and first Monday in April at the Einkaufzentrum Passage und Freigelände (shopping center and open space) in the suburb of Bonn-Tannenbusch. There's a selection of just about everything; finds can be made at this market if you look carefully. A large amount of furniture is on sale here, (unlike many flea markets), much dating from the turn of the century. The market takes place in a number of areas: the large inside passage (which is heated in winter), the inner courtyard, the parking lot, and just about anywhere else that place can be found. Organized by Hermann & Lampert, Hasselholzerweg 9, 5100 Aachen, telephone (0241) 7 20 21.

Antik- und Trödelmarkt (antique and junk market) third Saturday and Sunday of April and October at Wessel Werke, near the Autobahn-Verteilerkreises on the outskirts of the city. This large covered hall welcomes both dealers and private sellers, and has a special section for artisans. Though a relatively new market, it draws several hundred sellers. This hall is difficult to reach by public transit, but easy by car. Organized by Hermann & Lampert, Hasselholzerweg 9, 5100 Aachen, telephone (0241) 7 20 21.

Trödelmarkt (junk market) first Friday of the month at the Ellerbahnhof. Information from Franz Stefan, Mittelstrasse 5, 4820 Gevelsberg, telephone (02332) 21 87.

Musikbörse (music exchange) second Sunday of October at the Zentralmensa in the university district. Only music-related items, including instruments and sheet music, are offered. Information from Kogel & Lauber, Kornmarkt 10-12, 6900 Siegen, telephone (0271) 5 15 01.

Trödelmarkt (junk market) first Saturday of October at the Gelände am Herrendingert in the Bonn/Alfter district. A general junk market. Organized by L. Rau, Luitpoldstrasse 38, 4650 Gelsenkirchen, telephone (0209) 20 49 46.

Trödelmarkt (junk market) first Sunday of October at the Rathaus in the Alfter district. Organized by Junge & Schönenbrücher, Talbahnstrasse 4, 5190 Stolberg, telephone (02402) 8 27 67.

Antikmarkt (antique market) third Sunday in March and October and fourth Sunday in May at the Beethovenhalle. Organized by Theodore Wessling, Kurhausstrasse 31a, 4690 Herne 2, telephone (02325) 4 30 31.

Bornheim 5303

(Please also see Bonn, Bad Godesberg, and Saint Augustin.)

Trödelmarkt junk market) first Monday of October at the Rheinhalle. Organized by Christa Schelkowski, Hedwigstrasse 17, 5600 Wuppertal, telephone (0202) 30 08 48.

Borken 4280

Trödelmarkt (junk market) first Saturday of every month at the Co-op on Otto-Hahn-Strasse. Organized by Galerie G. Krencky, Heidestrasse 9a, 4900 Herford, telephone (04221) 5 67 41.

Floh- und Antiquitätenmarkt (flea and antique market) first Sunday of every month at the Edeka-Markt Wirtz. Organized by Friedhelm

Knoth, Stettinerstrasse 4, 3478 Zieghain-Schalmstadt, telephone (06691) 63 06.

Antikmarkt (antique market) first Sunday of February and September and last Sunday in April at the Stadthalle. Organized by Theodore Wessling, Kurhausstrasse 31a, 4690 Herne 2, telephone (02325) 4 30 31.

Bornheim 5303

Trödelmarkt (junk market) second Saturday of October on the Rathausplatz (city hall square). Organized by Hermann & Lampert, Hasselholzerweg 9, 5100 Aachen, telephone (0241) 7 20 21.

Bösenell 4403

Trödelmarkt (junk market) every Saturday year round at the Möbel Tacke (furniture center). Organized by L. Rau, Luitpoldstrasse 38, 4650 Gelsenkirchen, telephone (0209) 20 49 46.

Bramsche 4550

Trödelmarkt (junk market) first Saturday in September and October in the Innenstadt as part of the Erntedankfest (thanksgiving festival). Organized by A.M.V.V. Jörn Werber, Am Grossen Holz 9, 4817 Leopoldshöhe, telephone (05208) 14 23.

Trödelmarkt (junk market) third Saturday of October at the Parkplatz Einkaufzentrum (central city shopping garage). Information from Galerie G. Krencky, Heidestrasse 9a, 4900 Herford, telephone (05221) 5 67 41.

Braunschweig 3300

Trödelmarkt (junk market) every Saturday and Sunday at Am Schützenplatz 1. This is one of the larger markets in Germany, because it has been long-established and is the only one in the area. You'll find general flea market material, including minor porcelains, coins and medals, glassware, and a few pieces of furniture. Information from Sportzentrum Schützenplatz GmbH KG, Am Schützenplatz 1, 3300 Braunschweig, telephone (0531) 32 24 44.

Antikmarkt (antique market) first weekend of October in the Stadthalle. Only antiques may be sold. Organized by Avorga GmbH, Husarenstrasse 22, 3300 Braunschweig, telephone (0531) 33 14 15.

Bremen 2800

(Please also see Delmenhorst.)

Flohmarkt (flea market) every Sunday morning at the Bürgenwiede in the city center. Organized by Agentur Winkler, 2800 Bremen, telephone (04202) 8 11 62.

Antikmarkt (antique market) last Sunday of the every month at the Roland Zentrum. Information from Agentur Beinhorn, Husarenstrasse 22, 3300 Braunschweig, telephone (0531) 34 61 61.

Bremerhaven 2850

Musikmarkt (music market) second Sunday of October at the Stadhalle between Stresemannstrasse and Werftstrasse, 600 meters north of the city center. Only musically related items may be sold. Parking is available at the site. Organized by Galerie G. Krencky, Heidestrasse 9a, 4900 Hereford, telephone (05221) 5 67 41.

Brüggen 4057

(Please also see Mönchengladbach.)

Antiquitäten Fest (antiques fair) first weekend in October all over the town center. Information from the Stadt (city) Brüggen, Rathaus, 4057 Brüggen, telephone (02162) 2 22 73.

The same weekend, a private art market is held at Klosterstrasse 33, organized by Verkehrsverein Lebendiges Brüggen, at the same address, telephone (05910) 2 35 66.

Antikmarkt (antique market) third weekend of October in the town center. Information from Brass-Villegas, Gladbacherstrasse 32, 4060 Viersen 1, telephone (02162) 3 118 18.

Brühl 5040

(Please also see Hürth and Köln.)

Trödelmarkt (junk market) first Saturday (sometimes first Friday also) of each month at the Bleiche. Information from Georg Berens, Königstrasse 26, telephone (02232) 4 29 51. Occasionally other organizers have markets at this location.

Buchholz 2110

Antikmarkt (antique market) last Sunday of October at the Schützenhalle, organized by Inter-Antik, Michael Becker, Mommsenstrasse 10, 4006 Eckrath, telephone (02104) 41 61 52.

Büdelsdorf 2370

Flohmarkt (flea market) second Sunday of October and November in the village center. This is a small market. Information from P.A.M. Veranstaltungen, E. Köhler, Bornbrok 1-3, 2330 Eckernförde, telephone (04351) 29 80.

Burgau 8872

Flohmarkt (flea market) first Sunday of every month at the Volksfestplatz. Information from Messebüro Garon, Federmannweg 3, 7900 Ulm, telephone (0731) 3 05 74.

Castrup-Rauxel (Schwerin) 4620

(Please also see Bochum, Dortmund, and Herne.)

Trödelmarkt (junk market) every Wednesday and Saturday year round near the intersection of Megenderstrasse and Dortmundstrasse. Information from Bartels, Dortmund, telephone (0231) 67 02 87.

Antik- und Kunstmarkt (antique and artwork market) last weekend of October at the Europa-Halle. Organized by L. Rau, Luitpoldstrasse 38, 4650 Gelsenkirchen, telephone (0209) 20 49 46.

Trödelmarkt (junk market) first and weekend of October at the entrance to the Graf Schwerin mine. This weekend market has normal flea market items. Organized by Wolfgang Bartels, Osultweg 34, 4100 Dortmund 70, telephone (0231) 67 01 87.

Celle 3100

Trödelmarkt (junk market) first Sunday of every month year round at the Blau-Gelb Gelände. Organized by Veranstaltungsbüro A. Braun,

Amselweg 48, 2061 Bargfeld-Stegen, telephone (04532) 2 19 27.

Kunst- und Antiquitätentage (art and antique fair) first weekend in October at the Städtische Union. Information from Avorga GmbH, Husarenstrasse 22, 3300 Braunschweig, telephone (0531) 33 14 15.

Spielzeugbörse (toy exchange) first Saturday of November at the Stadliche Union-Restaurant. Organized by Klaus Graeber, Hohenstein 73, 5600 Wuppertal 1, telephone (0202) 55 05 89.

Cloppenburg 4590

Trödelmarkt (junk market) second Saturday of every month at the Münsterlandhalle. Organized by the Ordnungsamt der Stadt Cloppenburg, Rathaus, 4590 Cloppenburg, telephone (04471) 1 85 15.

Cochem 5590

Flohmarkt (flea market) second weekend of November in the center of town. Information from Rolf à Brassard, Rheinstrasse 4, 5434 Dernbach, telephone (02602) 7 08 38.

Coesfeld 4420

Antikmarkt (antique market) first or third Sunday of October in the Stadthalle. Information from Dieter Strauss, Wittumhof 4, 7140 Ludwigsburg, telephone (02332) 21 87, or Franz Stegan, An der Mühle 32, 4052 Korschenbroich 4, telephone (02166) 8 35 09.

Cologne

(Please see Köln.)

Crailsheim 7180

Trödelmarkt (junk market) second Saturday of October at the Grosso-Markt. Organized by Agentur Zelinka, Gmündstrasse 18, 7070 Schwäbisch Gmünd, telephone (07171) 8 52 32.

Antiquitäten- und Flohmarkt (antique and flea market) last weekend of October at Rossfeld in the Freimarktgelünde. Organized by CFM Verwaltungsgelellschaft MBH, Postfach 324, 7180 Crailsheim, telephone (07951) 2 10 12.

Darmstadt 6100

Antikmarkt (antique market) last weekend of October or first weekend of November at the Orangerie Garten south of the city center. Only true antiques may be sold here; reproductions and new items are strictly forbidden. Access by public transit on the Heidelgergererstrasse tram to Rudesheimerstrasse. Street parking is available in the vicinity. Information from Falk Anders, An der Martinspforte, 6719 Einselthum, telephone (06355) 22 94.

Deggendorf 8360

Antikmarkt (antique market) third Saturday of October at the Kolpinghaus. Organized by Werbe-Management F. Stock, Am Mühlring 7, 8202 Bad Aibling, telephone (09659) 7 01.

Deidesheim 6705

Antikmarkt (antique market) third Tuesday of October at the Stadthalle. Information from Manfred Kiefer, Leistader Strasse 7, 6701 Kallstadt, telephone (06322) 59 65. Other antique markets and collectors' exchanges are held at other times of the year in the Stadthalle.

Delmenhorst 2870

(Please also see Bremen.)

Antik- und Trödelmarkt (antique and junk market) first weekend of November at the Delmehalle. Information from Halina Müller GmbH, Kölnerstrasse 246, 4000 Düsseldorf 1, telephone (0211) 78 25 56.

Diesenhofen 8024

(Please also see München.)

Antikmarkt (antique market) third weekend of October at the Kugler-Alm. Organized by Alexander Dohn, Linprunstrassse 57, 8000 München 2, telephone (089) 18 75 55.

Diez/Lahn 6252

Flohmarkt (flea market) second Saturday and Sunday of October at the Toom-Markt or Eissporthalle (alternates year by year). Information from Rolf à Brassard, Rheinstrasse 4, 5434 Dernbach, telephone (02602) 7 08 39.

Dillenburg 6340

Antikmarkt (antique market) third Sunday of October at the Stadthalle. Organized by Norbert Junge, Talbahnstrasse 4, 5190 Stolberg, telephone (02402) 2 30 07.

Dillingen an der Donan 8880

Trödelmarkt (junk market) third Saturday of October at Am Kasernenplatz. Organized by Agentur Zelinka, Gmündstrasse 18, 7070 Schwäbisch Gmünd, telephone (07171) 8 52 32.

Dingolfing 8312

Trödelmarkt (junk market) first Saturday every month at the Stadion Stubn on Kerschensteinerstrasse. Organized by Hannelore Protz, telephone (08731) 14 90.

Dinslaken 4220

Antikmarkt (antique market) first Sunday of October at the Stadthalle. Information from Theodor Wessling, Kurhausstrasse 31a, 4690 Herne 2, telephone (02325) 4 30 31.

Antik- und Trödelmarkt (antique and junk market) third Sunday of October at the Hertie Parkplatz. Organized by Halina Müller GmbH, Kölnerstrasse 246, 4000 Düsseldorf 1, telephone (0211) 78 25 56.

Ditzingen 7257

(Please also see Rudesheim.)

Antik- und Trödelmarkt (antique and junk market) second or third Sunday of October at the Stadthalle. Organized by H. & H. K. Fischer, Uhlandstrasse 18, 7255 Rudesheim, telephone (07152) 5 43 77.

Dormagen 4047

Trödelmarkt (junk market) second Sunday in October at the Top-Markt building. Organized by Norbert Junge, Obersteinstrasse 51, 5190 Stolberg, telephone (02402) 2 30 07.

Antiquitätenmarkt (antique market) third weekend of October at the Bürgerhaus in the suburb of Dormagen-Zons. Organized by Brass-Villegas, Gladbacher Strasse 32, 4060 Viersen 1, telephone (021623) 2 22 73.

Dorsten 4270

(Please also see Gladbeck, Gelsenkirchen, and Marl.)

Trödelmarkt (junk market) second Sunday of October at the IKEA Parkplatz. Information from Marlies Scory, Schürenkampstrasse 23, 4390 Gladbeck, telephone (02043) 6 58 91.

Antik- und Trödelmarkt (antique and junk market) first Sunday of every month at the Lippetor Einkaufzentrum. Sometimes this market offers handicrafts, new paintings, and sculpture. Organized by Erich Radke, telephone (0209) 27 03 98.

Dortmund 4600

(Please also see Castrop-Rauxel, Schwerte, and Witten.)

Trödel- und Drammarkt (junk market) every Wednesday, Friday, and Saturday at 315-317 Bornstrasse. The same company also organizes the nearby market at the CEAG-Halle at Eberstrasse 11 on the same days. Organized by Walter Höning, H. von Kleist Strasse 9, 4714 Belm, telephone (02592) 2 01 41.

Trödelmarkt (junk market) every Saturday and Sunday at the Möbel Tacke building on Wittekindstrasse. Information from L. Rau, Luitpoldstrasse 38, 4650 Gelsenkirchen, telephone (0209) 20 49 46.

Trödelmarkt (junk market) first Saturday and Sunday of each month at the Westfalenhalle (Westfalia Hall). Sunday is the more interesting and better attended day. Organized by Allmedia-Klaus Goik, Wannestrasse 180, 4060 Dortmund 30, telephone (0231) 10 52 82. Information is also available from city press office, Presseamt der Stadt Dortmund, Postfach 907, 4600 Dortmund 1, telephone (0231) 54 22 21 30.

West-Antique (Westfalia antique show) second Thursday through following Sunday of November in the Westfalenhalle. This is one of the major fall antique shows. No reproductions or new items may be offered. Organized by Westfalenhalle GmbH, Rheinlanddamm 200, 4600 Dortmund 1, telephone (0231) 1 20 43 55.

Trödelmarkt (junk market) third Saturday of October at the Revierpark Wischlingen in the Wischlingen district. Information from Revierpark Wischlingen GmbH, Höfkerstrasse 12, 4600 Dortmund 1, telephone (0231) 17 19 91.

Trödelmarkt (junk market) second Sunday of the month at the Verkauf-Center. Organized by Hermann & Lampert, Hasselholzerweg 9, 5100 Aachen, telephone (0241) 7 20 21.

Mineralenbörse (mineral exchange) last Sunday of October at the Mehrzweckhalle in the Westfalenpark. Organized by Brigitte Püschel, Meisenstrasse 40, 4370 Marl, telephone (02365) 22 41 13. Information also available from Presseamt der Stadt Dortmund, Postfach 907, 4600 Dortmund 1, telephone (0231) 54 22 21 30.

Handwerkermarkt (artisans' market) first Sunday of May at the Alten Markt (old market place) right in the city center. This market is part of the Dortmunder Malermarkt (May festival). Access by public transit on any tram passing through Kampstrasse or Kleppeningstrasse. Parking during the festival is difficult, though there are parking garages under Hansaplatz and on Betenstrasse and Prinzenstrasse. Information from Herr Steinbeck, Presse- und Informationsamt der Stadt Dortmund, Postfach 907, 4600 Dortmund 1, telephone (0231) 54 22 21 30.

Comic-Tauschtag (comic day) second Sunday of October at the Gasthof Heimoth. Organized by Peter Köhler, Berghoferstrasse 149, 4600 Dortmund, telephone (0231) 77 32 58.

Sammlerbörse (collector's exchange) second Sunday of November at the Brauerei-Museum.

This exchange takes place in the old brewery museum; this bias is reflected in the items offered. Information from telephone (0231) 2 48 50.

Duisburg 4100

(Please also see Essen, Hamborn, Krefeld, Moers, Mühlheim, and Oberhausen.)

Duisburg is another of the Ruhr Valley industrial towns, rich in mid-to-late 19th-century and 20th-century items of all types.

Flohmarkt (flea market) every Wednesday through Sunday of the month at the Hamborner Markthalle in the Hamborn district. This is a regular business with several dozen dealers offering furniture, porcelain, glass, and early 20th-century items. The rest of the dealers change regularly. Information from Schneider und Partner & Co. KG, Hufstrasse 50, 4100 Duisburg 11, telephone (0203) 8 90 86.

Trödelmarkt (junk market) third Saturday of the month at the Marktplatz in the Bruckhausen district. Information from Schneider und Partner & Co. KG, Hufstrasse 50, 4100 Duisburg 11, telephone (0203) 8 90 86.

Trödelmarkt (junk market) fourth Sunday of April, third Sunday of July, and last Thursday of May at the Burgplatz and third Saturday of October on Königstrasse. This market is limited to used items and artisans' products; forbidden items include new or mass-produced products, guns and military items, and Nazi mementos. These are major markets, well attended in the area. Organized by Duisburger Werbe- und Touristik GmbH, Rathaus, 4100 Duisburg 1, telephone (0203) 2 83 21 89.

Floh- und Trödelmarkt (flea and junk market) second Sunday of November at the Rhein-Ruhr-Halle. Information from Duisburger Werbe- und Touristik GmbH, Rathaus, 4100 Duisburg 1, telephone (0203) 2 83 21 89.

Trödelmarkt (junk market), the second Sunday of the month at the Spicherplatz in the suburb of Duisburg-Mederich. Information from Schneider, Bahnhofstrasse 187, 4100 Duisburg 12, telephone (0203) 55 08 08.

Antikspielzeug und Phonomarkt (antique toy and phonograph market) third Saturday of October at the Mercatorhalle. Organized by Heesen & Kirchner, Goethestrasse 19, 4130 Moers, telephone (02845) 2 18 65.

Trödelmarkt (junk market) last weekend of every month and second weekend of August at the Wedau-Stadion in the Duisburg-Medan district. Information from Duisburger Werbe und Touristik GmbH, Rathaus, 4100 Duisburg, telephone (0203) 2 83 44 44.

Handwerkermarkt (handicraft workers' market) third Sunday of September on Hochheider Ladenstrasse. Only items made by the vendors may be offered for sale. Information from Duisburger Werbe- und Touristik GmbH, Rathaus, 4100 Duisburg 1, telephone (0203) 2 83 21 89.

Dülmen 4408

(Please also see Ludinghausen.)

Antikmarkt (antique market) first Sunday of November in the Dolpinghaus. Information from Galerie G. Krencky, Heidestrasse 9a, 4900 Herford, telephone (05221) 5 67 41.

Düren 5160

Trödelmarkt (junk market) irregularly held on Sunday mornings either at the Annakirmesplatz, Allkauf, or the Stadthalle. Information from Hermann & Lampert, Hasselholzerweg 9, 5100 Aachen, (0241) 7 20 21. Occasionally other organizers have markets at these locations, including Theodor Wessling,

Kurhaus 31a, 4690 Herne 2, telephone (02325) 4 30 31.

Düsseldorf 4000

(Please also see Neuss.)

This city is the largest in the Ruhr industrial area. While often thought of as grimy and depressing, it is in reality refreshing, visited by many business travelers but few tourists. It is particularly rich in 19th- and early 20th-century items.

The locations in parentheses are found on the map.

Antik- und Trödelmarkt (antique and junk market) (Uhlenbergstrasse) every Saturday year round from just after dawn until 2:30 p. m. (6:30 p. m. during Advent) at the fairgrounds on Uhlenbergstrasse in the Ulmerberg district. This is south of the Südring near the Düsseldorf-Neuss bridge. This is probably the largest market in Düsseldorf, luring thousands of potential buyers and hundreds of sellers. Lots of antiques and junk hide occasional gems and true finds. Access by public transit on tram 17 to Aachenerplatz, then walk east. Organized by Agentur Artur Gerke, Am Krummen Weg 7, 4000 Düsseldorf 11, telephone (0211) 59 39 36.

Flohmarkt (flea market) (Radschlägemarkt) every Saturday and the second Sunday of from May through October in the at Radschlägemarkt in the Innenstadt (city center) near the main Bahnhof. This market is reserved for private sellers only; antique dealers and vendors of mass-produced articles are strictly forbidden to set up shop, though many antique dealers find this market a good source of collectables. Organized by the Ordnungsamt der Stadt Düsseldorf, 4000 Düsseldorf, telephone (0211) 35 05 05.

Trödelmarkt (junk market) (Kartäuserstrasse) first Sunday of the month from May through December on Kartäuserstrasse in the Düs-

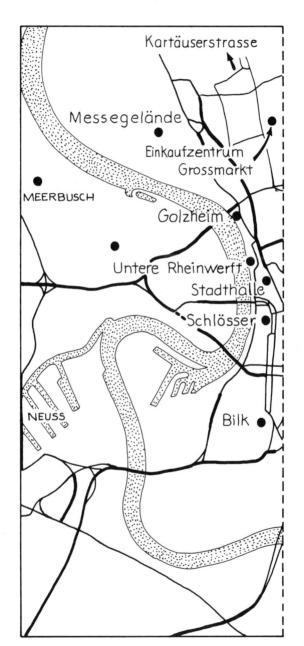

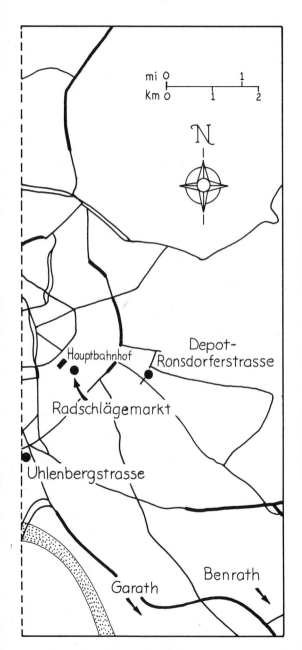

seldorf-Nord district. The market takes place in a field where about two hundred sellers offer everything from used clothes to junk, a few antiques, and other interesting items. Access by public transit on tram line 7 to Micklenburgerstrasse and then walk north on Kartauserstrasse to the market. Organized by Marktbüro S. J. Schmidt, Kartünserstrasse 25, 4000 Düsseldorf 30, telephone (0241) 41 11 77 or (0241) 42 30 48.

Trödelmarkt (junk market) (Einkaufzentrum Grossmarkt) third Saturday of every month at the Einkaufzentrum Grossmarkt on Ulmenstrasse in the Düsseldorf-Nord district, across the street from the Nordfriedhof cemetery. This market takes place near the Düsseldorf wholesale market district. Access by pubic transit on tram lines 2 and 7. Organized by Norbert Junge, Obersteinstrasse 51, 5190 Stolberg, telephone (02402) 2 30 07.

Puppen- und Spielzeugbörse (doll, puppet and toy exchange) (Schlösser) third Saturday of every month at the Schlössersaal in the Altstadt (city center). Parking is often difficult to find here; even the nearby parking garages are often full. Information from Nico Schweers, Gut Hommerich, 4030 Ratlingen 8, telephone (02102) 8 09 08. Other organizers use this hall on other weekends, mainly but not exclusively for toy markets.

Trödelmarkt (junk market) (Bilk) fourth Sunday of the month at the parking structure of the Möbel-Schaffrath in the suburb of Düsseldorf-Bilk, near the Bahnhof-Düsseldorf-Bilk. Access by public transit on tram lines 1, 4, and 17 to the Bilk Bahnhof, or by train. Information from Hermann & Lampert, Hasselholzerweg 9, 5100 Aachen, telephone (0241) 7 20 21.

Antikmarkt (antique market) one weekend every month or two at the Phillipshalle. This market is one of the largest and most worthwhile in Germany. Each one is a major event in the German antique trade calendar. About 200·

dealers offer the highest quality items (a good quantity of furniture, and too much more to describe). Organized by Komischke & Lange, Heiderweg 53, 4000 Düsseldorf 31, telephone (0203) 7 43 01.

Trödelmarkt (junk market) (Garath) second Sunday of March in the Fussgängerzone (pedestrian zone) of the S-Bahnhof in the southern suburb of Düsseldorf-Garath. Organized by Van Zütphen Direktmarketing, Frickestrasse 36, 5010 Bergheim, telephone (02271) 5 44 00.

Antik- und Trödelmarkt (antique and junk market) (Heerdt) first weekend in October at the Antik- und Trödelmarkt Heerdt. This is in the sales hall of this antique dealer. Organized by Komischke & Lange, Heiderweg 53, 4000 Düsseldorf 31, telephone (0203) 7 43 01.

Trödelmarkt (junk market) (Untere Rhein-werft) second Saturday and fourth Sunday of October at the Untere Rheinwerft and Rhein-terrassen (along the banks of the Rhine river) in the city center. Organized by Untere Rheinwerft, 4000 Düsseldorf, telephone (0211) 8 99 38 27.

Trödelmarkt (junk market) (Benrath) second weekend of October at the Schützenplatz in the Benrath district. Organized by Christel Diener, Erklerenzstrasse 73, 5138 Heinzburg-Dremmen, telephone (02452) 6 24 01.

Trödelmarkt (junk market) (Benrath) third Saturday of October at the Flora-Gartencenter in the southern suburb of Düsseldorf-Benrath. Access by public transit on the S-Bahn to the Bahnhof-Benrath, then walk. Information from Hermann & Lampert, Hasselholzerweg 9, 5100 Aachen, telephone (0241) 7 20 21.

Trödelmarkt (junk market) third Sunday of October at the Interspar-Parkplatz in the Reisholz district. Organized by Christel Deiner, Erklerenzstrasse 73, 5138 Heinzburg-Dremmen, telephone (02452) 6 24 01.

Trödelmarkt (junk market) (Ronsdorferstrasse) third Saturday of October at the Depot Einkaufzentrum on Ronsdorferstrasse east of the Hauptbahnhof. Access by public transit on tram line 7 to Ronsdorferstrasse. Information from Norbert Junge, Obersteinstrasse 51, 5190 Stolberg, telephone (02402) 2 30 07.

Schallplatten und Musikbörse (record and music exchange) (Stadthalle) third Sunday of October at the Stadthalle. Organized by Veranstaltungsbüro Norbert Junge, Obersteinstrasse 51, 5190 Stolberg, telephone (02402) 2 30 07.

Antik- und Sammlermarkt (antique and collector's market) second Sunday of October and November at the Wehrhahn-Center. Organized by Gabrielle Wallon, Postfach 39, Meerbusch 1, telephone (02105) 56 51.

Antikmarkt (antique market) (Golzheim) fourth Sunday of October in the Hilton Hotel at Georg-Gluck-Strasse 20 in the Golzheim district, north of the city center at the east end of the Theodore-Heuss bridge. Organized by Komischke & Lange, Heiderweg 53, Düsseldorf 31, telephone (0203) 7 43 01.

Antiquitäten Ausstellung (antique show) (Messegelände) for 10 days in March at the Neues Messegeläde (new fairgrounds) north of the city center along the river. The fairgrounds have parking available and are easily accessible by public transit. This is one of the major shows of the year. Only certified antiques may be shown: hundreds of dealers from Germany as well as some from other countries are present. Organized by Messegesellschaft, Novea 4, 4000 Düsseldorf 30, telephone (0203) 7 24 40.

Ebenhausen

(Please also see München.)

Antikmarkt (antiques market) second weekend of October at the Gasthof zum Post. Organized by Max Koch, Jakob-Hagenbucher-Strasse 16, 8000 München 50, telephone (089) 29 53 06.

Ebersbach (Fils) 7333

(near Gieslingen 7340.)

Antik- und Trödelmarkt (antique and junk market) most Sundays in November at the Marktschulhof. Organized by Agentur Floma, Industriesstrasse 15, 7340 Gieslingen, telephone (07331) 4 04 51.

Antik- und Trödelmarkt (antique and junk market) second Sunday of October at the Festhalle. Organized by Dieter Krauss, Pfarrweg 23, 7064 Remshalden, telephone (07181) 47 08.

Eching 8057

Trödelmarkt (junk market) second, third, and fourth Sunday of every month at the Bahnhofsgastätte. This market is much larger in summer and early fall than the rest of the year.

Eckernförde 2330

Flohmarkt (flea market) first and third Sunday of most months at the Fischmarkt or Stadthalle. Organized by P. A. M. Veranstaltungen E. Köhler, Bornbrok 1-3, 2330 Eckernförde, telephone (04351) 29 80.

Ehekirchen 8853

Flohmarkt (flea market) second Sunday of every month at the Zett/Hochzeitstadel. Information from Reiner Anlauf, Parkstrasse 6, 8070 Ingolstadt, (0841) 7 24 09.

Antik- und Flohmarkt (antique and flea market) second Sunday of October and November at the Hochzeitstadl. Organized by Rainer Anlauf,

Parkstrasse 6, 8070 Ingolstadt, telephone (0841) 6 41 66.

Ehingen 7930

Antikmarkt (antique market) third Sunday of October at the Stadthalle. Organized by Südorga Langlotz GdBR, Höllturm-Passage 1, 7760 Radolfzell, telephone (07732) 31 52.

Eisenberg 6719

Trödelmarkt (junk market) second Saturday of October and November (check for other months) at the Marktplatz in the town center. Organized by Horst Zehnpfennig, Pestalozzistrasse 54, 6504 Nierstein, telephone (06133) 5 85 11.

Eislingen an der Fils 7332

Flohmarkt (flea market) every Saturday on the Maibachgelände. Organized by Manfred Fritz, Postfach 280, 7320 Göppingen, telephone (07331) 4 38 49. Also, sometimes another flea market is held on Schumacherstrasse on Saturdays in the B-10 Center. Organized by Agentur Floma, Industriestrasse 15, 7340 Geislingen, telephone (07331) 4 04 51.

Ellwangen 7090

(Please also see Aalen.)

Trödelmarkt (junk market) first Saturday of October in the Grosso-Markt. Organized by Agentur Zelinka, Gmündstrasse 18, 7070 Schwäbisch Gmünd, (07171) 8 52 32.

Emmendingen 7830

Antikmarkt (antique market) second Saturday in October at the Fritz Boehl Halle. Organized

by Südorga Langlotz GdBR, Höllturm-Passage 1,
7760 Radolfzell, telephone (07732) 31 52.

Emmerich (Rhein) 4240

Trödelmarkt (junk market) third Sunday of
October at the Geistmarkt facing the Rathaus.
Organized by Relinda Schwabe, Schürenkampstrasse 23, 4390 Gladbeck, telephone
(02043) 6 20 51.

Enniger-Ennigerloh 4722

Antik- Trödel- und Handwerkermarkt (antique,
junk, and artisans' market) second Wednesday
in July throughout the village center. This is
part of the Kirmes- Kram- und Viehmarkt.
Organized by Stadt und Gilde Marktanschluss,
4722 Enniger, telephone (0254) 17 36.

Eppelborn 6686

Flohmarkt (flea market) August 15 in the town
center. This market is part of the annual
Children's Day celebration. Information from
Rathaus der Stadt Eppelborn, 6686 Eppelborn,
telephone (06881) 88 01 36.

Eppelheim 6904

(Four kilometers west of Heidelberg.)

Antik- und Trödelmarkt (antique and junk
market) second Sunday of October at the
Rhein-Neckar Halle. Information from WEWO
Antikmärkte, Rudi-Stefan-Allee 14, 6520
Worms, telephone (06241) 7 58 71.

Erding 8058

Flohmarkt (flea market) second Saturday of
every month at the Volksfestplatz (fairgrounds). Organized by Ernst Nowak, Wil-

helmstrasse 2, 8058 Erding, telephone (08122) 2 02 22.

Erklerenz 5140

Trödelmarkt (junk market) first weekend of October at the Gewerbegiet-Fest (trade festival grounds) throughout the town center. Organized by Hermann & Lampert, Hasselholzerweg 9, 5100 Aachen, telephone (0241) 7 20 21. The same weekend, there's also an Antikmarkt (antique market) in the Stadthalle, organized by Theodor Wessling, Kurhausstrasse 42, 4690 Herne 2, telephone (02325) 4 30 79.

Erlangen 8520

(Please also see Nürnberg.)

Flohmarkt (flea market) first Saturday of every month at the Bohlenplatz, a few blocks from the town center. If using the tram, go one block from the Bahnhof (train station) to where Friedrichstrasse meets Goethestrasse. Go about one hundred meters east to Bohlenplatz. Organized by D. K. Gerhard Stock, Am Hang 9, 8422 Riedenburg, telephone (09442) 22 49.

Antiquitätenmarkt (antique market) first Saturday of April, June, October, and November, and last Sunday of April and June, and a few other days during the year in the Stadthalle. Information from Günter Sitzmann GmbH, Abteilung Messen, Falknerweg 21, 8520 Erlangen, telephone (09131) 60 11 11.

Antik- und Sammlermarkt (antique and collectors market) first weekend of October in the Hotel Bayrischer Hof, on Schuhstrasse 16. Organized by Max Koch, Jacob-Hagenbacher-Strasse 16, 8000 München 50, telephone (089) 29 53 06.

Eschborn 6236

(Please also see Frankfurt-am-Main, Hofheim, Kelkheim, and Niedernhausen.)

Trödelmarkt (junk market) first Sunday of November at the Massa Einkaufzentrum (shopping center). Organized by Reinhard Preuss, Autoniusgasse 25, 6228 Eltville, telephone (06123) 7 46 11.

Eschweiler 5180

Trödelmarkt (junk market) second Thursday and Sunday of March and October at the Agros Parkplatz (town center parking structure) in the town center. Organized by Hermann & Lampert, Hasselholzerweg 9, 5100 Aachen, telephone (0241) 7 20 21.

Essen 4300

(Please also see Bochum, Buer, Gelsenkirchen, Heiligenhaus, Langenberg, and Mülheim.)

Antik- und Trödelmarkt (antique and junk market) every weekend year round at the Ruhrpromenade Halle in the Kettwig district, about 10 kilometers southwest of the city center. Organized by Thomas Märkte, L. Töllman, Kurt-Schumacher-Strasse 382, 4680 Gelsenkirchen, telephone (0209) 27 03 98.

Internationale Antiquitäten-Messe (international antiques fair) third week of November at the Messe Essen (fairgrounds). This is one of the major antique shows of the year. Only authentic, quality items may be offered. Naturally prices reflect the high quality. Organized by Messe Essen, Norbertstrasse, Postfach 100165, 4300 Essen, telephone (0201) 7 24 40.

Markets of various types take place almost every Sunday in the Saalbau about 300 meters south of the Hauptbahnhof (main rail station). For exact scheduling information, contact Herr Knocke, Arbeitsgemeinschaft der Markt- und Schausteller-Gewerbes, telephone (0201) 62 69 55 and 70 90 13. Some street parking; also several garages are in the area. Access by public transit: get to the Hauptbahnhof, then walk south on Huyssenallee about 300 meters. The Saalbau is in the third block on the left side of the street as you walk. For example, in October you'll find:

Schallplatten- und Musikbörse (record and music exchange) first Sunday. Organized by Norbert Junge, Obersteinstrasse 51, 5190 Stolberg, (02402) 2 30 07.

Antikmarkt (antique market) second Sunday of the month. Approximately 160 dealers offer all kinds of things. Only antiques and old items can be sold: new items and reproductions are forbidden. Often dealers come from distant parts of Germany to participate in this market. Prices are medium to very high, though quality is usually good. Organized by Komischke & Lange, Heiderweg 53, 4000 Düsseldorf 31, telephone (0203) 7 43 01.

Münzen- und Medallenbörse (coin and medals exchange) third Sunday. The organizer can be reached at telephone (0237) 7 17 83.

Esslingen am Neckar 7300

(Please also see Ost-Fildern and Stuttgart.)

Flohmarkt (flea market) second Sunday of October at the EZA-Marktplaza. Organized by Firma Syntis, Jacobsgasse 29, 7400 Tübingen, telephone (07071) 2 70 22.

Ettlingen 7505

(Please also see Forchheim and Karlsruhe.)

Antik- und Trödelmarkt (antique and junk market) second weekend of October at the Stadthalle. Information from Hans W. Nippen, Im Ferning 4, 7505 Ettlingen, telephone (07243) 1 21 06.

Eutin 2420

Trödelmarkt (junk market) last Sunday of August on the streets of the Innenstadt (town center). This market is part of the annual Stadtfest. Information from the Ostholsteiner Anzeiger, telephone (04521) 40 93.

Flehingen 7519

(Please also see Karlsruhe.)

Trödelmarkt (junk market) first Sunday of October in the Schlossgartenhalle. Organized by Margit Buzecki, Ausstellungsdienst, Stettfelderstrasse 7, 7526 Ubstadt-Weiher 3, telephone (07251) 6 33 94.

Forchheim 8550

Antik- und Trödelmarkt (antique and junk market) first and last Sunday of October at the Einkaufzentrum Beyer. Organized by Reinhard Preuss, Antoniusgasse 25, 6228 Eltville, telephone (06123) 7 46 11.

Forst 7521

(Please also see Karlsruhe.)

Trödelmarkt (junk market) first Sunday of October at the Waldseehalle. Organized by Hans W. Nippen, Im Ferning 4, 7505 Ettlingen, telephone (07243) 1 21 06.

Frankenthal 6710

Flohmarkt (flea market) first Tuesday of October and second Sunday of November at the Parseval-Platz. Information from Manfred Kiefer, Leistader Strasse 7, 6701 Kallstadt, telephone (06322) 59 65. Sometimes fairs here are organized by Person-Werbung, Wein- strasse Süd 20, 6702 Bad Dürkheim, telephone (06322) 6 66 00.

Trödelmarkt (junk market) third Sunday of October at the Basar Einkaufzentrum Parkplatz (shopping center parking garage). Organized by Hermann & Lampert, Hasselholzerweg 9, 5100 Aachen, telephone (0241) 7 20 21.

Frankfurt am Main 6000

(Please also see Bad Homburg, Eschborn, Hofheim, Kelkheim, Mülheim, Neu-Isenberg, Niedernhausen, and Offenbach. Offenbach, about 10 kilometers from Frankfurt's city center, has the best flea market in the area on a wonderful riverbank setting.)

The financial center of Germany, this city was seriously damaged in the Second World War. Most of the apparently old buildings (even in the city-center Römer district) were rebuilt completely after the Second World War. Old photographs formed the basis of the design. Nonetheless, it is one of the largest German antique centers, following only Munich and perhaps Berlin.

Though the Klienmarkthalle just off Berlinerstrasse in the city center sells beautiful fruit and vegetables, there are no antiques or collectables there.

Market locations are shown on the map by the names in parentheses.

Antik-Zentrum (antique center) (Antik-Zentrum) Monday through Saturday year round at Alte Gasse 5 in the city center, one block north of the Zeil U-bahn and S-bahn station. This is a building full of dozens of full-time dealers offering some fine items, often at very high prices. Organized by Antik-Center-Frankfurt-City, Alte Gasse 1-25, 6000 Frankfurt 1, telephone (069) 28 72 06.

Flohmarkt (flea market) (Deutschherrnufer) every Saturday on the Deustchherrnufer at the Schlacht- und Vierhof. This is along the river, east of the Sachsenhausen district, just south of the Flössbergerbrücke. Several hundred vendors of everything from tools to antiques, collectables, military medals, and used clothes. (Lots of Turks cluster around the clothes.) Not much furniture is found at this market. Sometimes amplified musicians play for the crowd. Street parking is available, as well as a pay parking lot, or in the parking garage on Heisterstrasse. Access by public transit on tram lines 11 and 16, or bus 46. Organized by Marktbetriebe der Stadt Frankfurt, Rückertstrasse, 6000 Frankfurt 1, telephone (0611) 2 12 36 97.

Antiquitätenwoche (antique week) (Alte Oper) usually the second and third weeks of October at the recently restored Alte Oper (Old Opera House). This is a major antique fair with scores of dealers coming from all over Germany and some from elsewhere in Europe with beautiful and expensive items of great quality. Street parking is difficult; there is a parking garage under the Opernplatz (access from Reuterweg). Access by public transit on the U-Bahn to the Opernplatz station. Information from Stadt Frankfurt am Main, Der Magistrat-Verkerhrsamt, Gutleutstrasse 7- 9, 6000 Frankfurt 1, telephone (060) 2 12 58 73.

Antikmarkt (antique market) (Höchst) on two or more Sundays per month at the Autokino Main-Taunus-Zentrum in the western suburb of Höchst. (The Autokino is a drive-in theatre.) Parking is available. Access by public transit on the S-Bahn line S3 to the Höchst station, then walk about two miles to the Main-Taunus-Zentrum (the busses don't run on Sundays). Information from Inter Antik, Mommsen-

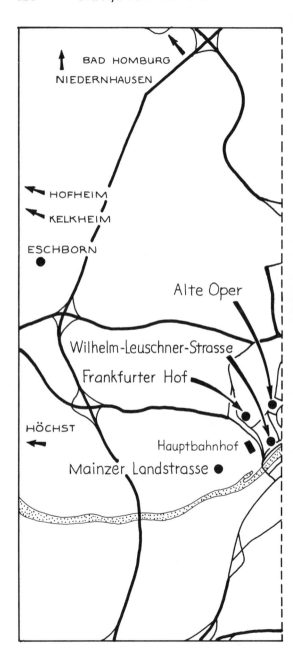

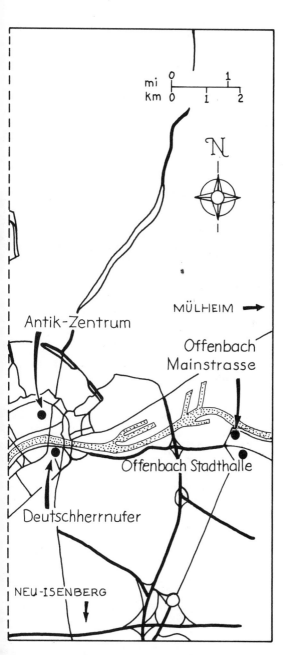

strasse 10, 4006 Ekrath, telephone (02104) 4
61 52. Several other organizers use this
location on weekends for antique fairs and flea
markets. The next market date is always
posted at the entrance to the drive-in.

Trödelmarkt (junk market) first Sunday of the
month at the Massa-Markt Maintal. Organized
by Komischke & Lange, Heiderweg 53, 4000
Düsseldorf 31, (0203) 7 43 01.

Sammler- und Münzenbörse (collectors' and coin
exchange) (Wilhelm-Leuchner-Strasse) first
Thursday of every month during business
hours at Wilhelm-Leuschner-Strasse 69-77,
between the Hauptbahnhof and the river.
Parking is difficult in this area. Access by public
transit to go to the Bahnhof and then walk.
Organized by Gesellschaft für Internationale
Geldgeschicte, Otto-Hahn-Strasse 9, 6082 Wall-
dorf, telephone (061) 05 52 34.

Spielzeugmarkt (toy market) (Höchst) first
Sunday of November at the Kasino
Jahrhunderthalle in the suburb of Höchst.
Organized by Toymania, N. Morneweg,
Bornweisenweg 53, 6000 Frankfurt, telephone
(069) 55 77 30.

Ansicht- und Postkartenmarkt (picture and
postcard market) (Wilhelm-Leuchner-Strasse)
last weekend of October at the Hotel-
Intercontinental at Wilhelm-Leuchner-Strasse
43, between the Hauptbahnhof and the river.
Several organizers jointly sponsor this event.
Information available from the hotel at (069)
23 05 61, or the Frankfurter Magistrat der
Verkehrsamt at (069) 2 12 58 73.

Antikmarkt (antique market) (Höchst) fourth
Sunday in October at the Kasino Jahr-
hunderthalle in the Frankfurt suburb of Höchst.
Access by public transit on S-Bahn line S3 to the
Höchst station. Organized by Firma Blank,
Friedrich-Ebert-Strasse 2, 6368 Bad Vilbel,
telephone (0601) 82 12.

Puppenbörse (puppet exchange) (Frankfurter Hof) first Sunday in October at the city-center Frankfurter Hof Hotel conference halls at Bettmanstrasse 33, facing Friedrich-Ebert-Anlage, between the Hauptbahnhof and Messegeläde (fairgrounds). Another puppet fair takes place at the Alte Oper on the third Sunday of October. Organized by M. Wanke AG, in der Stolzweise 25, 6243 Idstein, telephone (06431) 82 13. Information also available from Stadt Frankfurt am Main, Der Magistrat-Verkehrsamt, Gutleutstrasse 7-9, 6000 Frankfurt 1, telephone (069) 3 23 58 73.

Flohmarkt (flea market) (Mainzer Landstrasse) every Sunday near the Massa-Markt on Mainzer Landstrasse 200. The market is small (about 80 vendors) selling old clothes, used plumbing, household gadgets, but few antiques or collectables. Turks are numerous at the market. No toilets are available. Access by tram on Mainzer Landstrasse. Parking on the street is easy to find.

Frechen 5020

(Please also see Brühl, Hürth, Kerpen, and Köln.)

St. Martinsmarkt (St. Martin's Market) October 10 and 11 throughout the Fuss- gängerzone (pedestrian zone) in the town center. This fair is a celebration offering food as well as junk, antiques, new items, etc. Information from the Stadt Frechen, Rathaus, 5020 Frechen, telephone (02234) 5 40 01.

Trödelmarkt (junk market) second weekend of March and November throughout the Fussgängerzone and on the Rathausplatz in the town center. Organized by Hermann & Lampert, Hasselholzerweg 9, 5100 Aachen, telephone (0241) 7 20 21.

Antik- und Trödelmarkt (antique and junk market) first Saturday of February and second Sunday of March in the Antik- und Trödelhallen in the Grosskönigsdorf district. Organized by Hermann & Lampert, Hasselholzerweg 9, 5100 Aachen, telephone (0241) 7 20 21.

Freiburg-im-Breisgau 7800

(Please also see Emmendingen.)

Spielzeugmarkt (toy market) first Sunday of October at the Waldsee restaurant terrace. Information from the organizer at telephone (0761) 71 17 63.

Antikmarkt (antique market) first Thursday through following Sunday of October at the Messehalle. Organized by M. Peich, Markt-strasse 5, 7270 Nagold, telephone (07452) 6 61 44.

Photobörse (photo exchange) first Saturday of November in the Stadthalle-Halle 2. Photo equipment, old cameras, and photos are available at this exchange. Organized by Axel Breitzler, Schumannstrasse 22, 7030 Böblingen 4, telephone (07031) 7 19 88.

Freidberg 6360

Antikmarkt (antique market) first Sunday of November in the Stadthalle. Organized by Firma Blank, Friedrich-Ebert-Strasse 2, 6308 Bad Vilbel, telephone (0601) 82 12.

Freising 8050

(Please also see Erding and Garching.)

Flohmarkt (flea market) fourth Saturday of every month from February through December at the Lindenkeller. Organized by D. K. Gerhard Stock, Am Hang 9, 8422 Riedenburg, telephone (09442) 22 49.

Fridingen 7203

Floh- Trödel- und Antikmarkt (flea, junk, and antique market) second Sunday of September throughout the Innenstadt (old city center). This market is part of the annual fall festival. Organized by the Bürgermeisteramt der Stadt Fridingen, Rathaus, 7203 Fridingen, telephone (07463) 10 11.

Fuecht 8501

(Please also see Nürnburg.)

Antikmarkt (antique market) second weekend in October at the Reichswaldhalle. Organized by Messebüro Garon, Federmannweg 3, 7900 Ulm, telephone (0731) 3 05 74.

Fulda 6400

Trödelmarkt (junk market) third Sunday of every month year round near the church in the Fulda-Trötzhof district. Organized by H. Grösch, telephone (0661) 7 55 17.

Flohmarkt (flea market) last Sunday of October and first Sunday of November at the Löhertor Zentrum. Information from Gabrielle Wallon, Postfach 39, 4005 Meerbusch 1, telephone (02105) 56 51.

Fürstenfeldbruck 8080

Antik- und Trödelmarkt (antique and junk market) first weekend of October at the Jahnhalle. Organized by Suzanne Honold, Messebüro, Kolpingstrasse 12, 7910 Neu-Ulm, telephone (0731) 71 17 63.

Gaggenau 7560

Trödelmarkt (junk market) first Sunday in November at the Jahnhalle. Organized by Klaus Sheppe, KS-Management, Fidel-Fischer-Strasse 1, 7580 Bühl, telephone (07223) 48 95.

Garching 8046

(Please also see München.)

Antikmarkt (antique market) last weekend of October at the Bürgerhaus. Organized by Alexander Dohn, Linprunstrasse 58, 8000 München, telephone (089) 55 31 31.

Garbsen 3008

Trödelmarkt (junk market) first Sunday of October at the Nordwest-Zentrum parking lot. Organized by Novema Hannover, Hahnensteig 22, 3000 Hannover 91, telephone (0511) 41 41 14.

Gärtringen 7034

(Please also see Stuttgart.)

Flohmarkt (flea market) second Sunday of October in front of the Rathaus in the town center. Organized by Veranstaltungen Gertrud Birkenbach, Blücherstrasse 11, 7031 Gärtringen, telephone (07034) 2 16 43.

Geesthacht 2054

Flohmarkt (flea market) second Sunday of October in the Magnet-Parkplatz. Organized by Helmut Brassat, Nachtigallenweg 7, 2054 Geesthacht, telephone (04152) 7 51 25.

Gelnhausen 6460

Antikmarkt (antique market) third weekend of October at the Kinzighalle in the Roth district. Organized by Firma Weber, Semmelstrasse 42, 8700 Würzburg, telephone (0931) 1 37 03.

Gelsenkirchen 4650

Antik- Trödel- und Handwerkermarkt (antique, junk, and artisans market) first Friday and every weekend year round at the Bahnhofzentrum on Bahnhofstrasse in the Altstadt (old city). Parking can be difficult, though there are a couple of parking garages in the neighborhood. Access by public transit: walk from the Bahnhof. Organized by Agentur Erich Radke, Bahnhofstrasse 5, 4650 Gelsenkirchen, telephone (0209) 27 03 98.

Spielkartebörse (playing card exchange) last Sunday of October at the Revierpark Neinhausen. Information from (0209) 5 55 05.

Mineralenbörse (mineral and rock exchange) second weekend of November in the Revierpark Nienhausen. Organized by Brigitte Püschel, Meisenstrasse 40, 4370 Marl, telephone (02365) 22 41 13.

Antikmarkt (antique market) third Saturday in February at the Hans-Sachs Haus. Organized by Theodor Wessling, Kurhausstrasse 31a, 4690 Herne 2, telephone (02325) 4 30 31.

Gelsenkirchen-Buer 4660

(This is a separate town north of Gelsenkirchen.)

Trödelmarkt (junk market) every weekend year round at the Autokino am Verkehrshof (drive-in movie theatre). Saturdays the sellers are both dealers and individuals; Sundays the sellers must be private parties. The market site is large, and the size of market depends on the season and the weather. Toilets and parking are available on the grounds. Organized by Relinde Schwabe, Schürenkampstrasse 23, 4390, Gladbach, telephone (02043) 6 20 52.

Flohmarkt (flea market) every Sunday at the Plaza-Warenhaus. On most market days, this is the biggest flea market in this town. Organized by Flohdom Veranstaltungs-GmbH, Klosterallee 106a, 2000 Hamburg 13, telephone (040) 48 88 21.

Gensingen 6531

Trödelmarkt (junk market) third Sunday of October and second Sunday of November at the Globus Handelshof parking lot. Organized by Reinhard Preuss, Antoniusgasse 25, 6228 Eltville, telephone (06123) 7 46 11.

Gensungen 3582

Floh- und Antikmarkt (flea and antique market) fourth Sunday in October at the Edeka Markt Wirtz. Information from Friedhelm Snoth, Stettinerstrasse 4, 3578 Ziegenhain-Schwalm-stadt, telephone (06691) 63 06.

Georgsmarienhütten 4504

Trödelmarkt (junk market) fourth Sunday of October at the Möbel-Meyer parking lot. Organized by M. Nordmann, Leconskamp 18, 4513 Belm, telephone (05406) 40 41.

Gerlingen 7016

(Please also see Böblingen and Stuttgart.)

Antik- und Trödelmarkt (antique and junk market) first Sunday in November at the Stadthalle. Information from H. & H. K. Fischer, Uhlandstrasse 18, 7255 Rutesheim, telephone (07152) 5 29 84. Other organizers use this site on other Sundays.

Germering 8034

(Please also see München.)

Flohmarkt (flea market) third Saturday of every month at the Volksfestplatz. Information from the Marktamt der Stadt Germering, Rathaus, 8034 Germering, telephone (089) 84 10 91.

Flohmarkt (flea market) first Saturday of every month on Max-Roger-Strasse. This market is limited to private sellers only—no dealers are permitted to sell, though this is sometimes their source. Interesting items of all kinds are found. Information from the Marktamt der Stadt Germering, Rathaus, 8034 Germering, telephone (089) 84 10 91.

Germersheim 6728

Antikmarkt (antique market) first Sunday of November at the Stadthalle. Organized by Antiquariat Peter Kiefer GmbH, Eberstein-strasse 14, 7530 Pforzheim, telephone (07231) 1 72 72.

Gernsbach 7562

Antik- und Sammlermarkt (antique and collectors' market) second weekend in November at the Stadthalle. Information from Hans W. Nippen, Im Ferning 4, 7505 Ettlingen, telephone (07243) 1 21 06.

Gerolstein 5530

Antik- Trödel- und Handwerkermarkt (antique, junk, and artisans' market) second weekend of June. This market in the old center of town is part of the celebration anniversary of the town's founding. Organized by Claudia Wand, Platiss 11, 5374 Hellenthal, telephone (02482) 20 95.

Giesenfeld 8069

(Please also see München.)

Trödelmarkt (junk market) second Sunday of every month year round at the Sportgelände on Johanstrasse. This market also has small animals for sale, including dogs, cats, pigeons, and rabbits. Organized by Agentur Röttinger, telephone (08452) 28 42.

Flohmarkt (flea market) second Sunday of the month at the Sportgelände (sports grounds) on Jahnstrasse. Organized by the Heimatverein Stadt Geisenfeld, 8169 Giesenfeld, telephone (08452) 28 42.

Giessen 6300

Antiquitätentage (antique days) first weekend in October at the Kongresshalle. Organized by Firma Blank, Friedrich-Ebert-Strasse 2, 6368 Bad Vilbel, telephone (06101) 82 12. This hall is used on other weekends for antique fairs, organized by other firms.

Trödelmarkt (junk market) third Sunday of October at the Wertkauf-Center parking garage. Organized by Hermann & Lampert, Hasselholzerweg 9, 5100 Aachen, telephone (0241) 7 20 21.

Antikmarkt (antique market) second Sunday of October at the Hessenhalle. Organized by Galerie G. Krenky, Heidestrasse 9a, 4900 Herford, telephone (05221) 5 67 41.

Gifhorn 3170

Trödelmarkt (junk market) fourth Sunday of October near the Möbel Schifski building in the town center. Information from Veranstaltungsbüro A. Braun, Amselweg 48, 2061 Bargfeld-Stegen, telephone (04532) 2 19 27.

Gladbeck 4390

Antik- und Kunstmarkt (antique and art market) first weekend of October at the Möbel-Tacke building. Organized by L. Rau, Luitpoldstrasse 38, 4650 Gelsenkirchen, telephone (0209) 20 49 46.

Glückstadt 2208

Trödelmarkt (junk market) last Sunday in every month at the Fischmarkt. Organized by Gerhard Bauer, Wallgraben 44, 2100 Hamburg 90, telephone (040) 77 46 24.

Göppingen 7320

Floh- und Trödelmarkt (flea and junk market) first and third Saturday of every month at the B-10 Center, Schuh Mayer building, and first and third Sunday at the Nerckarwerke. Organized by Agentur Floma, Industriestrasse 15, 7340 Geislingen, (07331) 4 04 51.

Modellbahn- und Speilzeugmarkt (model railway and toy market) second Sunday of October beginning at 1 p.m. in the Stadthalle on Lutherstrasse, about 500 meters northeast of the Bahnhof. Park in the street or in a parking garage at the hall. Information from W. Frieden Benedikt, Weiserweg 2, 7959 Mietingen 3, telephone (07353) 21 81.

Goslar 3380

Trödelmarkt (junk market) first Sunday in February and second Sunday in March at the Hotel Lindenhof. Organized by Hasse Alfeld, telephone (05181) 2 37 79.

Antiquitäten- und Kunsttage (antiques and art days) second weekend of October at the Neues Schützenhaus. Informedia, Renate Maemeke, Leiferdesstrasse 15, 3300 Braunschweig, telephone (0531) 61 20 80.

Göttingen 3400

Flohmarkt (flea market) every Saturday year round at Düstere Strasse 1. This is one of the largest markets in east-central Germany and is well worth a visit. Organized by Herr Döll, Kramer Landstrasse 39, 3400 Göttingen, telephone (0551) 5 51 44.

Antikmarkt (antique market) third weekend of October in the Stadthalle. Organized by Avorga GmbH, Husarenstrasse 22, 3300 Braunschweig, telephone (0531) 33 14 15.

Graben-Neudorf 7523

Flohmarkt (flea market) second Sunday of November in the village center. Organized by Dieter Pille, Hardtstrasse 3, 7523 Graben-Neudorf, telephone (07255) 44 30.

Grevenbroich 4048

Antik- und Trödelmarkt (antique and junk market) third Sunday of most months at the Mantanushof Einkaufzentrum in the town center. Organized by Hermann & Lampert, Hasselholzerweg 9, 5100 Aachen, telephone (0241) 7 20 21.

Gröbenzell 8038

(Please also see München.)

Antikmarkt (antique market) second weekend of October at the Mehrzweckhalle. Information from telephone (08141) 1 85 81.

Gross-Zimmern 6112

Antik- und Trödelmarkt (antique and junk market) first Sunday of October at the Plaza Einkaufzentrum. Organized by Reinhard Preuss, Antoniusgasse 25, 6228 Eltville, telephone (06123) 7 46 11.

Grünwald 8022

(Also please see München.)

Antik- und Sammlermarkt (antique and collectors' market) third weekend of October at the Bürgerhaus Römerschanz. Organized by Max Koch, Jakob-Hagenbucher-Strasse 16, 8000 München 50, telephone (089) 29 53 06.

Gütersloh 4830

Kinder Flohmarkt (children's flea market) first Saturday of every month. In the winter from December through April it is held at the Kaufhaus Hertie; the rest of the year it is held at the Berlinerplatz. Information from Herr Grönheit, Verkehrsverein der Stadt Gütersloh, 4830 Gütersloh, telephone (05241) 82 27 49.

Antikmarkt (antique market) on occasional Sundays at the Stadthalle (city convention hall). Organized by Komischke & Lange, Heiderweg 53, 4000 Düsseldorf 31, telephone (0203) 743 01; sometimes by Theodor Wessling, Kurhausstrasse 31a, 4690 Herne 2, telephone (02325) 4 30 31; and sometimes by A.M.V.V. Jörn Weber, Am Grossen Holz 9, 4817 Leopoldshohe, telephone (05208) 14 23. For details about the forthcoming schedule, contact the Verkehrsverein der Stadt Gütersloh, 4830 Gütersloh, telephone (05241) 82 27 49.

Gummersbach 5270

Trödelmarkt (junk market) second Sunday of October at the Extra Parkplatz. Organized by Hans Theodor Lampert, Hasselholzer Weg 9, 5100 Aachen, telephone (0241) 17 20 21.

Trödelmarkt (junk market) third Sunday of October in the Platz an der Stadthalle (city convention hall square). Organized by Norbert Junge, Obersteinstrasse 51, 5190 Stolberg, telephone (02402) 2 30 07.

Flohmarkt (flea market) first Sunday after the 15th of every month in the Dieringhausen district at the Güterbahnhof (rail freight terminal). Organized by Gabrielle Wallon, Postfach 39, 4005 Meerbusch 1, telephone (02105) 56 51.

Antiktage (antique days) first weekend in November at the Aggerhalle in the Diereingshausen district. Information from Alida Schleusener, Waldfriedstrasse 1, 5000 Köln 60, telephone (0221) 71 34 14.

Gunzenhausen 8820

Tauschtreff der Militaria (military item meeting) first weekend of October at the Turnhalle. Organized by Reinhold Siebentritt, Negelein-strasse 32, 8820 Gunzenhausen, telephone (09831) 25 97.

Hagen 5800

Kunstmarkt (art market), Musikbörse (music exchange), and other antique-related events the first Sunday of every month in the Stadthalle. Information from Theodor Wessling, Kurhausstrasse 31a, 4690 Herne 2, telephone (02325) 4 43 03. Other organizers use this hall on weekends irregularly for toy markets, antique shows, and similar events.

Trödelmarkt (junk market) first Sunday of the month in the town center. This is a small outdoor market.

Hamburg 2000

The ancient free city of Hamburg is one of the largest urban areas in Germany. Unfortunately it has less charm than villages, since much of the city was virtually leveled during World War II. But the many flea markets are as interesting as any in Germany; most are on Sunday, and a few (including the largest) are on Saturday.

Market locations shown on the map are shown in parentheses in the listings.

Flohmarkt (flea market) (St. Pauli Fischmarkt) every Saturday year round (first Saturday of the month is the best and the market is largest from May through October) at the Speicher am Fischmarkt along the Elbe river about a kilometer west of the city center. This is the largest and most interesting market in the area. During the week, this is the fish market and fish auction. There are two public toilets in the market area. Two parking garages are available at the Fischmarkt, but street parking is scarce. Access by public transit on the S-Bahn to Nobistor station, walk south to the river on Pepermuhlenstrasse. Organized by Lübke GmbH, telephone (040) 31 41 51.

Antikmarkt (antique market) (Antik-Center Klosterwall) at the Antik-Center Tuesday through Saturday at Klosterwall 9-21. This is an indoor dealers' market with dozens of small shops. Parking is limited in this area. Access by public transit is from the U-bahn to the Steinstrasse station, or walk one block south from the Hauptbahnhof-Sud. The retail market district, with vegetable and meat markets in large market halls, is in the vicinity as well. Information from the antique center at the same address, telephone (040) 33 88 89.

Flohmarkt (flea market) (Farmsen) first (and sometimes second) Sunday of every month at the

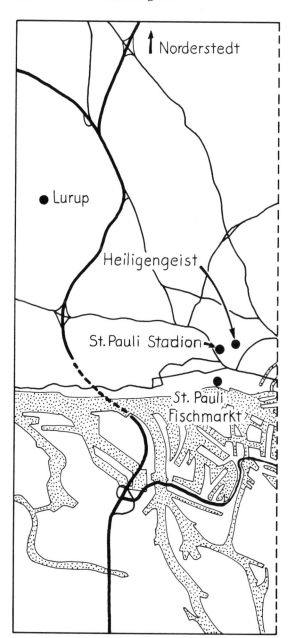

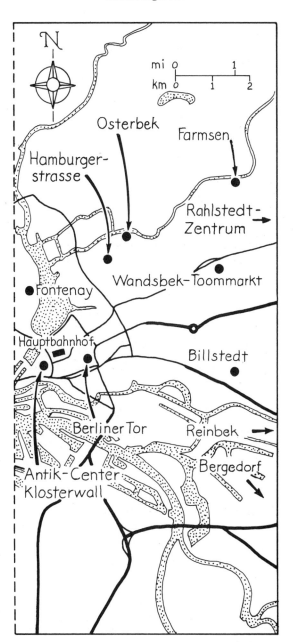

N

mi 0 ... 1
km 0 ... 1 ... 2

Osterbek
Farmsen
Hamburger-
strasse
Rahlstedt-
Zentrum
Fontenay
Wandsbek–Toommarkt
Hauptbahnhof
Billstedt
Berliner Tor
Reinbek
Antik-Center
Bergedorf
Klosterwall

Einkaufzentrum Farmsen (postal zone 72) in the Farmsen district northeast of the city center. Some street parking is available, in part because this market is one of the few things to do on Sunday in Hamburg. Access by public transit on U-Bahn lines 1 or 2 to the Trabrennbahn or Farmsen station. Organized by Hennings, Weissenhof 7e, 2000 Hamburg 72, telephone (040) 6 43 31 81.

Flohmarkt (flea market) (Billstedt) second and occasionally third Sunday of every month, Billstedt Einkaufzentrum (postal zone 74) in the Billstedt district east of the city center. Park on the street or the park-and-ride lot on Legierstrasse. Access by public transit on S-Bahn line S2 to the Billstedt station, then walk. Organized by Hennings, Weissenhof 7e, 2000 Hamburg 72, telephone (040) 5 43 31 81.

Flohmarkt (flea market) (Heiligengeist) first Sunday of every month at the Plaza-Gelände Heiligengeist (fairgrounds) west of the city center. Ample parking on the grounds. Public restrooms are relatively plentiful here, but cost 40 pfennigs. Access by public transit on U-Bahn line U2 to the Feldstrasse station, then walk south onto the grounds, or to the St. Pauli station and walk north. Information from P. Lakenmacher & Co., Klosterallee 106a, 2000 Hamburg 13, telephone (040) 48 88 21. The second Sunday of November the Messehallen (fairgrounds halls) are used for a market; information from Melan-Initiativ GmbH, Am Hasenberge 27, 2000 Hamburg 63, telephone (040) 5 40 40 40.

Flohmarkt (flea market) (Berliner Tor) second Saturday from May through October at the Berliner Tor about a kilometer east of the city center (postal zone 1). Several public toilets are available in the district. This area a major intersection which was at one time one of the old city gates. Parking is available in pay garages. Access by public transit by U-Bahn or S-Bahn to the Berliner Tor station. Organized by Hennings, Weissenhof 7e, 2000 Hamburg 72, telephone (040) 5 43 31 81.

Flohmarkt (flea market) (Wandsbek-Toom-markt) fourth Thursday of every month at the Wandsbek-Toommarkt and third Sunday at the Big Bör in the Wandsbek district east of the city center. Access by public transit on the U-Bahn to the Wandsbek Markt station, then walk. Information from Uwe Flick, Kanalstrasse 34b, 2000 Hamburg 76, telephone (040) 2 20 00 54.

Trödelmarkt (junk market) (Lurup) fourth Saturday from April to November at the Einkaufzentrum Eckhoffplatz in the Hamburg-Lurup district northwest of the city center. Organized by Burmeister, Norderstedt, telephone (040) 5 22 39 98.

Flohmarkt (flea market) (Hamburgerstrasse) first Sunday of October at the Hamburgerstrasse Einkaufzentrum in the Barmbek district east of the Ausser-Alster lake, northeast of the city center. Access by public transit on U-Bahn line U3 or 31 to the Mundsberg station and walk, or tram 15 to Hamburgerstrasse. Information from Melan-Initiativ GmbH, Am Hasenberge 27, 2000 Hamburg 63, telephone (040) 5 40 40 40.

Flohmarkt (flea market) (Bergedorf) first Sunday of October at the Fachhochschule Bergedorf in the suburb of Bergedorf (postal zone 80) about 10 kilometers southeast of the city center. Access by car southeast on Billstedter Hauptstrasse past the Hamburg-Billstedt interchange with the Autobahn. Street parking is available. Access by public transit on S-Bahn line S2 to Bergedorf, then walk about half a mile to the school. Organized by C. Hochberg, Waltreiterweg 30, 2070 Grosshandsdorf, telephone (041 02) 6 50 83.

Flohmarkt (flea market) third Sunday of October in the S- Einkaufzentrum in the Neugraben district. Organized by Hennings, Weissenhof 7e, 2000 Hamburg 72, telephone (040) 6 43 31 81.

Flohmarkt (flea market) (St. Pauli Stadion) third Sunday of every month at the St. Pauli

Stadion. Organized by Hennings, Weissenhof 7e, 2000 Hamburg 72, telephone (040) 6 43 31 81.

Flohmarkt (flea market) (Osterbek) second Saturday of October on Osterbekstrasse along the south side of the Osterbek canal. Street parking is possible. Access by public transit on U-Bahn line U3 to the Stadtpark station (don't mistake this for the different S-Bahn Stadtpark station!) or U-Bahn or S-Bahn to the Barmbek station on U3, U312, or S1, then walk south until you cross the canal. Information from Hennings, Weissenhof 7e, 2000 Hamburg 72, telephone (040) 5 43 31 81.

Flohmarkt (flea market) (Reinbek) fourth Sunday of October at the Reinbek Einkaufzentrum (shopping center) about 13 kilometers southeast of the city center. Parking is available in the shopping center. Access by public transit by S-Bahn line S2 to the Reinbek station, then bus 237 or 332 west until you pass under the pedestrian bridge of the center. The bus stops at the next corner upon request. Organized by Hennings, Weissenhof 7e, 2000 Hamburg 72, telephone (040) 6 43 31 81.

Flohmarkt (flea market) (Norderstedt) first Sunday of October at the Herold-Center in the suburb of Hamburg-Norderstedt. Information from Melan-Initiativ GmbH, Am Hasenberge 27, 2000 Hamburg 63, telephone (040) 5 40 40 40.

Flohmarkt (flea market) (Rahlstedt-Zentrum) first and third Sunday of October at the Rahlstedt-Zentrum northeast of the city center. Street parking or the park-and-ride lot at the Rahlstedt S-Bahn station is available. Access on public transit by S-Bahn to the Rahlstedt station, then take bus 32 to the center. Organized by Alfred Spott, Bahnhofstrasse 21, 2000 Hamburg 73, telephone (040) 6 77 09 70.

Antikmarkt (antique market) last Sunday in March and first Sunday of October at the Elbe-Einkaufzentrum (postal zone 52). Organized by Inter Antik, Michael Becker,

Mommsenstrasse 10, 4006 Ekrath, telephone
(02104) 4 61 52.

Modellbahn- und Spielzeugmarkt (model railroad and toy market) fourth Sunday in October
at the Besenbinderhof. Organized by G. Gall,
Tegelbergstrasse 12, 7343 Kuchen, telephone
(07331) 8 21 24.

Puppenbörse (doll and puppet exchange)
(Fontenay) first Sunday of November at the
Hotel Intercontinental at Fontenay 10 (postal
district 36) along the west bank of the
Aussenalster. Organized by Ulrich Gierse, St.
Nicolaistrasse 1, 2280 Westerland/Sylt, tele-
phone (04651) 10 57.

Hameln 3250

Antik- und Trödelmarkt (antique and junk
market) two Saturdays a month (usually first
and third one month, then second and fourth the
next) at the Bügergarten on Ritter-Passage in
the center of town, near the city theatre on
Kastanien Wall (where the ancient city walls
stood until they were demolished about 100
years ago). Park on the street or in the theatre's
garage. Organized by Novema Hannover,
Hahnensteg 22, 3000 Hannover 91, telephone
(0511) 41 41 14.

Hamlin

(Please see Hameln.)

Hamm 4700

Antikmarkt (antique market) third Sunday in
January at the Maximilianhalle. Organized by
Inter-Antik, Michael Becker, Mommsenstrasse
10, 4006 Eckrath, telephone (02104) 4 61 52.

Antikmarkt (antique market) first Sunday in
October at the Westenschützenhof. Organized by

Galerie G. Krenky, Heidestrasse 9a, 4900 Herford, telephone (05221) 5 67 41.

Kunstmarkt (art market) second Sunday of October at the Zentralhallen, about 1500 meters south of the Bahnhof on Richard Wagnerstrasse. Organized by Theodor Wessling, Kurhausstrasse 31a 4690 Herne 2, telephone (02325) 4 30 31.

Other markets, including flea and antique markets are held irregularly on other Sundays at the same location.

Antik- und Sammlermarkt (antique and collectors market) first Sunday of October at the Bürgerhalle in the Delkum district, about 5 kilometers southwest of the city center. Organized by Hedwig Langer, Kastanienstrasse 37, 4712 Werne, telephone (02389) 13 75.

Hanau 6450

Antikmarkt (antique market) first weekend in October at the Kurhaus Wilhelmsbad. Organized by Falk Anders, An der Martinspforte, 6719 Einselthum, telephone (06355) 22 94.

Hannover 3000

(Please also see Altwarmbüchen and Barsighausen.)

Flohmarkt (flea market) every Saturday year round beginning at 7 a. m. on the Liebnizufer and Hohenufer. This market has one of the best market settings in Germany, along the Leine river under the trees near the old city center. This market is known for encouraging private sellers, though dealers also sell here. During the annual Altstadtfest (Old City Festival) (exact dates vary from year to year), over 100,000 people visit the old city and market. Park on the street; it may be difficult. Access by public transit on any tram to Friederickenplatz, then walk north along the river. Information from Stadtverwaltung

Hannover, 3000 Hannover, telephone (0511) 1 68 23 19.

Antikmarkt (antique market) second Sunday of every month in the Leine Einkaufzentrum in the Laatzen district, about 10 kilometers south of the city center. Organized by Hennings, Weissenhof 7e, 2000 Hamburg, telephone (040), 6 43 31 81.

Flohmarkt (flea market) first Sunday of every month at the City-Centrum of Langenhagen, a town about 10 kilometers north of the Hannover city center. Organized by Karin Pöschel, Pfarrer-Hottenrott Strasse 9, 3209 Schellerten 6, telephone (05123) 85 94.

Antikmarkt (antique market) second weekend of every month at the Antikhalle. (This site is used for doll and puppet shows during the rest of the year.) Organized by Dipl. Georg F. Eigend, Klogesmarkt Postkamp 10, 3000 Hannover 1, telephone (0511) 32 32 66.

Antikmarkt (antique market) first Sunday of October in the Hotel Maritim conference halls at Hildesheimerstrasse 34. Organized by Maren Fischer, Ot Wenden 26, 3071 Stöckse, telephone (05026) 15 75.

Trödelmarkt (junk market) third Sunday of October in the Zentrum-Passage in the city center. Organized by Novema Hannover, Hahnensteig 22, 3000 Hannover 91, telephone (0511) 41 41 14.

Puppenbörse (doll and puppet exchange) first Sunday of October at the Hotel Inter-continental at Freidrichswall 11. Organized by Ulrich Gierse, St. Nicolaistrasse 1, 2280 Westerland/Sylt, telephone (04651) 10 57.

Antikmarkt (antique market) third weekend of October in the Blumengrossmarkt (wholesale flower market building). Organized by Agentur Beinhorn, Husarenstrasse 22, 3300 Braun-schweig, telephone (0531) 34 61 61.

Antik- und Trödelmarkt (antique and junk market) fourth Sunday of October in the Riethorpassage. Information from Novema Hannover, Hahnensteg 22, 3000 Hannover 91, telephone (0511) 41 41 14.

Antiktage (antique days) first weekend of November in the city center. Organized by Dipl. Georg F. Eigend, Klagesmarkt Postkamp 10, 3000 Hannover 1, telephone (0511) 32 32 66.

Hasbergen 4507

Trödelmarkt (junk market) first Sunday of October at the Dorfplatz in the town center. Organized by M. Nordmann, Leconskamp 18, 4513 Belm, telephone (05406) 40 41.

Hassfurt 88728

Antikmarkt (antique market) second Sunday of October at the FC- Stadion. Organized by Firma Weber, Semmelstrasse 42, 8700 Würzburg, telephone (0931) 1 37 03.

Hattingen 4620

Trödelmarkt (junk market) first Sunday of October in the town center. The market is part of the Altstadtfest, the annual old town festival. Organized by Theodor Wessling, Kurhausstrasse 31a, 4690 Herne 2, telephone (02325) 4 30 31.

Heidelberg 6900

Antikmarkt (antique market) second weekend in October in the Stadthalle, which is at Neckarstaden 24. Information from Falk Anders, An der Martinspforte, 6719 Einselthum, telephone (06355) 22 94.

Antik- und Puppenmarkt (antique doll and puppet market) second Sunday of November at

the Stadthalle, at Neckarstaden 24. Organized
by Irmgard Wolfermann, Obere Pfannen-
steigstrasse 14, 8540 Schwabach, telephone
(0911) 63 53 83.

Flohmarkt (flea market) second Saturday in
November at the Neue Messeplatz (new
fairgrounds). Information from M. Lukas,
Mönchhofstrasse 14a, 6806 Viernheim, telephone (0621) 72 15 03.

Antik- und Puppenmarkt (antique and puppet
market) third Sunday in October at the Stadthalle. Information from Irmgard Wolfermann,
Obere Pfaffensteigstrasse 14, 8540 Schwabach,
telephone (0911) 63 53 83. Other events such
as record exchanges also take place on some
weekends at this location.

Heidenheim-Schnaitheim 7920

Trödelmarkt (junk market) first Saturday of
every month at the Preisfux Einkaufzentrum
in Ritterpark. Organized by Agentur Zelinka,
Gmündstrasse 18, 7070 Schwäbisch Gmünd,
telephone (07171) 8 52 32.

Heidenheim-Hattheim 7921

Antik- und Trödelmarkt (antique and junk
market) third Sunday of October at the
Sporthalle and adjacent Gemeindehalle.
Organized by Dieter Krauss, Pfarrweg 32, 7064
Remshalden, telephone (0781) 47 08.

Heilbronn 7100

Trödelmarkt (junk market) first Sunday of the
month in the Kaufland shopping center in the
Neckarsulm district and fourth Sunday of
October at the Flachsmann Parkplatz in the city
center. Organized by Firma Syntis, Jakobgasse
29, 7400 Tübingen, telephone (07071) 2 70 22.
This firm organized other Sunday markets
around Heilbronn; call for exact locations.

Flohmarkt (flea market) second Sunday of every month at the Depot parking lot. Organized by RAS Dew. Raspe, Flohmarkt Antik, Bergstrasse 21, 7100 Heilbronn, telephone (0731) 6 06 26.

Eisenbahn- Spielzeug- und Puppenmarkt (railway, toy, and puppet market) first Sunday of October in the Bürgerhaus in the Böckingen district. Organized by Hermann Bauder, Hebelstrasse 9, 6921 Hüffenhardt, telephone (06268) 7 19.

Heilingenhaus 5628

Trödelmarkt (junk market) second weekend of October in the Bahnhof (train station) and its parking lot. Organized by Zensen, Hülsenbergweg, 4030 Ratingen/Lintorf, telephone (02102) 3 79 24.

Heiligenroth 5431

Trödelmarkt (junk market) third Sunday of October at the Allkauf parking lot. Organized by Reinhard Preuss, Antoniusgasse 25, 6228 Eltville, telephone (06123) 7 46 11.

Heinsberg 5138

Trödelmarkt (junk market) second Sunday of every month in the Allkauf shopping center parking structure, except from December until March at the Stadthalle. Organized by Hermann & Lampert, Hasselholzerweg 9, 5100 Aachen, telephone (0241) 7 20 21.

Trödelmarkt (junk market) last Sunday of October at the Marktplatz in the town center. Organized by Christel Diener, Erklerenzstrasse 73, 5738 Heinsberg-Dremmin, telephone (02452) 6 24 01.

Hemeldirchen-Dabringhausen 5632

Antikmarkt (antique market) last weekend in January in the Mehrzweckhalle. Organized by Hermann & Lampert, Hasselholzerweg 9, 5100 Aachen, telephone (0241) 7 20 21.

Herborn im Dillkreis 6348

Antik- und Trödelmarkt (antique and junk market) first Saturday of July at the Kornmarkt and Holzmarkt. Organized by Stadt Herborn.

Herford 4900

Antikmarkt (antique market) first Sunday of every month at the Firlefanzmarkt in the Hiddenhausen district. Organized by Galerie G. Krenky, Heidestrasse 9a, 4900 Herford, telephone (05221) 5 67 41.

Brauereisouvenir-Tausch (brewery souvenir exchange) third Friday of October at the Gasthaus Schony. Organized by Ingolf Held, Goebenstrasse 29, 4900 Herford, telephone (05221) 5 01 42.

Herne 4690

(Please also see Castrop-Rauxel, Bochum, and Gelsenkirchen.)

Antikmarkt (antique market) first Saturday of January and last Sunday of October in the Kulturzentrum. Organized by Theodor Wessling, Kurhausstrasse 31a, 4690 Herne 2, telephone (02325) 4 30 31.

Trödelmarkt (junk market) third Saturday of October in the CityCenter parking garage. Organized by Marlies Scory, Schürenkampstrasse 23, 4390 Gladbeck, telephone (02043) 6 58 91.

Herrsching am Ammersee 8036

Antikmarkt (antique market) fourth weekend of October at the Bildingszentrum der Bayerisches Bauernverbandes (building center of the Bavarian farmers' union). Organized by Max Koch, Jakob-Hagenbucher-Strasse 16, 8000 München 50, telephone (089) 29 53 06.

Herzogenrath 5120

Trödelmarkt (junk market) first weekend of every month at the Idealkauf Einkaufzentrum. Organized by Hermann & Lampert, Hasselholzerweg 9, 5100 Aachen, telephone (0241) 7 20 21.

Trödelmarkt (junk market) second Sunday of every month in the Marktplatz on Bargstrasse. Organized by Norbert Junge, Obersteinstrasse 51, 5190 Stolberg, telephone (02402) 2 30 07.

Hilden 4010

(Please also see Düsseldorf.)

Trödelmarkt (junk market) first Sunday of most months at the Vonnahme-Möbelcenter Parkplatz (parking lot), though locations may be elsewhere in the town's central area. The market held in the Stadthalle has more antiques than the other locations. Information from Hermann & Lampert, Hasselholzerweg 9, 5100 Aachen, telephone (0241) 7 20 21.

Antikmarkt (antique market) third Sunday in February, May Day, and the second Sunday of October at the Stadthalle. This market has more antiques than other markets in this town. Organized by Komischke & Lange, Heiderweg 53, 4000 Düsseldorf 31, telephone (0203) 7 43 01.

Hildesheim 3200

Antik- und Trödelmarkt (antique and junk market) second Sunday of every month in the fall on the Andreas-Passage. Organized by Karin Pöschel, Pfarrer-Hottenrott Strasse 9, 3209 Schellerten 6, telephone (05123) 85 94.

Hilzingen 7709

(Near Singen, closest reference on the maps.)

Kunst- und Trödelmarkt (art and junk market) third Sunday and Monday of October at the Festplatz.

Hochheim 6203

Antikmarkt (antique market) second Sunday in January and last Sunday of October at the Stadthalle. Organized by Reinhard Preuss, Antoniusgasse 25, 6228 Eltville, telephone (06123) 46 11.

Hockenheim 6832

Antikmarkt (antique market) third Sunday of October in the Festhalle. Organized by Peter Fuchs, Bahnhofstrasse 5, 6940 Weinheim, telephone (06201) 1 22 32.

Höhr-Grenzhausen 5410

Flohmarkt (flea market) third Sunday of October at the Mini-Mall. Organized by Helene Schmitt, Karl-Marx-Strasse 35, 5450 Neuwied 12, telephone (02631) 7 66 44.

Hofheim am Taunus 6238

Antik- und Sammlermarkt (antique and collectors' market) second weekend of every month at the Stadthalle. Organized by WEWO

Antikmärkte, Rudi-Stefan-Allee 14, 6520 Worms, telephone (06241) 7 58 71.

Holzminden 3450

Trödelmarkt (junk market) the last Thursday, Friday, and Saturday in June in the Fussgängerzone (pedestrian zone) and Marktplatz in the town center. This market is part of the annual summer festival. Organized by the Ordnungsamt der Stadt Holzminden.

Homburg am Saar 6650

Flohmarkt (flea market) first Saturday of the month from April through October from 8 a. m. to 6 p. m. at the Christian-Weber-Platz. This market offers only antiques, old junk, trinkets, jewelry, and artwork. New items (except artisans' work) is strictly forbidden. Thousands of people visit this market, which also brings hundreds of sellers. Organized by the Werbegemeinschaft der Stadt Homburg am Saar, 6650 Homburg, telephone (06841) 20 66.

Hürth 5030

Antik- und Trödelmarkt (antique and junk market) the third weekend in January, February, and May, the Monday after Easter, and the first Thursday and first weekend of October at the Hürth-Park Einkaufzentrum in the underground parking garage. Also there is another market in the Bürgerhaus on the second weekend of February and October. Both organized by Hermann & Lampert, Hasselholzerweg 9, 5100 Aachen, telephone (0241) 7 20 21.

Flohmarkt (flea market) third weekend in October on the Strasse am Hürth-park. Organized by Rita Schneider, Wipperfürther Strasse 45, 5060 Bergisch Gladbach 1, telephone (02204) 5 61 28.

Husum 2250

Antik- und Trödelmarkt (antique and junk market) second Sunday of October at the Nordseehalle. Organized by C. Hochberg, Waltreiterweg 30, 2070 Grosshansdorf, telephone (04102) 6 50 83. On the first Sunday of each month, other organizations sometimes use this hall for antique and junk markets.

Huttenheim 7522

(near Karlsruhe)

Flohmarkt (flea market) second of Saturday every month in the Vorteilkauf. Information from Dieter Pille, Hardtstrasse 3, 7523 Graben-Neudorf, telephone (07255) 44 30.

Ibbenbüren 4530

Antikmarkt (antique market) second Sunday of October at the Bürgerhaus. Information from Galerie G. Krenky, Heidestrasse 9a, 4900 Herford, telephone (05221) 67 41.

Illertissen 7918

Flohmarkt (flea market) first Sunday of October at the Marktplatz in the village center. Organized by Peter Gailer, Eberhardstrasse 49, 7000 Stuttgart 1, telephone (0711) 24 43 80.

Ingelheim am Rhein 6507

Trödelmarkt (junk market) second Sunday of October at the Möbel Hunsch lot. Organized by Reinhard Preuss, Antoniusgasse 25, 6228 Eltville, telephone (06123) 7 46 11.

Antikmarkt (antique market) first weekend of November at the Alte Markthalle (old market hall) in the town center. Organized by WEWO

Antikmärkte, Rudi-Stefan-Allee 14, 6520 Worms, telephone (06241) 7 58 71.

Ingolstadt 8070

Flohmarkt (flea market) first Sunday of every month at the Kreutztor on Friedhofstrasse 3. This is one of the better market settings, since it is near the park that surrounds the center of this town, between now-demolished city walls and the ring boulevard. Organized by Peter Kraus, Ottstrasse 2, 8071 Ingolstadt, telephone (08456) 89 35.

Trödelmarkt (junk market) third Sunday of every month at the Gut Herrenschwaige. Organized by Firma Schönacher, telephone (0841) 7 14 31.

Iserlohn 5860

Antikmarkt (antique market) first weekend of November at the Parkhalle Alexanderhöhe. Organized by WEWO Antikmärkte, Rudi-Stefan-Allee 14, 6520 Worms, telephone (02332) 21 87.

Itzehoe 2210

Flohmarkt (flea market) second Sunday of October at the Einkaufzentrum (shopping center) in the town center. Organized by Firma Kingmann, Holstenstrasse 52, 2216 Schenefeld, telephone (04892) 2 67.

Jülich 5170

Trödelmarkt (junk market) third Sunday of August at the Flussufer (riverbank). Organized by Harry Owens Flohmarkt GmbH, Blaubach 38, 5000 Köln, telephone (0221) 23 53 65.

Kaiserslautern 6750

Antik- und Trödelmarkt (antique and junk market) first weekend in October at the Barbarossahalle. Information from Hans W. Nippen, Im Ferning 4, 7505 Ettlingen, telephone (07243) 1 21 06.

Flohmarkt (flea market) first Sunday of October at the Messeplatz in the east side of town, off Altenwoogstrasse. The following Saturday the market is held on Martinsplatz. Information from Organisation A. Hövelmeyer, Altenwoogstrasse 41, 6750 Kaiserslautern, telephone (0631) 4 04 77.

Trödelmarkt (junk market) last Sunday of October in the parking lot in front of the Hauptbahnhof (main railway station). Organized by Gabrielle Wallon, 4005 Meerbusch 1, telephone (02105) 56 51.

Kalkar 4192

Flohmarkt (flea market) second Sunday of May and October in the Marktplatz vor dem Rathaus in the village center. This market has been held on the same days for many years at the same location. Organized by Gabrielle Wallon, Postfach 39, 4005 Meerbusch 1, telephone (02105) 56 51.

Kaltenkirchen 2358

Trödelmarkt (junk market) last Sunday of every month at the IKEA-Familia Einkaufzentrum (shopping center). Organized by Burmeister, 2000 Hamburg/Norderstedt, telephone (040) 5 22 39 98.

Kamen 4708

Trödelmarkt (junk market) last Sunday of October at the IKEA Einkaufzentrum parking lot. Organized by Norbert Junge, Talbahnstrasse 4, 5190 Stolberg, telephone (02402) 2 30 07.

Kamp-Linfort 4132

Trödelmarkt und Handwerkmarkt (junk and artisans' market) first weekend in October takes place as part of the Stadtfest (city festival) throughout the center of the town. Information from Werbegemeinschaft Kamp-Linfort e. V., Postfach 19 02, 4132 Kamp-Linfort, telephone (02842) 8 15 93.

Karlsruhe 7500

(Please also see Flehingen, Forch, and Huttenheim.)

Kunsthandwerkmarkt (art and handicrafts market) second weekend of October at the Oststadthalle. Organized by Hans W. Nippen, Im Ferning 4, 7505 Ettlingen, telephone (07243) 1 21 06.

Münzbörse (coin exchange) one Sunday of October (sometimes first, other years third) at the Nancyhalle. Organized by Günter Wolf, Am Pfinztor 20, 7500 Karlsruhe 41, telephone (0721) 40 14 14.

Kunst- und Antikmarkt (art and antique market) first weekend of November in the Stadthalle. Information from Hinte Messe und Ausstellungs GmbH, Postfach 2948, 7500 Karlsruhe 1, telephone (0721) 2 29 01.

Spielzeugmarkt (toy market) last Sunday of October in the foyer of the Konzertshaus. Organized by Kirschner & Patarek GmbH, Ostwall 39, 4150 Krefeld 1, telephone (02841) 2 62 60.

Eisenbahn- Puppen- und Spielzeugbörse (railway, puppet, and toy exchange) first Sunday of November at the Festhalle in the suburb of Karlsruhe-Durlach, about 7 kilometers east of the city center. Easy access from the Autobahn

(Karlsruhe-Durlach exit). Parking is available. Information from Hannelore Püttner, Volzstrasse 8, 7500 Karlsruhe, telephone (0721) 68 26 64.

Kassel 3500

Flohmarkt (flea market) first Saturday of every month (but when the first is on a Sunday, the following weekend) at the Kurhessenhalle. Information from Rode Messen, Schloss Sickendorf, 6420 Lauterbach 7, telephone (06641) 30 26.

Flohmarkt (flea market) second and fourth weekends of most months at the Messehallen (fairgrounds) across the Fuldabrücke from the main city center. Information from Rode Messen, Schloss Sickendorf, 6420 Lauterbach 7, telephone (06641) 30 26.

Antik- und Kunst Woche (antique and art week) first weekend in October every year at the Stadthalle on Friedrich-Ebert-Strasse. Easily accessible by tram. Parking garage is across the street. This is one of the larger fall events, with large quantities of furniture, silver, porcelain, and other miscellaneous items. Information from Rode Messen, Schloss Sickendorf, 6420 Lauterbach 7, telephone (06641) 30 26.

Kaufbeuren 8950

Flohmarkt (flea market) last Saturday of October at the Tänzfestplatz. Organized by Veranstaltungsagentur Schuller, Magnusstrasse 22, 8960 Kempten, telephone (0831) 6 58 27.

Kaunitz-Verl 2 4837

Handwerkermarkt (artisans' market) first Saturday at every month at the Ostwestfalenhalle. Information from Herr Graffunder,

Marktamt der Stadt Verl, Rathaus, 4837 Kaunitz-Verl, telephone (05246) 5 02 16.

Kehl 7640

Antikmarkt (antique market) last Sunday of October at the Stadthalle. Organized by Antiquariat Peter Kiefer GmbH, Ebersteinstrasse 14, 7530 Pforzheim, telephone (07231) 1 72 72.

Kelheim 8420

Flohmarkt (flea market) fourth Sunday of every month from March through October at the Rennstrecke (Langkeller Little Apple) parking lot. Organized by D. K. Gerhard Stock, Am Hang 9, 8422 Riedenburg, telephone (09442) 22 49.

Kelkheim 6233

Antik- und Trödelmarkt (antique and junk market) first Sunday of January, second Sunday of April, and fourth Sunday of October at the Stadthalle. Information from Eberhard Neumann, Am Grünen Graben 22a, 6000 Frankfurt, telephone (069) 51 11 95.

Kelkheim 8420

Trödelmarkt (junk market) last Sunday of May, August, September, and October at the Rennstrecke. Organized by D. K. Gerhard Stock, Am Hang 9, 8422 Riedenburg, telephone (09442) 22 49.

Kempen 4152

Trödelmarkt (junk market) first Saturday of October on the Burgparkplatz and nearby Thomasstrasse in the town center. Organized by Norbert Junge, Obersteinstrasse 51, 5190 Stolberg, telephone (02402) 2 30 07.

Kempten (Allgäu) 8960

Trödelmarkt (junk market) first Saturday of October in the Allgäuhalle. Organized by Veranstaltungsagentur Schiller, Magnusstrasse 22, 8960 Kempten, telephone (0831) 6 58 27.

Kerpen 5014

Trödelmarkt (junk market) last weekend of September in the Innenstadt of the Kerpen-Horren district. This location is also used for the Adventsmarkt (Advent market) the first weekend of December. The second weekend of December, the market moves to the square in front of the Alte Kirch (Old Church) in the Sindorf district. Organized by R. Grossman, Johann-Sebastian-Bach-Strasse 20, 5014 Kerpen-Mödrath, telephone (02237) 5 20 66.

Trödelmarkt (junk market) first Sunday in October at the Kaufhalle Parkplatz (parking garage). Information from Hermann & Lampert, Hasselholzerweg 9, 5100 Aachen, telephone (0241) 7 20 21.

Antik- und Trödelmarkt (antique and junk market) second Sunday of October at the Kaufhalle Parkplatz. Organized by Halina Müller GmbH, Kölnerstrasse 246, 4000 Düsseldorf 1, telephone (0211) 78 25 56.

Kiel 2300

Flohmarkt (flea market) first Sunday of every month at the Rathausplatz in the city center. Public parking in garages behind the city hall and under nearby squares. Information from Kulturamt der Stadt Kiel, Holstenstrasse 88, 2300 Kiel, telephone (0431) 9 01 34 04.

Flohmarkt (flea market) third Saturday of January and February, third Sunday of October in the Ostseehalle, a few hundred meters south of the Rathaus. Parking on the street, in paid lots, or in an underground garage. Information from EXPO Management GmbH, Eichenweg 59, 2300 Kiel 17, telephone (0431) 80 40 10.

Trödelmarkt (junk market) fourth Friday, Saturday, and Sunday of February at the Kieler Innenstadt Umschlag. Information from Bauverwaltung der Stadt Kiel, 2300 Kiel, telephone (0431) 9 01 25 87.

Spielzeugbörse (toy exchange) third Sunday of October at the Kieler Yacht Club Hotel, at Hindenbergerufer 70, along the shore two kilometers north of the city center. Organized by Klaus Graeber, Hohenstein 73, 5600 Wuppertal 2, telephone (0202) 55 05 89.

Kierspe 5883

Flohmarkt (flea market) second weekend of October at the Schulzentrum (school center). Organized by Rolf à Brassard. Rheinstrasse 4, 5434 Dembach, telephone (02602) 7 08 39.

Kirchheimbolanden 6719

Trödelmarkt (junk market) first Sunday of October and November at the Kreisverwaltung (local government offices). Organized by Horst Zehnpfennig, Pestalozzistrasse 54, 6504 Nierstein, telephone (06133) 5 85 11.

Kitzingein 8710

Antikmarkt (antique market) first weekend of October in the Florian-Geyer-Halle. Organized by Firma Weber, Semmelstrasse 42, 8700 Würzburg, telephone (0931) 1 37 08.

Kleve 4190

Flohmarkt (flea market) first Sunday of October at in front of the Rathaus in the town center. Information from Gabrielle Wallon, Postfach 39, 4005 Meerbusch 1, telephone (02105) 56 51.

Klingen bei Aichach 8891

(An outlying village of Aichach.)

Flohmarkt (flea market) the second Saturday of every month at the Gastwirtschaft Haus Harti in the Ortsmitte (village center). Organized by Gastwirtschaft Haus Harti, at the same address, telephone (08251) 28 61.

Koblenz 5400

(Please also see Landstein and Mülheim.)

Flohmarkt (flea market) first weekend every month at Am Primus. Organized by Helene Schmitt, Karl-Marx-Strasse, 5450 Neuwied 12, telephone (02631) 7 66 44.

Schallplatten- und Musikbörse (record and music exchange) third Sunday in October at the Rhein-Mosel-Halle, near the Schloss (castle) and the Rhine bridge. Parking is available near the hall. Information from Kogel & Lauber, Kornmarkt 10-12, 6900 Siegen, telephone (0271) 5 15 01. This hall is also frequently used for antique fairs throughout the year on a sporadic basis (not always on weekends).

Antik- und Flohmarkt (antique and flea market) first Sunday of October and November at the Nutzviehhalle. Information from Fotis Nikolopoulos, Im Sayntal 65, 5413 Bendorf/Rhein, telephone (02622) 60 29.

Antik- und Trödelmarkt (antique and junk market) last Sunday in February, March, and August, and second Sunday in March at the Löhr- Center in the Löhr district. Organized by Hermann & Lampert, Hasselholzerweg 9, 5100 Aachen, telephone (0241) 7 20 21.

Kochel am See 8113

Oberland-Flohmarkt (highland flea market) second and fourth Sunday in October at the Gastätte Heimatbühne. Information from Manfred Laemmerer, Preysingstrasse 53/II, 8000 München 80, telephone (089) 4 48 59 68.

Köln 5000

(Please also see the nearby towns of Bensburg, Bergisch-Gladbach, Brühl, and Dormagen, since markets there are accessible on the local public transit network.)

This large city is best known for its soaring cathedral, which though immense is rather sober inside. It's also a commercial and industrial center which was heavily bombed in the Second World War.

A large number of flea markets and shows take place in and around this city. Markets move from week to week in a monthly cycle, rather than using the same locations all the time. Therefore, the regular markets are listed in the order that they occur during the month; the irregularly held markets are listed at the end.

The number in parenthesis in each listing corresponds to the market location on the map.

Antik- und Trödelmarkt (antique and junk market) (20) every weekend of year round at the Deutzer Bahnhof in the suburb of Köln-Deutz, just across the Rhine from the city center. A parking garage is available; street parking is limited. Access by public transit to the Deutzer Bahnhof. Organized by Hermann & Lampert, Hasselholzerweg 9, 5100 Aachen, telephone (0241) 7 20 21.

Trödelmarkt (junk market) (14) first Saturday in each month on Berlinerstrasse in the suburb of Köln-Mulheim. This market has few antiques, some collectables, a large amount of household goods, and cheap porcelains. A good place to buy tools. Toilets on site cost 40 pfennig. Street parking is available in the surrounding streets along the Clevischer Ring. Access by public transit is on tram line 5 to the Sparrstrasse stop, then walk north to Berlinerstrasse, or take bus lines 43 and 52 to the intersection of the Clevischer Ring and Berlinerstrasse. Organized by Waltraud Kopp, Postfach 52 03 06, 5000 Köln 51, telephone (0221) 36 55 00.

Flohmarkt (flea market) (22) first and second Sunday of October at the Hagenwork in the Kalk district. This is a relatively new market. Organized by NS-Service, Reinhard Schmale, Teichstrasse 16, 5000 Köl6, telephone (0221) 53 43 14.

Trödelmarkt (junk market) first Sunday of every month at the Autokino (drive-in movie theatre) in the suburb of Köln-Pulheim. (See Köln-Dösseldorf detail map.) Organized by Waltraud Kopp, Postfach 52 03 06, 5000 Köln 51, telephone (0221) 36 55 00.

Trödelmarkt (junk market) (5) first Sunday from April through December at the Depot-Markt in the suburb of Köln-Ehrenfeld. Organized by Waltraud Kopp, Postfach 52 03 06, 5000 Köln 51, telephone (0221) 36 55 00.

Trödelmarkt (junk market) (22) first Sunday (except June through September) and fourth Sunday of (except September) at the Markt-platz in the Köln-Gremberg district. Information from Waltraud Kopp, Postfach 52 03 06, 5000 Köln 51, telephone (0221) 36 55 00.

Trödelmarkt (junk market) (23) first Sunday in February through October, and third Sunday in January, at the Marktplatz on Ostheim-erstrasse in the Köln-Vingst district. Organized by Van Zütphen Direktmarketing, Fricke-strasse 36, 5010 Bergheim, telephone (02271) 5 44 00.

Antik- und Trödelmarkt (antique and junk market) (16) second Saturday of the month from June through October and first weekend of January at the Markplatz in front of the

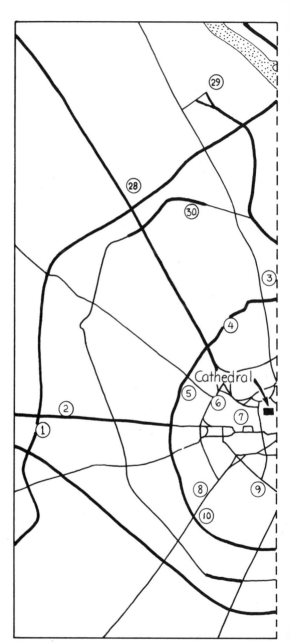

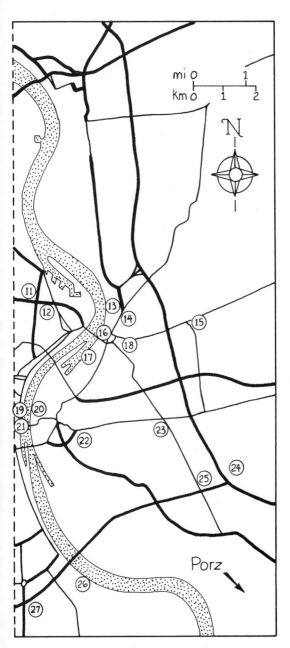

Arbeitsamt (government employment office) in the Köln-Mülheim district. Organized by Van Zütphen Direktmarketing, Frickestrasse 36, 5010 Bergheim, telephone (02271) 5 44 00.

Trödelmarkt (junk market) (15) second Saturday of the month from March through October at the Marktplatz on Piccolominstrasse in the Köln-Holweide district. Organized by Van Zütphen Direktmarketing, Frickestrasse 36, 5010 Bergheim, telephone (02271) 5 44 00.

Antikmarkt (antique market) second Sunday of every month year round in the center of the Ladenstadt district. Organized by Harry Owens Flohmarkt GmbH, Blaubach 30, 5000 Köln, telephone (0221) 23 53 65.

Antik- und Trödelmarkt (antique and junk market) (24) second Sunday of every month year round at the OBI on Rosrätherstrasse in the Merheim district. This can be reached by tram on the Rath line. Organized by Galow, telephone (02203) 2 26 96.

Trödelmarkt (junk market) (11) second Sunday of the month from March through December at the Interspar on Boltensternstrasse in the Köln-Niehl district. From June through September the market moves a short distance away and is held on the first Sunday of the month at Wirichs Baumarkt on Escherstrasse. Organized by NS-Service, Reinhard Schmale, Teichstrasse 16, 5000 Köln, telephone (0221) 53 43 14.

Antik- und Trödelmarkt (antique and junk market) (18) second Sunday of the month from April through December at the Extra- Bau- und Hobby-Markt in the Köln-Buchheim district. Organized by Waltraud Kopp, Postfach 52 03 06, 5000 Köln 51, telephone (0221) 36 55 00.

Flohmarkt (flea market) (19) third Saturday of the month from March through October and the four Advent Sundays (usually last of November through the Sunday before Christmas) in the Altstadt (old town) in the city center. Organized by Harry Owens Flohmarkt GmbH, Blaubach 30, 5000 Köln, telephone (0221) 23 53 65.

Trödelmarkt (junk market) (30) on the Sunday nearest the 18th of the month from March through September at the Marktplatz on Schlackerstrasse in the Köln-Longerich district. Organized by NS-Service, Reinhard Schmale, Teichstrasse 16, 5000 Köln 30, telephone (0221) 53 43 14.

Trödelmarkt (junk market) third Sunday the month from of March through October at the IKEA-Parkplatz in the suburb of Köln-Godorf. Information from Waltraud Kopp, Postfach 52 03 06, 5000 Köln 51, telephone (0221) 36 55 00.

Antik- und Trödelmarkt (antique and junk market) (16) third Sunday of every month at the Festplatz under the Mühlhausen Bridge in the suburb of Köln-Mülheim. Park on the street. Access by public transit is by trams 5 and 15 to Wienerplatz and then walk. on the same day, organized by Müller Musik, 5000 Köln, telephone (0221) 61 56 29. Another market takes place at the nearby Stadhalle on the same day from September through April and the first Sunday of January October at the Stadthalle. Organized by Christa Schalkowski, Hedwigstrasse 19, 5600 Wuppertal 1, telephone (0202) 3008 48.

Antikmarkt (antique market) third Sunday of February, May, September, and October, and first Sunday of December at Gürtzenich auction sales rooms at Unter Fettenbrennen 19. Information from Stadtverwaltung Köln, Verkehrsamt, at the same address, telephone (0221) 2 21 33 43.

Trödelmarkt (junk market) (18) fourth Sunday of every month from March through December in the PS-Markt parking lot in the suburb of Köln-Mülheim. Plentiful parking is available. Access by public transit on tram lines 5 and 15 or busses 5, 16, 38, and 59 to Wienerplatz, then walk. Organized by Waltraud Kopp,

Postfach 52 03 06, 5000 Köln 51, telephone (0221) 36 55 00.

Trödelmarkt (junk market) (25) last Saturday of the month from March through October at the Sportpark on Frankfurterstrasse in the Köln-Höhenberg district. Organized by Van Zütphen Direktmarketing, Frickestrasse 36, 5010 Bergheim, telephone (02271) 5 44 00.

Also a market takes place the third weekend in February and September and last weekend of May at the Sporthalle organized by Hermann & Lampert, Hasselholzerweg 9, 5100 Aachen, telephone (0241) 7 20 21.

Antik- und Trödelmarkt (antique and junk market) (11) last weekend of every month from February through November at the Pferderennbahn (racetrack) in the Köln-Wiedenpech district. Organized by Nicholas Dollmann, Teichstrasse 16, 5000 Köln 30, telephone (0221) 53 17 44.

Trödelmarkt (junk market) (4) fourth Sunday of March, second and fourth Sunday of through October on the Niehler Gürtel and Wilhelmsplatz in the suburb of Köln-Nippes, about two kilometers north of the cathedral. Street parking available, but places are often difficult to find find. Access by public transit on the U-Bahn to Nippes-Florastrasse, then walk toward the cathedral two blocks and turn right for one more block. Organized by Harry Owens Flohmarkt GmbH, Blaubach 30, 5000 Köln, telephone (0221) 23 53 65. and occasionally by Udo Potzeldt, Wickuhl 35, 5204 Lohmar 21, telephone (02205) 64 77.

Trödelmarkt (junk market) (10) last Sunday in March, May, July, and September at Auerbachplatz in the Köln-Sulz district. Organized by Van Zütphen Direktmarketing, Frickestrasse 36, 5010 Bergheim, telephone (02271) 5 44 00.

Irregularly Held Markets—Call to confirm before you go.

Antik- und Trödelmarkt (antique and junk market) first weekend of January at the Alte Mensa and the second weekend of January at the Neue Mensa. Organized by Hermann & Lampert, Hasselholzerweg 9, 5100 Aachen, telephone (0241) 7 20 21.

Trödelmarkt (junk market) (10) last Sunday of June, August, and October on the Kletterburg-Gürtel in the Köln-Klettenburg district. Organized by Van Zütphen Direktmarketing, Frickestrasse 36, 5010 Bergheim, telephone (02271) 5 44 00.

Antikmarkt (antique market) second weekend of October under the Fernsehturm (television transmission tower). Organized by Alida Schleusener, Waldfriedstrasse 1, 5000 Köln 60, telephone (0221) 71 34 14.

Antiquitätentage (antique days) (26) second weekend of October at the Bildungzentrum in the southern suburb of Köln-Rodenkirchen, past the Autobahn. Access by public transit on tram line 16 to the end, or bus line 26 and get off at Rodenkirchnen-Zentrum. Organized by Brass-Villegas, Gladbacher Strasse 32, 4060 Viersen 1, telephone (02162) 2 22 73.

Trödelmarkt (junk market) (Porz) second Sunday of October at the Autokino (drive-in theatre) in the southern suburb of Köln-Porz. Parking available at the site. This market is not easily accessible by public transit. Organized by Waltraud Kopp, Postfach 52 03 06, 5000 Köln 51, telephone (0221) 36 55 00.

Antik- und Trödelmarkt (antique and junk market) (29) second Sunday of November at the City-Center-Passage in the Chorweiler district. Organized by Waltraud Kopp, Postfach 52 03 06, 5000 Köln 51, telephone (0221) 36 55 00.

Trödelmarkt (junk market) (21) third weekends of May and October at the Neumarkt in the old city center. Parking is available in a garage under the square. Organized by Freizeit und

Hobby GmbH, Riehlerstrasse 11, 5000 Köln 1, telephone (0221) 73 59 09.

Trödelmarkt (junk market) Easter Sunday and Monday (also a holiday) at the Tiefgarage (underground garage) in the Köln-Park district. Organized by Hermann & Lampert, Hasselholzerweg 9, 5100 Aachen, telephone (0241) 7 20 21.

Antik- und Trödelmarkt (antique and junk market) (2) second Sunday of January and October at the Einkaufzentrum on Aachenerstrasse in the Köln-Wieden district. Parking available; also accessible by the Braunsfeld tram line. Organized by Inter- Antik, Michael Becker, Mommsenstrasse 10, 4006 Eckrath, telephone (02104) 4 61 52.

Trödelmarkt (junk market) (5) fourth weekend of October in the Reisen-Gewerbehalle at Venloerstrasse 41 in the Ehrenfeld district. Organized by Hermann & Lampert, Hasselholzerweg 9, 5100 Aachen, telephone (0241) 7 20 21.

Flohmarkt (flea market) (27) first Sunday of October on Vorgebirgstrasse in the suburb of Köln-Süd. Organized by Harry Owens Flohmarkt GmbH, Blaubach 30, 5000 Köln, telephone (0221) 23 53 65.

Trödelmarkt (junk market) (28) fourth Sunday of October at the Agros in the suburb of Köln-Pesch. Organized by Lothar Schneider, Bahnhofstrasse 187, 4100 Duisburg 12, telephone (0203) 55 08 08.

Trödelmarkt (junk market) (1) first weekend of October at the Kirmesplatz in the Köln-Junkersdorf district. This is near where Aachenerstrasse crosses the Autobahn west of the city center. This irregular market is organized by Karl Heinz Müller, Regentenstrasse 97, 5000 Köln 80, telephone (0221) 62 15 58.

Trödelmarkt (junk market) (12) second Sunday of October along the Neihler Gurtel, north of the city center. Organized by Udo Potzeldt, Wickuhl 35, 5204 Lohmar 21, telephone (02205) 64 77.

Antiktag (antique day) (7) second Sunday of October in the Intercontinental Hotel at Helenenstrasse 14, near the Römer Turm in the city center. This show offers only certified antiques. Organized by Brass-Villegas, Gladbacherstrasse 32, 4060 Wiergen 1, telephone (02162) 3 18 18.

Trödelmarkt (junk market) (23) third Sunday of October at the Co-op Center in the Höln-Dellbrück district. Organized by Waltraud Kopp, Postfach 520306, 5000 Köln 51, telephone (0221) 36 55 00.

Köln Königsdorf 5020

Antik- und Trödelmarkt (antique and junk market) third weekend of October at the ASKO-Möbelhaus Antikhallen in the Cologne (Köln) suburb of Köln/Königsdorf. Organized by Hermann & Lampert, Hasselholzerweg 9, 5100 Aachen, telephone (0241) 7 20 21.

Königsbrunn 8901

(Please also see Augsburg.)

Antik- und Trödelmarkt (antique and junk market) second Sunday of January and second weekend of October and November on the Blumenallee and adjoining Sportpavilion. Information from Helmuth Müller, Donauwörtherstrasse, 8901 Königsbrunn, telephone (08231) 55 89.

Konstanz 7750

Kunst- und Trödelmarkt (art and junk market) second Saturday of October at the Domhotel

St. Johann. Organized by Bruno Konrad, Falkenstrasse 21, 7965 Ostrach 8, telephone (07558) 10 10.

Korntal 7015

(Please see Stuttgart.)

Korb 7054

(Please also see Stuttgart.)

Antik- und Trödelmarkt (antique and junk market) second Sunday of November in the Remstalhalle. Organized by H. & H.K. Fischer, Uhlandstrasse 18, 7255 Rutesheim, telephone (07152) 5 43 77.

Korbach 3540

Antik- und Trödelmarkt (antique and junk market) third weekend of every month year round and the fourth Sunday of June, August, and November at the Halle Waldeck. Organized by Lamm & Ende, telephone (05631) 6 21 09.

Krefeld 4150

Flohmarkt (flea market) every Sunday year round on Ritterstrasse in the city center. Information from Gabrielle Wallon, Postfach 39, 4005 Meerbusch 1, telephone (02105) 56 51.

Flohmarkt (flea market) every Sunday year round at the Guterbahnhof in the suburb of Krefeld-Uerdingen. Organized by Gabrielle Wallon, Postfach 39, 4005 Meerbusch 1, telephone (02105) 56 51.

Flohmarkt (flea market) first and second weekend of the month from March through November on Schönwasserstrasse in the Oppum district. Information from Lothar

Schneider, Bahnhofstrasse 187, 4100 Duisburg 12, telephone (0203) 55 08 08.

Flohmarkt (flea market) first Sunday of October at Wirichs and Havelstrasse in the suburb of Krefeld-Fischeln. Organized by Norbert Junge, Obersteinstrasse 51, 5190 Stolberg, telephone (02402) 2 30 07.

Antikmarkt (antique market) first weekend of October at the Kolpinghaus. Organized by Brass-Villegas, Gladbacherstrasse 32, 4060 Viersen 1, telephone (021 62) 3 18 18.

Antik- und Trödelmarkt (antique and junk market) second weekend of October at the Golopprenbahn (racetrack), off the Nord-tangente. Organized by Komischke & Lange, Heiderweg 53, 4000 Düsseldorf 31, telephone (0203) 55 08 08.

Antikmarkt (antique market) second Sunday of February, fourth Sunday in March, and first Sunday of November in the Hansa- Centrum-und Passage indoor shopping center. Organized by Hermann & Lampert, Hasselholzerweg 9, 5100 Aachen, telephone (0241) 7 20 21.

Trödelmarkt (junk market) last Sunday in February at the Allkauf Einkaufzentrum. Organized by Hermann & Lampert, Hassel-holzerweg 9, 5100 Aachen, telephone (0241) 7 20 21.

Kreutztal 5910

Trödelmarkt (junk market) fourth Sunday of October at the Minimal Einkaufzentrum on Marburger Strasse. Organized by Kogel & Lauber, Kornmarkt 10-12, 6900 Siegen, telephone (0271) 5 15 01.

Kröv am Mosel 5563

Antik- und Trödelmarkt (antique and junk market) first weekend of May, September, and

October, and second weekend of July and December at the Weinbrunnehalle und Vorplatz. Organized by Marktveranstaltungen Albert Becker, Händelstrasse 46, 5560 Wittlich, telephone (06571) 6 99 50.

Künzelsau 7118

Antikmarkt (antique market) third Sunday of October at the Stadthalle in the town center. Information from Antiquitariat Peter Kiefer GmbH, Ebersteinstrasse 14, 7530 Pforzheim, telephone (07231) 1 72 72.

Ladenburg 6802

Altstadtfest (old city festival) flea market, second weekend of September in the town center. Organized by the Stadt Ladenburg.

Spielzeugmarkt (toy market) second Sunday of October in the Neues Rathaus (new city hall). Organized by Götz Chalkidis-Seidel, Hauptstrasse 5, 6802 Ladenburg, telephone (06203) 1 30 14.

Langenhagen 3012

(Please see Hannover.)

Lahr-Reichenbach 7630

Trödelmarkt (junk market) second Sunday of October at the Geroldsecker-Halle. Organized by Klaus Sheppe, KS-Management, Fidel Fischer Strasse 1, 7580 Bühl, telephone (07223) 48 95.

Lampertheim 6840

Flohmarkt (flea market) first Saturday of October at the Selbsbedienungs Kaufhof Riedkauf. Organized by Agentur M. Lukas,

Mönchhofstrasse 142, 6806 Viernheim, telephone (0621) 72 15 03.

Landau 6740

Antikmarkt (antique market) third weekend of
October at the Festhalle. Organized by Falk
Anders, An der Martinspforte, 6719 Einselthum,
telephone (06355) 22 94. This hall is used
sporadically for markets throughout the year,
usually on weekends.

Flohmarkt (flea market) second Sunday of
October at the Plaza shopping center parking
lot. Organized by Person-Werbung, Weinstrasse Süd 20, 6702 Bad Durkheim, telephone
(06322) 6 66 00.

Landshut 8300

Flohmarkt (flea market) third Saturday in
March through December at Kennedyplatz,
and in October at Leiderersall. Organized by
D. K. Gerhard Stock, Am Hang 9, 8422
Riedenburg, telephone (09442) 22 49.

Landstein 5420

(A village near Koblenz.)

Antikmarkt (antique market) first weekend of
November in the Stadthalle. Organized by Rolf à
Brassard, Rheinstrasse 4, 5434 Dernbach,
telephone (02602) 7 08 39.

Langenberg 5602

*(Please also see Essen, Heilingenhaus, and
Wüppertal.)*

Handwerkermarkt (artisans' market) third
Sunday of October in the town center. This
market is part of the annual Stadtfest (city

festival) celebration. Information from telephone (02161) 18 63 86.

Langenfeld 4018

Funk- Radio und Trödelmarkt (television, radio, and junk market) second Sunday of October in the Stadthalle. Information from Necker Radiomuseum, Hauptstrasse 83, 4018 Langenfeld, telephone (02173) 1 21 27.

Lauf an der Regnitz 8560

Antikmarkt (antique market) first weekend of October at the Wollnersaal. Information from Wolfgang Meissner, Panorama 27, 8481 Leuchtenberg, telephone (09659) 7 01.

Laufen (Oberbayern) 8229

Floh- und Trödelmarkt (flea and junk market) every Saturday year round in the Untere Altstadt (lower old town). Information from R. Tiedemann, Rottmayrstrasse 26, 8229 Laufen, telephone (08682) 16 34.

Laufenburg (Baden) 7887

Flohmarkt (flea market) last Friday of October at the MAM-Market parking lot. Organized by Patric Hartwig, Bahnhofstrasse 21a, 7778 Marktdorf, telephone (07544) 66 09.

Lauterbach 6420

Flohmarkt (flea market) first Sunday of every month at the Schloss Sickendorf (Sickendorf Castle). This market is also called the Pferdemarkt (translates to horse market). Information from Rode Messen, Schloss Sickendorf, 6420 Lauterbach 7, telephone (06641) 30 26.

Lehrte 3160

Trödelmarkt (junk market) first Saturday of October in the Innenstadt (old city center). Organized by M. Nordmann, Leconskamp 18, 4513 Belm, telephone (05406) 40 41.

Lemgo 4920

Antikmarkt (antique market) fourth Sunday of October at the Schlossscheune. Organized by Galerie G. Krencky, Heidestrasse 9a, 4900 Herford, telephone (05221) 5 67 41.

Lengerich 4540

Trödelmark (junk market) first Saturday of October in the Innenstadt (old town center). Organized by Galene G. Krencky, Heidestrasse 9a, 4900 Herford, telephone (05221) 5 67 41.

Leonburg 7250

Antik- und Trödelmarkt (antique and junk market) second weekend in June and November at the Leo-Center Ladenpassage. Organized by WEWO Antikmärkte, Rudi-Stefan-Allee 14, 6520 Worms, telephone (06241) 7 58 71.

Antiktage (antique days) second weekend of October in the Stadthalle. Organized by Peter Fuchs, Bahnhofstrasse 5, 6940 Weinheim, telephone (06201) 1 22 32.

Trödelmarkt (junk market) second Sunday of November at the TSV-Halle in the Eltingen district. Organized by H. & H. K. Fischer, Uhlandstrasse 18, 7255 Rutesheim, telephone (07152) 5 43 77.

Leverkusen 5090

(Please also see Köln.)

Antik- und Trödelmarkt (antique and junk market) first and third Sunday of April through November at the Super 2000 in the Küppersteg district about one kilometer west of the Autobahnkreutz Leverkusen. Organized by NS-Service, Reinhard Schmale, Teichstrasse 16, 5000 Köln 30, telephone (0221) 53 43 14.

Sommerfest (summer festival) second weekend of June at the Königsbergerplatz in the Leverkusen-Reindorf district. Organized by Werner Nolden, Altstadtstrasse 196, 5090 Leverkusen 3, telephone (02171) 4 55 92.

Volksfest (people's festival) flea market third weekend of June at the Wappermann Park Marktplatz in the Leverkusen-Schlebusch district. Organized by Werner Nolden, Altstadtstrasse 196, 5090 Leverkusen 3, telephone (02171) 4 55 92.

Spielzeugmarkt (toy market) first Sunday of October at the Forum in the town center. Organized by M. Cremer, Bismarckstrasse 16, 4010 Hilden, telephone (02103) 5 11 33.

Flohmarkt (flea market) third Sunday of October in front of the Bahnhof (train station) in the Schlebusch district. Organized by Gabrielle Wallon, Postfach 39, 4005 Meerbusch 1, telephone (02105) 56 51.

Weinachtsmarkt (Christmas market) from the first day of December to the third Sunday of December at the Zentrum of the Leverkusen-Schlebusch district. Organized by Werner Nolden, Altstadtstrasse 196, 5090 Leverkusen 3, telephone (02171) 4 55 92.

Seefest (lake festival) third weekend of July on lake on Oulustrasse. Organized by Werner Nolden, Altstadtstrasse 196, 5090 Leverkusen 3, telephone (02171) 4 55 92.

Lichtenfels 8620

Antik- und Trödelmarkt (antique and junk market) second weekend in October. Contact the organizer at telephone (09561) 6 97 72.

Limburg an der Lahn 6250

Flohmarkt (flea market) first weekend of September in the Innenstadt at the City-Ring, the first weekend of October in the Markthalle (market hall), the last weekend of October in the Buderus-Werke building, and second weekend of November at the Markthalle. Organized by Rolf à Brassard, Rheinstrasse 4, 5434 Dernbach, telephone (02602) 7 08 39.

Lindlar 5253

Antik- und Trödelmarkt (antique and junk market) first weekend of September and last weekend of November at the Sport- und Freizeit Park. Organized by Richard Altmann, Mediaschergasse 13, 5276 Siel 3, telephone (02262) 18 66.

Linz am Rhein 5460

Münzen- Briefmark- und Postkartenmarkt (coin, stamp, and postcard market) fourth weekend of January in the town center. Organized by Agentur W. Demandt, Domackerstrasse 29, 5010 Bergheim 3, telephone (02271) 9 54 94.

Lippstadt 4780

Weinachtsmarkt (Christmas market) second weekend of November and third weekend of December in the Südliche Schützenhalle. This market has antiques, junk, and arts and crafts. Organized by A. M. V. V. Jörn Werber, Am Grossen Holz 9, 4817 Leopoldshöhe, telephone (05208) 14 23.

Lohmar 5204

Kunst- und Töpfermarkt (art and pottery market) first weekend of October in the Jabach-Halle and last weekend of October in the Hauptschule Aula (main school auditorium). Information from Alida Schleusener, Waldfriedstrasse 1, 5000 Köln 60, telephone (0221) 71 34 14.

Antik- und Trödelmarkt (antique and junk market) third weekend of October at the Jabach-Halle. Organized by Franz Stefan, An der Mühle 32, 4052 Korsenbroich 4, telephone (02166) 8 35 09.

Lü—
is alphabetized as Lue—

Ludwigsburg 7140

(Please also see Stuttgart.)

Trödelmarkt (junk market) first Sunday of October at the Gemeindehalle in the Neckarweihingen district. Organized by Antiquitariat Peter Keifer GmbH, Ebersteinstrasse 14, 7530 Pforzheim, telephone (07231) 1 72 72.

Trödelmarkt (junk market) third Sunday of October and first Sunday of November in the Mehrzweckhalle in the Eglosheim district, about two kilometers northwest of the main rail station. Information from Agentur Walter GmbH, Postfach 1171, 7140 Ludwigsburg, telephone (07141) 2 76 01.

Antikmarkt (antique market) last Friday, Saturday, and Sunday of October at the Musikhalle. Organized by Falk Anders, An der Martinspforte, 6719 Einselthum, telephone (06355) 22 94.

Ludwigshafen 6700

Trödelmarkt (junk market) first Saturday of the month from April through June and September through November and the third weekend of December at the Haus der Jugend on Bahnhofstrasse. Information from Stadtjugendamt, Haus der Jugend, Bahnhofstrasse 30, 6700 Ludwigshafen 3, telephone (0621) 5 04 28 80.

Antiktage (antique days) third Friday, Saturday, and Sunday of October at the Pfalzbau. This is a major regional fair. Organized by Organisation Märkte-Messen Mezger, Zeppelinstrasse 4, 7770 Donaueschingen, telephone (0771) 1 39 39.

Antik- und Trödelmarkt (antique and junk market) first Saturday of October at the Rathaus-Center. Information from WEWO Antikmärkte, Rudi-Stefan-Allee 14, 6520 Worms, telephone (06241) 7 58 71.

Lübbecke 4990

Antik- und Trödelmarkt (antique and junk market) second weekend of August as part of the Bierbrennfest throughout the Innenstadt (old city center) and the first Sunday of October at the Marktkauf. The third weekend of October this market is held again in the Innenstadt. Information from A. M. V. V. Jörn Werber, Am Grossen Holz 9, 4817 Leopoldshöhe, telephone (05208) 14 23.

Lübeck 2400

Trödelmarkt (junk market) first Saturday of every month in the Stadtmitte (central market place), fronting the Rathaus. This centuries-old market in the center of the old Hanseatic League city has an interesting setting and variety. Street parking is difficult; several underground garages are in the neighborhood. Information from Büro Altstadt-Trödelmarkt

Lübeck, Thiel & Nickel, Halmweg 16, 2400
Lübeck 14, telephone (0451) 39 22 04.

Flohmarkt (flea market) first Sunday of most
months at the Plaza shopping center.
Organized by Gerhard Bauer, Wallgraben 44,
2100 Hamburg 90, telephone (040) 77 46 24.

Flohmarkt (flea market) second Sunday of
October at the Magnet Gelände (fairgrounds).
The third Sunday of October this market is held
at the Neukauf on Ziegelstrasse, southwest of
the city center. Organized by C. Hochberg,
Waltreiterweg 30, 2070 Grosshandelsdorf,
telephone (04102) k6 50 83.

Lüdenscheid 5880

Antikmarkt (antique market) second Sunday of
February and October at the Kulturhaus.
Organized by Theodor Wessling, Kurhausstrasse
31a, 4690 Herne 2, telephone (02325) 4 30 31.

Trödelmakt (junk market) first Sunday of
September in the Innenstadt. Organized by
Isenmeyer & Seltmann, telephone (02358) 74 01.

Antik- unt Trödelmarkt (antique and junk
market) last weekend of December through the
December 23 at the Stemplatz. This is part of
the annual Wiehnachtsmarkt (Christmas fair).
Organized by Cultura, 4000 Düsseldorf, telephone (0211) 67 27 22.

Lüdinghausen

Antikmarkt (antique market) fourth Sunday of
October at the Seppenrade-Festhalle. Organized by Galerie G. Krencky, Heidestrasse 9a,
4900 Herford, telephone (05221) 5 67 41.

Lüneburg 2120

Antik- und Trödelmarkt first Sunday (and
occasionally second Sunday) of every month at

the Schützenhaus. Information from Firma
Bona, Frankenberger Strasse 32, 3380 Goslar im
Harz, telephone (05321) 2 27 54.

Flohmarkt (flea market) second Saturday of
every month on the Am alten Kran. Only private
parties, not dealers, are permitted to sell at
this market. Information from Schul- und
Kulturamt, 2120 Lüneburg, telephone (04131)
3 22 00.

Antikmarkt (antique market) first Friday,
Saturday, and Sunday of January at the
Seminaris. Organized by Avorga GmbH,
Husarenstrasse 22, 3300 Braunschweig,
telephone (0531) 33 14 15.

Mainz 6500

(Please also see Ingelheim, Nieder Olm, and Raunheim.)

Flohmarkt (flea market) third Saturday of every
month year round on the Rheinufer/
Rheinpromenade (tree-shaded walk on the
bank of the Rhine in the city center downstream
about 100 meters from the bridge). Parking is
sometimes available at the site. Information
from the Ordnungsamt der Stadt Mainz, An
der Krimm 21, 6500 Mainz-Gonzenheim,
telephone (06131) 12 24 33.

Antikmarkt (antique market) second Sunday of
October in the Rheingoldhalle, which is along
the bank of the Rhine in the city center, just
south of the bridge. Parking is available in a
nearby lot. Organized by Michael Becker, Inter
Antik, Mommsenstrasse 10, 4006 Ekrath,
telephone (02104) 4 61 52. Other organizers
use this hall irregularly during the year.

Antik- und Trödelmarkt (antique and junk
market) first Sunday of October at the Massa
Einkaufzentrum in the suburban Bretzenheim
district. Organized by Reinhard Preuss,
Antoniusgasse 25, 6228 Eltville, telephone
(06120) 87 44.

Antiktage (antique days) first weekend of November in the Kurfürstliches Schloss. Organized by Michael Becker, Inter- Antik, Mommenstrasse 10, 4006 Eckrath, telephone (02104) 4 61 52.

Mannheim 6800

(Please also see Lampertheim, Ludwigshafen, and Mutterstadt.)

Trödelmarkt (junk market) every Saturday at Keppenheimerstrasse 53. Organized by M. Lukas, Mönchhofstrasse 14a, 6806 Viernheim, telephone (0021) 72 15 03.

Antikmarkt (antique market) second Sunday of April and last Sunday of October at the Kongresszentrum in the Rosengarten. Organized by Theodor Wessling, Kurhausstrasse 31a, 4690 Herne 2, telephone (02325) 4 30 31.

Antik- und Trödelmarkt (antique and junk market) first Saturday of October at the Autokino (drive-in theatre) on Friedrichstrasse. Organized by Reinhard Preuss, Antoniusgasse 25, 0228 Eltville, telephone (06123) 7 46 11.

Münzbörse (coin exchange) first Sunday of October in the Rosengarten (rose garden) building on Friedrichsplatz and Friedrichsring. Parking is available in lots and garages, and sometimes on the surrounding side streets. Information from Günter Wolf, Am Pfinztor 20, 7500 Karlsruhe 41, telephone (0721) 40 14 14.

Antikmarkt (antique market) second weekend of October in the Rosengarten. Organized by Falk Anders, An der Martinspforte, 6719 Einselthum, telephone (06355) 22 94.

Antik- und Trödelmarkt (antique and junk market) third weekend of October or second weekend in November (varies year by year) in the Rhein-Neckar-Halle. Organized by Hans

W. Nippen, Im Ferning 4, 7505 Ettlingen, telephone (07243) 1 21 06.

Marbach am Neckar 7142

Antik- und Trödelmarkt (antique and junk market) first weekend of November in the Stadthalle. Organized by Hans W. Nippen, Im Ferning 4, 7505 Ettlingen, telephone (07243) 1 21 06.

Marburg 3550

Flohmarkt (flea market) first Saturday of every month on the of the castle and old center of town on the Plantage am Steinweg. Underground parking is available in a garage off of Ketzerbachstrasse. Organized by the Stadtverwaltung, 3550 Marburg, telephone (06421) 20 13 36.

Antikmarkt (antique market) first Sunday of October at the Bürgerhaus in the Cappel district. Organized by Galerie G. Krencky, Heidestrasse 9a, 4900 Herford, telephone (05221) 5 67 41.

Trödelmarkt (junk market) first and last weekend of October at the Marburg-Wehrda Einkaufzentrum. Organized by Nicholas Dollmann, Teichstrasse 16, 5000 Köln 30, telephone (0221) 53 17 44.

Antikmarkt (antique market) second weekend of October in the Stadthalle between Bürgerstrasse and the Lahn river. Organized by Firma Weber, Semmelstrasse 42, 8700 Würzburg, telephone (0931) 1 37 03.

Marienheide 5277

Trödelmarkt (junk market) second weekend of July in the Marktplatz in the village center. Organized by Richard Altmann, Mediaschergasse 13, 5276 Siel 3, telephone (02262) 18 66.

Marktdorf 7778

Antikmarkt (antique market) first Sunday in November at the Stadthalle. Information from Südorga Langlotz GdBR, Höllturm-Passage 1, 7760 Radolfzell, telephone (07732) 31 52.

Marl 4370

Trödelmarkt (junk market) first Saturday of every month at the Marler Stern Einkaufzentrum (shopping center) at the Rathausplatz. Organized by WOBS GmbH, Unnaerstrasse 2, 4700 Hamm 1, telephone (02381) 8 49 19.

Massenhausen 8051

(Please also see München.)

Flohmarkt (flea market) fourth Sunday in October at the Neufahm. Information from D. K. Gerhard Stock, Am Hang 9, 8422 Riedenburg, telephone (09442) 22 49.

Meckenheim 5309

Antikmarkt (antique market) first weekend of October in the Never Markt. Organized by Nikolaus Dollmann, Teichstrasse 16, 5000 Köln 30, telephone (0221) 2 12 25.

Antikmarkt (antique market) last Sunday of October in the Mehrzweckhalle. Organized by Norbert Junge, Talbahnstrasse 4, 5190 Stolberg, telephone (02402) 2 30 07.

Meerbusch-Büderich 4005

(Please also see Düsseldorf and Krefeld.)

Antikmarkt (antique market) second weekend of November in the Bürgersaal. Organized by

Gabrielle Wallon, Postfach 39, 4005 Meerbusch 1, telephone (02105) 56 51.

Meinerzhagen 5882

Antikmarkt (antique market) last Sunday of October at the Stadthalle. Organized by Halina Müller GmbH, Kölnerstrassse 246, 4000 Düsseldorf 1, telephone (0211) 78 25 56.

Melle 4520

Trödelmarkt (junk market) first Sunday of October at the Allkauf Parkplatz (parking lot). Organized by Galerie G. Krencky, Heidestrasse 9a, 4900 Herford, telephone (05221) 5 67 41.

Melsungen 3508

Floh- und Trödelmarkt (flea and junk market) second Sunday of October in the Stadthalle. Information from Friedhelm Knoth, Stettinerstrasse 4, 3578 Ziegenhain-Schwalmstadt, telephone (06691) 63 06.

Memmingen 8940

Kunst- und Antiktage (art and antique days) first Sunday of November in the Stadionhalle or Neue Stadthalle. Organized by Ernst Marser, Reutlinger Messebüro, Rathausstrasse 12, 7410 Rentlingen, telephone (07072) 82 41.

Meschede 5778

Flohmarkt (flea market) first Saturday of every month in the Schützenhalle or in the Innenstadt (city center). Information from Karl Hennebohl, Zeughausstrasse 18b, 5778 Meschede, telephone (0291) 63 44, between 2 to 5 p.m. Occasionally this organizer uses these locations on other weekends during the month.

Mettmann 4020

Antik- und Trödelmarkt (antique and junk market) second Sunday of September on Freiheitstrasse. This market is part of the annual city festival. Information from Herr Küppermann, Kulturamt, 4020 Mettmann, telephone (021 04) 79 54 48.

Antikmarkt (antique market) first Sunday of October at the Stadthalle. Organized by Komischke & Lange, Heiderweg 53, 4000 Düsseldorf 31, telephone (0203) 7 43 01.

Metzingen 7430

Antik- und Trödelmarkt (antique and junk market) fourth Sunday of October in the Stadthalle. Organized by H. & H. K. Fischer, Uhlandstrasse 18, 7255 Rutesheim, telephone (07152) 5 43 77.

Minden 4950

Antik- und Trödelmarkt (antique and junk market) first and third Sunday of October in the Obermarktpassage. Information from Novema Hannover, Hahnensteg 22, 3000 Hannover 91, telephone (0511) 41 41 14.

Kunstmarkt (art market) first weekend of October in the Stadthalle. For further information, telephone (05534) 20 62.

Mönchengladbach 4050

Trödelmarkt (junk market) some Saturdays and every Sunday morning year round, but in various places around the town. Locations include the Mönchengladbach town center, Farmka Einkaufzentrum, Marktplatz in the Rheydt district (two kilometers south of the Hauptbahnhof), Giesenkirchen Markt (one kilometer east of Rheydt), and Massa 1 shopping center on Krefeldstrasse (northwest of the Hauptbahnhof). Most Sunday markets are organized by R. Leines, Talstrasse 32, 4050 Mönchengladbach 3, telephone (02166) 60 25 10. Some Sunday markets are organized by Norbert Junge, Talbahnstrasse 4, 5190 Stolberg, telephone (02402) 2 30 07.

Antikmarkt (antique market) last weekend of October in the Kaiser-Friedrich-Halle. Organized by Komischke & Lange, Heiderweg 53, 4000 Düsseldorf 31, telephone (0203) 7 43 01.

Moers 4130

(Please also see Duisburg and Krefeld.)

Trödelmarkt (junk market) second Sunday of October at the Divi-Markt in the Asberg district. Organized by Schneider & Partner & Co. GmbH KG, Hufstrasse 50, 4100 Duisburg 11, telephone (0203) 8 90 86.

Spielzeugmarkt (toy market) third Sunday of October at the Hans Kliver. Organized by Kirchner & Patarek GmbH, Ostwall 39, 4150 Krefeld 1, telephone (02841) 2 62 60.

Monheim 4019

Antik- und Trödelmarkt (antique and junk market) last weekend of May in the Altstadt (old city center). This market is pat of the annual Gänselieselmarkt celebration. Organized by the Ordnungsamt, 4019 Monheim, telephone (02173) 59 73 23.

Montabauer 5430

Flohmarkt (flea market) last weekend of October on the Eichweise. Organized by Rolf à Brassard, Rheinstrasse 4, 5434 Dernbach, telephone (02602) 7 08 39.

Mössingen 7406

Floh- und Trödelmarkt (flea and junk market) at the EZA-Markt. Organized by Agentur Floma, Industriestrasse 15, 7340 Geislingen, telephone (07331) 4 04 51.

Mosbach

Trödelmarkt (junk market) third Sunday of October at the Stadthalle. Organized by Antiquariat Peter Kiefer GmbH, Ebersteinstrasse 14, 7530 Pforzheim, telephone (07231) 1 72 72.

Much 5023

Trödelmarkt (junk market) last weekend of June in the village center. Organized by Richard Altmann, Mediascher Gasse 13, 5276 Siel 3, telephone (02262) 18 66.

Mühlheim 5403

(Please also see Koblenz.)

Flohmarkt (flea market) second Sunday of October at the Baesch. Organized by Helene Schmitt, Karl-Marx-Strasse 35, 5450 Neuwied 12 telephone (02631) 7 66 44.

Antik- und Trödelmarkt (antique and junk market) second weekend of November at the Massa Einkaufzentrum in the Karlich district. Organized by Nikolaus Dollmann, Teichstrasse 16, 5000 Köln 30, telephone (0221) 53 17 44.

Mülheim am Main 6052

Altes Spielzeug Markt (old toy market) first Sunday of October in the Bürgerhaus. Information from Antiquitäten Wagner, Bieberestrasse 84, 6050 Offenbach, telephone (069) 88 70 60.

Mülheim am Ruhr 4330

(Please also see Essen, Düsseldorf, and Duisburg, which are not far away and easily accessible by public transit as well as by road.)

Antikmarkt (antique market) second Sunday of every month year round in the City-Center. This large market offers all kinds of antiques and junk, and draws thousands of potential buyers. The market space covers several acres. This is one of the largest monthly markets in Germany. Parking is available only in parking garages, since there is virtually none on the street. Organized by Veranstaltungsbüro Norbert Junge, Obersteinstrasse 51, 5190 Stolberg, telephone (02402) 2 30 07.

Trödelmarkt (junk market) second and fourth Sunday of the month at the Rhein-Ruhr-Zentrum. Organized by Komiscke & Lange, Heiderweg 53, Düsseldorf 31, telephone (0203) 7 43 01.

Antik- und Trödelmarkt (antique and junk market) first Saturday of the month at the Interhome Parkplatz. Organized by Halina Müller GmbH, Kölnerstrasse 246, 4000 Düsseldorf 1, telephone (0211) 78 25 56.

Spielzeugmarkt (toy market) first Sunday of fall months in the Stadthalle across the Ruhr River on the opposite bank from the town center. Organized by Kirchner & Patarek GmbH, Ostwall 39, 4150 Krefeld 1, telephone (02841) 2 62 60.

Antikmarkt (antique market) third Sunday of October in the Stadthalle on the bank of the Ruhr river across from the center of the city. Organized by Theodor Wessling, Kurhausstrasse 31a, 4690 Herne 2, telephone (02325) 4 30 31. Other organizers use this hall irregularly during the year. (For example, see the next listing.)

Antik- und Spielzeugmarkt (antique and toy market) fourth Sunday of October in the Stadthalle. Organized by Heesen & Kirchner, Goethestrasse 19, 4130 Moers, telephone (02845) 2 18 65.

Müllheim 7840

Antik- und Trödelmarkt (antique and junk market) first Saturday of October at the Bügerhaus. Organized by Peter Gailer, Eberhardstrasse 49, 7000 Stuttgart 1, telephone (0711) 24 43 80.

München 8000

(Please also see Ebenhausen, Germering, Griesing, Massenhausen, and Planegg.)

The gracious capital of Bavaria is also the center of the German antique trade (as well as the publishing trade). Opulent shops compete with some of the largest and well-stocked flea markets in Germany. The colorful Viktualienmarkt (food market) in the city center doesn't have antiques or collectables.

Market locations are listed on the map with the names in parentheses following the name.

Flohmarkt (flea market) (Dachauerstrasse 128) every Friday, Saturday, and Sunday at Dachauerstrasse 128, just past the Landshuter-Allee ring road. This is by far the largest and best flea market in the Munich area. A large open lot is full of hundreds of sellers on any day that isn't rainy. Friday is not as good as the other days. About 250 sellers have permanent booths in old and rundown warehouses at the back. Toilets are back by the permanent buildings and are free. This market is a good place to find used Eurostyle plumbing and faucets, mounds of china both old and new, and some inexpensive and good-quality crystal, but only a bit of furniture (though quality can be acceptable and prices cheap), and a few paintings. Permanent dealers in the buildings have more expensive items (though not necessarily better quality). Parking is on nearby streets on the opposite side of Dachauer Strasse, since on-site parking is reserved for sellers. Access by public transit is on tram lines 1 and 27 to the first stop past the underpass at Landshuter Allee. Organized by Firma Spitzbarth, Dachauer Strasse 128, 8000 München 19, telephone (089) 1 57 33 88.

Flohmarkt (flea market) (Aschauerstrasse 28) every Friday, Saturday, and Sunday at Aschauerstrasse 26. This is a newer, smaller market and has the standard odds and ends expected at a flea market. Access by public transit on U-bahn to Giesing or Unter-bergstrasse and walk, or from line 27. Organized by Hermann Ponta (Geisinger Trödelmarkt), Wilhelmstrasse 43, 8000 München 80, telephone (089) 49 32 24.

Flohmarkt (flea market) (Truderingerstrasse 265) every Saturday and Sunday morning at Truderingerstrasse 265 in the suburb of München-Trudering. This market takes place on a vacant lot and in small halls visible just east of the Trudering railway station, which is the first stop on milk-run trains going toward Salzburg. Access by public transit on the S-Bahn to the Trudering station, then walk away from the city for about 100 meters. Access by car is by the airport road until you see signs for Trudering to the right (at the start of the Autobahn), then follow Truderingerstrasse under the railway tracks and stay on the street for about 2 more kilometers. About 50 vendors. Sometimes good finds can be made here early on Saturday mornings. No toilets are available. Stay off the railroad tracks; there are no fences and the express trains rush by at about 100 miles (160 kilometers) per hour. Organized by Firma V. Riederer, Truderingerstrasse 128, 8000 München, telephone (089) 42 11 10.

Trödelmarkt (junk market) (Kirchenstrasse 15) every Saturday year round from about 7 a.m. to about 2 p.m. at Kirchenstrasse 15 in the suburb of München-Haidhausen (southeast of

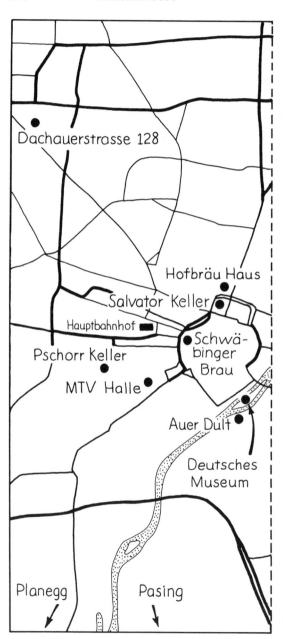

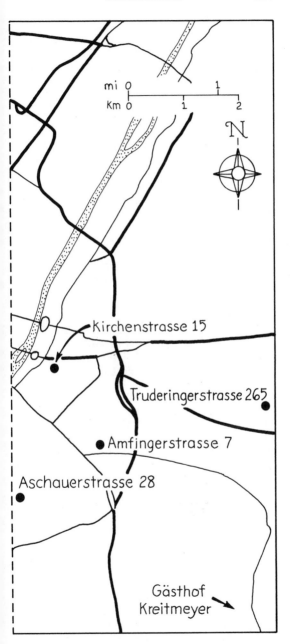

Maximilianstrasse). There are about 200 dealers
in three old warehouse buildings, and other
sellers in the courtyard. Watch out for uneven
floors and crumbling stairs. Lots of furniture, old
stoves, bric-a-brac, etc. Toilets available on
site. Access by public transit on tram line 1 or
9 to Max-Weber-Platz, then walk down
Kirchstrasse. This market will be only a block
from the Einsteinstrasse station on the new
U-Bahn subway line when it is finished. By
car, go to the Einstein-Zentrum, then on right on
Kirchenstrasse. Street parking only, which will
usually be hard to find. Organized by Firma
Vorocek, Klenzestrasse 64, 8000 München 5,
telephone (089) 4 70 54 22.

Antikmarkt (antique market) (Amfingerstrasse
7) Tuesday through Sunday at Amfingerstrasse
7 at the corner of Grofingerstrasse. Lots of
dealers of all kinds of junk in an old
three-story warehouse. This area is being
considered for redevelopment, which may
change its nature. Accessible by car and by
public transit on bus line 44, Müldorferstrasse
stop, or tram lines 19 or 29 to Amfingerstrasse
trolley line, or by subway U-bahn to Karl- Preiss
Platz and walk north two blocks.

Auer Dult (a festival of religious origin) (Auer
Dult) takes place three times a year for ten days
each fair at Mariahilfplatz, surrounding the
church, about one mile (1500 meters) southeast
of the city center. The Maidult takes place at the
end of April and beginning of May, the
Jacobidult takes place at the end of July and
beginning of August, and the Kirchwiedult takes
place at the end of October. This market is an
interesting combination of religious celebration,
county fair, remnant sale (mainly of new
porcelain), lederhosen, and about 90 antique
dealers. Bavarian bands provide music, and
large crowds celebrate the occasion. Few
bargains to be had but it's lots of fun. The
dealers bring in more items as the initial stock is
sold. Toilets are available on site; charge is 40
pfennigs. Access by public transit by tram lines
7, 15, 25, 27; they are clearly marked "Auer
Dult" during the fair. Street parking is difficult

to find; there are no garages or parking lots in the vicinity. Organized by Landeshauptstadt München, Fremdenverkehrsamt, Bindermarkt 5, 8000 München telephone (089) 2 39 11.

Antiquitäten- und Trödelmarkt (antique and junk market) (Salvator Keller) first and third weekend of every month at the Salvatorkeller am Nockherberg. Information from Messebüro M. Ebert, Linienstrasse 33, 8024 Oberhaching, telephone (089) 6 13 40 14.

Trödelmarkt (junk market) second Sunday of every month from April through October at the Wertkauf-Center parking garage. Organized by Hermann & Lampert, Hasselholzerweg 9, 5100 Aachen, telephone (0241) 7 20 21.

Antik- und Trödelmarkt (antique and junk market) (Gästhof Kreitmayr) first Sunday of the month from June through October at the Gästhof Kreitmayr in the Kieferloh district south of the central city. This market has lots of small and interesting items, but only a small quantity of large items such as furniture. This market takes place on a large vacant field around the inn. The restaurant and beer garden offer far better food than is found at most flea markets. Access by public transit to the Haar S-bahn station, then wait for a special market bus. Parking is available. Organized by Firma Vorocek, Klenzestrasse 64, 8000 München 5, telephone (089) 4 70 54 22.

Antik- und Kunstwoche (antique and art week) (Deutsches Museum) mid October at the Deutsches Museum. This quality show is part of the Munich fall antiques season. Access by public transit by S-bahn to Isartorplatz and walk on Zweibückerstrasse to the bridge, then upstream to the Museum. Parking is difficult: parking garages are found on Banderstrasse and Rosenheimerstrasse. Organized by Rode Messen, Schloss Sickendorf, 6420 Lauterbach 7, telephone (06641) 30 26.

Filmbörse (film exchange) (Löwenbraukeller) third Sunday of October in the Löwenbraukeller. Information from telephone (08131) 1 39 22.

Ansichtskartetausch (postcard exchange) (Hauptbahnhof) second Monday of November at Marsstrasse 5, two streets north of the Hauptbahnhof (main railway station). Walk west on Marsstrasse. Access by public transit to Hauptbahnhof, then walk. Organized by Werner Metzig, Demollstrasse 15, 8000 München 19, telephone (089) 1 57 50 54.

Fotobörse (photography exchange) (MTV Halle) first weekends of February and October at the MTV-Halle on Häberstrasse or Vereinsheim TSV-1960. Access by public transit by S-Bahn to Göetheplatz, then walk to the hall. Parking available on the nearby streets or in a lot. Organized by Foto Beck, Ludwigstrasse 53, 8500 Nürnberg, telephone (0911) 22 60 88.

Antikmarkt (antique market) one weekend a month (it varies irregularly between second, third, and fourth) at the Schwäbinger Bräu brewery, in postal district 40. This market is held at other locations on other weekends, such as the Augustiner Keller. Organized by Alexander Dohn, Linprunstrasssse 57, 8000 München 2, telephone (089) 42 11 10. The Schabinger Bräu hall is also used about six times a year for period clothing markets. Organized by Cultura Verlags GmbH und Vertriebs KG, Münchner Freiheit 20, 8000 München 40, telephone (089) 33 40 51.

Ansichtskartenbörse (view and post card exchange) first Sunday of February, May, and October, and second Sunday of November at the Kultursaal Arbeiterwohlfart at Strösserstrasse 14. Organized by Franz Miexner Ansichtskartenbörsen, Floriansmühle 1 d, 8000 München, telephone (089) 32 87 12. At other times, this organizer sponsors weekday evening postcard exchanges.

Medallienbörse (medal and coin exchange) second weekend of October at the

Mathänser-Festsaal. Organized by R. Rahn Numismarkt, 8904 Friedburg, telephone (0821) 60 11 32.

Antiquitätenmarkt (antique market) (Pschorr Keller) last week of October and first few days of November from 10 a.m. to 7 p.m. at the Pschorr-Keller at the Theresienhöhe. This is the finest-quality market in Munich: strictly antiques and usually high prices. Only dealers are permitted to sell. This is one of the antique trade's high points of the year, and the market is worth a visit. Information from Münchner Antiquitätenmarkt e.V., Türkenstrasse 24, 8000 München 32, telephone (089) 22 98 90.

Antikmarkt (antique market) third (Hofbräu Haus and also Pasing) Saturday of October at the Hofbräuhaus and first Saturday of November at the Postsaal in the Gasthof Post in the suburb of München-Pasing. Access by public transit on the S-bahn to Pasing or tram 19 and walk. Organized by Max Koch, Jakob-Hagenbucher-Strasse 16, 8000 München 50, telephone (089) 27 53 06.

Briefmarken-Tauschbörse (postage stamp trading exchange) every other Saturday in October and November at the Vollmar-Haus. Stamps and related material only! For details and directions, call the organizer at (089) 26 44 36.

Kunst- und Antiquitätenmesse (art and antiques fair) second half of October at the Regingehaus. This is another of the major fall antique fairs in Munich: the quality of items is high. Organized by Messebüro Ulrich Hölzermann, Mühltalstrasse 16, 8184 Gmünd-Dürnbach, telephone (08022) 7 43 50.

Münster 4400

Flohmarkt (flea market) third Saturday of the month from April through October at the Promenade am Hindenburgplatz, in front of the Residenz-Schloss west of the town center.

Since the market place is used the rest of the time as a parking lot, street parking is usually difficult. Information from Stadtverwaltung Münster, Postfach 5909, 4400 Münster, telephone (0251) 49 21.

Trödelmarkt (junk market) last Sunday of every month at the Hit-Markt. Information from A. M. V. V. Jörn Werber, Am Grossen Holz 9, 4817 Leopoldshöhe, telephone (05208) 14 23.

Trödelmarkt (junk market) first Saturday of every month at the Aasee Einkaufzentrum, second Sunday in the parking structure of the Haus Pröbsting in the suburb of Handorf and fourth Sunday at the Co-op Parkplatz in the city center. Since the markets move from place to place, month by month, check with the organizer or city tourist office before going. Organized by Galerie G. Krencky, Heidestrasse 9a, 4900 Herford, telephone (05221) 5 67 41.

Schallplatten- und Musikbörse (record and music exchange) fourth Sunday of October at the Münsterlandhalle, southeast of the town center, across (and under) the railroad tracks from the Hauptbahnhof on Albersloher Weg. Organized by Kogel & Lauber, Kornmarkt 10-12, 6900 Siegen, telephone (0271) 5 15 01. This hall is used irregularly on weekends for antique and specialized collectors markets throughout the year.

Mutterstadt 6704

(Please also see Mannheim.)

Schmuckwoche (decoration week) first 10 days of October at Henry's Auktionzentrum. This show and sale is a collection of curios, antiques, and furniture held in the organizer's sales hall. Organized by Henry's Auktionzentrum GmbH, An der Fohlenweide 30, 6704 Mutterstadt, telephone (06234) 8 01 10.

Neckarsulm 7107

(Please also see Heilbronn.)

Antikmarkt (antique market) second or third weekend on October (varies year by year) at the Ballei. Organized by Peter Fuchs, Bahnhofstrasse 9, 6949 Weinheim, telephone (06201) 1 22 32.

Neckarenzlingen 7449

Floh- und Trödelmarkt (flea and junk market) first Sunday of October at the Adler. Organized by Sacha Brennessel, Klopstockstrasse 89, 7410 Reutlingen, telephone (07121) 5 34 24.

Neckarweihingen 7140

Trödelmarkt (junk market) first Sunday of October at the Gemeinlandehalle in the Ludwigsburg district. Organized by Antiquariat Peter Kiefer GmbH, Ebersteinstrasse 14, 7530 Pforzheim, telephone (07231) 1 72 72.

Nieder-Olm 6501

Antikmarkt (antique market) second Sunday of October at the Festhalle. Organized by Reinhard Preuss, Antoniusgasse 25, 6228 Eltville, telephone (06123) 46 11.

Neuburg an der Donau 8858

Flohmarkt (flea market) first Saturday of every month at Monheimerstasse 5. Organized by Angelika Jeschek, Monheimerstasse 5, 8898 Neuberg, telephone (8431) 4 73 00.

Neuenstadt am Kocher 7106

Flohmarkt (flea market) fourth weekend of October in the Stadthalle. Information from the organizers at telephone (07139) 71 72.

Neuenstein 6431

Antik- und Flohmarkt (antique and junk market) second Sunday of every month except December in Halle and Freigelände (hall and grounds) of the Domäne (estate). Organized by Reinhold Hess, Domäne, 6431 Neuenstein 1, telephone (06677) 4 72.

Neu-Isenberg 6078

(Please also see Frankfurt-am-Main.)

Trödelmarkt (junk market) fourth Sunday of January and October in the Einkaufzentrum (shopping center) in the town center. Organized by Inter-Antik, Michael Becker, Mommsenstrasse 10, 4006 Eckrath, telephone (02104) 4 61 52.

Neumarkt in der Oberpfalz 8430

Flohmarkt (flea market) second Saturday or Sunday every month (day varies) year round at the Parkplatz Alde on Dammstrasse. Information from Karl Götz, Schönwerthstrasse 48, 8430 Neumarkt, telephone (09181) 2 09 59.

Neumünster 2350

Trödelmarkt (junk market) first, second, or third Sunday (varies month by month) once a month from April through October at the Parkplatz Hertie in the town center. Organized by Dieter Burmeister, Rendsburgerstrassae 1, 2362 Wahlstedt, telephone (04554) 34 00.

Antiquitätentag (antique day) last Sunday of October at the Stadthalle. Organized by Dieter Groneberg, Rethfelder 1, 2200 Elmshorn, telephone (04121) 14 76.

Neunkirchen 5908

(Please also see Siegen.)

Trödelmarkt (junk market) third Sunday of October at Rathausplatz in the town center. Organized by Kogel & Lauber, Kornmarkt 10-12, 6900 Siegen, telephone (0271) 5 15 01.

Neunkirchen am Saar 6680

Antik- und Trödelmarkt (antique and junk market) second Monday of every month (though once or twice a year the third Sunday) year round in the Fussgängerzone (pedestrian zone) in the town center. Information from the Verkehrsverein, 6680 Neunkirchen, telephone (06821) 20 21.

Neuss 4040

(Please also see Düsseldorf.)

Flohmarkt (flea market) every Sunday year round at the Güterbahnhof (railway freight station) in the center of town, and second and fourth weekend in the Südpark in the Reuschenberg district. Organized by Gabrielle Wallon, Postfach 39, 4005 Meerbusch 1, telephone (02105) 56 51.

Trödelmarkt (junk market) first weekend of October at Kirmesplatz in the Furth district. Organized by Norbert Junge, Talbahnstrasse 4, 5190 Stolberg, telephone (02402) 2 30 07.

Flohmarkt (flea market) second Sunday of October at the Rheincenter Parkplatz, behind the Huma building. Information from Gisela

Schaake, Kaiserstrasse 69a, 4018 Langenfeld, telephone (02173) 7 62 11.

Trödelmarkt (junk market) second Sunday of October at the Möbelhaus Knuffman parking lot in the Hafen (harbor) district, toward the Rhine from the city center. Organized by Hermann & Lampert, Hasselholzerweg 9, 5100 Aachen, telephone (0241) 7 20 21.

Modellspielzeugmarkt (model toy market) last Sunday of October at the Stadthalle. Organized by M. Kremer, Bismarckstrasse 16, 4010 Hilden, telephone (02103) 5 11 33.

Trödelmarkt (junk market) first Sunday of November at the Kaufpark shopping center on Römerstrasse. Organized by Norbert Junge, Talbahnstrasse 4, 5190 Stolberg, telephone (02402) 2 30 07.

Neustadt 3057

Trödelmarkt (junk market) first Saturday of October at Kirchplatz in the town center. Organized by Novema Hannover, Hahnensteg 22, 300 Hannover 91, telephone (0511) 41 74 02.

Neustadt an der Weinstrasse 6730

Antik- und Sammlermarkt (antique and collectors' market) third Saturday of November in the Saalbau. Organized by WEWO Antikmärkte, Rudi-Stefan-Allee 14, 6520 Worms, tele- phone (06241) 7 58 71.

Neu-Ulm 7910

(Please also see Senden and Ulm.)

Antikmarkt (antique market) fourth Saturday of October at the Edwin-Scharff-Haus. Information from Messebüro Garon, Federmannweg 3, 7900 Ulm, telephone (0731) 3 05 74.

Neuwied 5450

Antik- und Trödelmarkt (antique and junk market) first Sunday of October in front of the Agros shipping center. Organized by Nikolaus Dollmann, Teichstrasse 16, 5000 Köln 30, telephone (0221) 53 17 44.

Flohmarkt (flea market) second Sunday of October at the Toom-Markt. Organized by Helene Schmitt, Karl-Marx-Strasse 35, 5450 Neuwied 12, telephone (02631) 7 66 44.

Niederhausen 6272

Trödelmarkt (junk market) last Sunday of October at the Rathaus. Organized by M. Kriegel, Kirchhohl 36, 6200 Wiesbaden 41, telephone (06127) 49 06.

Nördlingen 8860

Trödelmarkt (junk market) fourth Sunday of October at the Ankerbräuhalle (Anchor beer hall) in the Kaiserwiese. (Have a beer while you browse the junk!) Organized by Agentur Zelinka, Gmündstrasse 18, 7070 Schwäbisch Gmünd, telephone (07171) 8 52 32.

Antikmarkt (antique market) first Friday of November in the Klösterle. Organized by Messebüro Garon, Federmannweg 3, 7900 Ulm, telephone (0731) 3 05 74.

Nörhen-Hardenburg 3412

Trödelmarkt (junk market) second Sunday of January at the Saalbau. Organized by Hasse Alfeld, telephone (05181) 2 37 79.

Nuremberg

(Please see Nürnberg.)

Nürnberg 8500

(Please also see Feucht.)

Trempelmarkt (junk market) second weekends (including Fridays) of May, September, and November in the Altstadt Hauptmarkt. These markets are part of centuries-old celebrations, quite colorful and interesting. This market is the largest and most interesting market held in this largely reconstructed medieval city. Information from the Marktamt und Landschaftbehörde, Altstadt, Hauptmarkt, 8500 Nürnberg, telephone (0911) 16 26 93.

Trödelmarkt (junk market) first Sunday of the month from April through December at the Parkcafe Wanner in the Dutzenteich district southeast of the city center. This station is near the parks, Volksfestplatz, and Zeppelinwiese. Parking is available. Organized by D. K. Gerhard Stock, Am Hang 9, 8422 Riedenberg, telephone (09442) 22 40.

Antik- und Trödelmarkt (antique and junk market) first weekend of October as the Gesellschaftshaus in the Gartenstadt district. Organized by Max Koch, Jakob-Hagenberger-Strasse 16, 8000 München, telephone (089) 29 53 06.

Trödelmarkt (junk market) first and third Saturday of October in the Bahnhof in the Dutzenteich district. Organized by M. Bogner, Rothenburgerstrasse 32, 8500 Nürnberg 70, telephone (0911) 26 47 49.

Antikmarkt (antique market) first Sunday of October in the Grand Hotel, less than 200 meters from the Hauptbahnhof (main railway station.) Other markets (such as puppet markets and coin shows) also take place here on weekends. Information from Rhein-Main-

Taunus Antiquitäten, Hasenspitz 19, 6200 Wiesbaden, telephone (06121) 46 71 09.

Flohmarkt (flea market) first Sunday of October in the Saalbau in the Buchenbühl district, and first and third Sunday of October at the Hummelsteiner Park. Organized by D. K. Gerhard Stock, Am Hang 9, 8422 Riedenberg, telephone (09442) 22 40.

Puppenmarkt (doll and puppet market) first Sunday of October at the Kulturverein. Organized by Irmgard Wolfermann, Obere Pfaffensteigstrasse 14, 8540 Schwabach, telephone (0911) 63 53 83.

Mineralen- und Fossilienbörse (rock and fossil exchange) second weekend of October in the Messezentrum (fairgrounds). Information from Nürnberger Messe- und Ausstellungs Gesellschaft mbH, telephone (0911) 8 60 60.

Münzbörse (coin exchange) third Sunday of October at the Meistersingerhalle in the Gleisskammer on My9nchenerstrasse. This is about two kilometers southeast of the Hauptbahnhof (main rail station). Information from (0911) 44 43 52.

Antikmarkt (antique market) fourth Sunday of October in the Heilige-Geist Spital. Organized by Messebüro Garon, Federmannweg 3, 7900 Ulm, telephone (0731) 3 05 74.

Spielzeug- und Sammlerbörse (toy and collectors' exchange) fourth Sunday of October at the Festhalle TSV. Organized by Walter Beck, Herzogstandstrasse 4, 8500 Nürnberg, telephone (0911) 26 88 89).

This hall is used for other specialized markets, such as photo and camera markets.

Ansichtkarten- und Papierbörse (picture and paper exchange) second Sunday of October at the Gesellschaftshaus in the Gartenstadt district. Organized by Norbert Graf, Hüttenbacherstrasse 26, 8500 Nürnberg 30, telephone (0911) 57 15 38.

Nürtingen 7440

Flohmarkt (flea market) third Saturday of October in the Topkauf-Center. Organized by Agentur Floma, Industriestrasse 15, 7340 Geislingen, telephone (07331) 4 04 51.

Antik- und Trödelmarkt (antique and junk market) third Saturday of October in the Stadthalle. Organized by H. & H. K. Fischer, Uhlandstrasse 18, 7255 Rutesheim, telephone (07152) 5 43 77.

Oberaudorf/Oberbayern 8203

Flohmarkt (flea market) first Sunday of May and second Sunday of October in the town's central area. Organized by the Kur- und Verkehrsamt, Postfach 38, 8203 Oberaudorf.

Oberhausen 4200

(Please also see Duisburg, Essen, and Mülheim an der Ruhr.)

Antik- und Trödelmarkt (antique and junk market) first Sunday of every month in the Bero-Center Passage und Parkplatz, second Sunday of October at the Revierpark in the Vonderort district. Information from Lothar Schneider, Bahnhofstrasse 187, 4100 Duisburg 12, telephone (0203) 55 08 08.

Trödelmarkt (junk market) every Sunday of October at the Interspar shopping center on Luchsstrasse in the Sterkrade district, about five kilometers north of the Bahnhof (rail station) and town center. Organized by L. Rau, Luitpoldstrasse 38, 4650 Gelsenkirchen, telephone (0209) 20 49 46.

Antikmarkt (antique market) last Sunday of October in the Stadthalle. Organized by Komischke & Lange, Heiderweg 53, 4000 Düsseldorf 31, telephone (0203) 7 43 01.

Oberstdorf 8980

Antikmarkt (antique market) last Friday through following Sunday of October in the Festhalle. Organized by Organisation Märkte-Messen Mezger, Zeppelinstrasse 4, 7710 Donaueschingen, telephone (0771) 1 39 99.

Oberwesel 6532

Trödelmarkt (junk market) third Sunday of October around the Rathaus. Organized by WEWO Antikmärkte, Rudi-Stefan-Allee 14, 6520 Worms, telephone (06241) 7 58 71.

Ochtrup (Westfalia) 4434

Trödelmarkt (junk market) second Saturday of October at the Einkaufszone in the town center. Information from the organizers at telephone (02442) 27 17.

Odenthal 5068

Antikmarkt (antique market) third weekend of October at the Pfarrhaus. Organized by Alida Schleusener, Waldfriedstrasse 1, 5000 Köln 60, telephone (0221) 71 34 14.

Offenbach 6050

(Please also see Frankfurt.)

Trödel- und Antikmarkt (junk and antique market) every Saturday year round from about 8 a.m. through early afternoon along the Main River on Mainstrasse for about two kilometers east of the Carl-Ulrich-Brücke. This is by far the best market in the Frankfurt area; hundreds of vendors line both sides of the tree-lined embankment on the banks of the Main river.

They sell everything (strong on brass doorknobs and fittings, furniture, and beer steins) for relatively reasonable prices. Bargaining is encouraged. No toilets are on the site. Access by public transit from Frankfurt: S-bahn to Offenbach, then walk north to the river, or take bus 46 or tram 16 to the end, then walk to two blocks north to the river. Parking is available on the street or under the bridge. Organized by the Stadt Offenbach, Verkehrsbüro, Am Stadthof, telephone (0611) 80 65 29 46.

Antikmarkt (antique market) first and third Sunday of most months in the Stadthalle in the town center. About half a mile toward the river from the Bahnhof. Street parking should be available; a parking garage is adjacent to the hall. Organized by Firma Blank, Friedrich-Ebert-Strasse 2, 6368 Bad Vilbel, telephone (0601) 82 12.

Oldenburg 2900

Trödelmarkt (junk market) second Saturday of the month year round from April through November at the Schlossplatz in the old central area and from December through March in the Weser-Ems-Halle, which is found under the railroad to Pferdemarkt and then about 500 meters on the Donnerschweer. There is ample parking on the fairgrounds where the hall is located. Organized by the Stadt Oldenburg; information from the Verkehrsverein, Lange Strasse 3, 2900 Oldenburg, telephone 2 50 92.

Opladen 5090

Antikmarkt (antique market) first Sunday of October in the Stadhalle. Organized by Christa Schalkowski, Hedwigstrasse 19, 5600 Wuppertal 1, telephone (0202) 30 08 48.

Osnabrück 4500

Flohmarkt (flea market) second Saturday of May and September throughout the Altstadt (old city in the city center). Organized by the Amt für Öffentliche Ordnung, Gewerbeabteilung—Herr Lindtke, 4500 Osnabrück, telephone (0541) 3 23 41 62.

Münzbörse (coin exchange) first Sunday of October in the Stadthalle on Schlosswall, near the Schloss (castle) in the central part of the city. Organized by Galerie G. Krenky, Heidestrasse 9a, 4900 Herford, telephone (05221) 5 67 41.

Trödelmarkt (junk market) second Sunday of October at the Marktkauf in the Nahne district about 2 kilometers south of the city center, third Sunday of October at the Halle Gartlage. Organized by Galerie G. Krenky, Heidestrasse 9a, 4900 Herford, telephone (05221) 5 67 41. Halle Gartlage is also used the third weekend of May for an Antik- Trodel- und Handwerkemarkt organized by A. M. V. V. Jörn Werber, Am Grossen Holz 9, 4817 Leopoldshöhe, telephone (05208) 14 23.

Trödelmarkt (junk market) first Sunday of June at the Dixi Discount shopping center in the Sutthausen district south of the city center. Organized by Firma Nordmann, Belm, telephone (05406) 40 41.

Modellspielzeugmarkt (model toy market) second Sunday of November at the Stadthalle. Organized by M. Cremer, Bismarckstrasse 16, 4010 Hilden, telephone (02103) 5 11 33.

Osterode am Harz 3360

Trödelmarkt (junk market) third Sunday of January and February in the Stadthalle. Organized by Hasse, 3220 Alfeld, telephone (05181) 2 37 79.

Ostfildern 7302

Flohmarkt (flea market) third Sunday of October in the Stadthalle in the Nellingen district. Organized by Heinz Weber, Plochinger Strasse 33, 7302 Ostfildern-Ruit, telephone (0711) 41 52 50.

Ottmarsbucholt/Senden 4403

Antik- und Trödelmarkt (antique and junk market) second Saturday of every month at the Mehrzweckhalle. Organized by Anita Pressel, Hermann-Lons-Weg, 4670 Lünen, telephone (02306 5 01 72.

Paderborn 4790

Antikmarkt (antique market) third Sunday of February at the Schützenhalle. Organized by Theodor Wessling, Kurhausstrasse 31a, 4690 Herne 2, telephone (02325) 4 30 31.

Antiktage (antique days) first Friday through following Sunday of October at the Schützenhalle. Organized by Organisation Märkte-Messen Mezger, Zeppelinstrasse 4, 7710 Donaueschingen, telephone (0771) 1 39 99.

Schallplatten- und Musikbörse (record and music exchange) first and last Sunday of October in the Paderhalle. Organized by Kogel & Lauber, Kornmarkt 10-12, 6900 Siegen, telephone (0271) 5 15 01.

Antikmarkt (antique market) second Sunday of October in the Schützenhalle. Organized by Galerie G. Krencky, Heidestrasse 9a, 4900 Herford, telephone (05221) 5 67 41.

Papenburg 2990

Antikmarkt (antique market) second weekend of February at the Mehrzweckhalle in Herbrun district 6 kilometers southwest of the city center.

Organized by Hermann & Lampert, Hasselholzerweg 9, 5100 Aachen, telephone (0241) 7 20
21 or 4 81 88.

Trödelmarkt (junk market) first Sunday of
October at the Ems- Center. Organized by
Galerie G. Krencky, Heidestrasse 9a, 4900
Herford, telephone (05221) 5 67 41.

Passau 8390

Antikmarkt (antique market) fourth Friday
through following Sunday of October in the
Nibelungenhalle; follow the signs to the tourist
information office, which is located in this hall.
Organized by Liekeim, Adelheidstrasse 18,
8000 München 40, telephone (089) 2 72 18 60.

Pfafferhofen an der Ilm 8068

Trödelmarkt (junk market) last Sunday of
February, July, August, October, and Novem-
ber at the Volksfestplatz and adjacent
Hofenhalle. Organized by Thomas Seitzmeier,
Enthofstrasse 35, 8068 Pfaffenhofen, telephone
(08443) 4 53.

Pforzheim 7530

Flohmarkt (flea market) second Saturday of
October and first Saturday of November at the
Festplatz in the Eutingen district about three
kilometers of the Hauptbahnhof (main rail
station). Information from Dieter Krauss,
Pfarrweg 32, 7064 Remshalden, telephone
(07181) 47 08.

Philippsburg 7522

(Please also see Karlsruhe.)

Trödelmarkt (junk market) first Sunday of
October in the Festhalle. Organized by Antiquariat Peter Kiefer GmbH, Kirchstrasse 4, 7537

Remchingen-Wilferdingen, telephone (07231) 1 72 72.

Pirmasens 6780

(Please also see Zweibrücken.)

Antikmarkt (antique market) third Sunday of October at the Messehalle 1 at the fairgrounds on Zeppelinstrasse. Parking is available at the fairgrounds. Organized by Organisation A. Hövelmeyer, Altenwoogstrasse 41, 6750 Kaiserslautern, telephone (0631) 4 04 77.

Briefmarken- und Münzen Sammlerbörse (postage stamp and coin collectors' exchange) fourth Sunday of the month at the Wasgauhalle. Information from Stadtverwaltung Pirmasens, Postfach 2763, telephone (06331) 8 42 73.

Planegg 8033

(Please also see München.)

Antikmarkt (antique market) the third weekend of February and first weekends April, June, October, and November at the Heide-Volm. Organized by Alexander Dohn, Linprunstrasse 57, 8000 München 2, telephone (089) 18 75 55.

Plankstadt von Schwetzingen 6831

Kunsthandwerkermarkt (artisans' market) first Sunday of November in the Mehrzweckhalle. Organized by Hans W. Nippen, Im Ferning 4, 7505 Ettlingen, telephone (07243) 1 21 06.

Plettenberg 5970

Maimarkt (May market) the first weekend of May, and Weinachtsmarkt (Christmas market) the first weekend of December in the town center. Organized by Langhoff, telephone (02391) 5 32 35 and 1 06 48.

Preussisch Oldendorf 4994

Trödelmarkt (junk market) first Sunday of November at the Fleugzeug Café in the Holsing district. Organized by M. Nordmann, Leconskamp 18, 4513 Belm, telephone (05406) 40 41.

Pulheim/Geyen 5024

(Please also see Bergheim and Köln.)

Flohmarkt (flea market) third Sunday of October at the Marktplatz in the town center. Information from the organizer at telephone (02238) 5 72 06.

Quackenbrück 4570

Flohmarkt (flea market) as part of the May market festival the third Sunday of May at the Marktplatz in the town center. Organized by the Stadtdirektor, Rathaus, 4570 Quackenbrück, telephone (05431) 20 41.

Radolfzell 7760

Trödelmarkt (junk market) second Sunday of October in the Höllturm-Passage. Organized by Südorga Langlotz GdBR, Höllturm-Passage 1, 7760 Radolfzell, telephone (07732) 31 52.

Ramstein 6792

Flohmarkt (flea market) first Sunday of October at the Autokino (drive-in theatre). Organized by Organisation A. Hövelmeyer, Altenwoogstrasse 41, 6750 Kaiserslautern, telephone (0631) 4 04 77.

Ratingen 4030

(Please also see Düsseldorf.)

Antikmarkt (antique market) first Sunday of January, first weekends of May, September, and December, and second Sunday of October in the Stadthalle. Organized by Komischke & Lange, Heiderweg 53, 4000 Düsseldorf 31, telephone (0203) 7 43 01. This hall is used on other Sundays for other markets including model railroad and puppet markets.

Trödelmarkt (junk market) last Sunday of October at the Ratio-Markt. Organized by Norbert Junge, Talbahnstrasse 4, 5190 Stolberg, telephone (02402) 2 30 07.

Raunheim 6096

(Please also see Hochheim and Neu-Isenberg.)

Floh- und Trödelmarkt (flea and junk market) every Saturday year round at the Mainspitze Einkaufzentrum parking garage. Organized by Helmut Schuster, Frankfurterstrasse 84, 6054 Rodgau 3, telephone (06106) 7 16 28.

Antik- und- Trödelmarkt (flea and junk market) first Sunday of October at the Wertkauf-Center. Organized by Reinhard Preuss, Antoniusgasse 25, 6228 Eltville, telephone (06123) 7 46 11.

Ravensburg 7980

Flohmarkt (flea market) second Saturday of May, June, and September in the Rathausgasse in the Innenstadt (old inner city). Organized by the Stadtkämmerei der Stadt Ravensburg, 7980 Ravensburg, telephone (0751) 8 23 53.

Recklinghausen 4350

Antikmarkt (antique market) fourth Sunday of February and of October at the Saalbau. Organized by Theodor Wessling, Kurhausstrasse 31a, 4690 Herne 2, telephone (02325) 4 30 31.

Antik- und Kunstmarkt (antique and art market) first and fourth weekend of October at the Vestlandhalle. Organized by L. Rau, Luitpoldstrasse 38, 4650 Gelsenkirchen, telephone (0209) 20 49 46.

Spielzeug- und Modelleisenbahnmarkt (toy and model railway market) second Sunday of November at the Festspielhaus. Organized by Kirchner & Patarek GmbH, Ostwall 39, 4150 Krefeld, telephone (02841) 2 62 60.

Rees 4122

Trödelmarkt (junk market) first Sunday of October at the Marktplatz in the town center. Organized by Lothar Schneider, Bahnhofstrasse 187, 4100 Duisburg 12, telephone (0203) 55 08 08.

Regensburg 8400

Flohmarkt (flea market) second Sunday of the month from April through December at the Kneitinger Keller. This market specializes in small art work and hobby items. Organized by D. K. Gerhard Stock, Am Hang 9, 8422 Riedenburg, telephone (09442) 22 49.

Flohmarkt (flea market) last Saturday of every month year round at the Schwerdnermüle in the Lappersdorf district. Organized by Herr von Radny, Antiqutäten in der Schwerdnermühle, 8411 Regensburg-Lappersdorf, telephone (0941) 8 28 77.

Antik- und Trödelmarkt (antique and junk market) first weekend of October at Lilienstrasse 5. Organized by Gero Fritz,

Lilienstrasse 5, 8400 Regensburg, telephone (0941) 3 27 24.

Antikmarkt (antique market) second Saturday of October at Antoniushaus. Organized by Wolfgang Meissner, Panorama 27, 7500 Karlsruhe 41, telephone (09659) 7 01.

Antikmarkt (antique market) first Sunday of November in the Hotel Maximilian. Organized by Firma Leikheim, Adelheidstrasse 16, 8000 München 40, telephone (089) 2 72 18 60.

Reidlingen 7940

Antik- und Trödelmarkt (antique and junk market) first Friday of November at the Riethalle. Organized by Dieter Krauss, Pfarrweg 32, 7064 Remshalden, telephone (07181) 47 08.

Remagen 5480

Töpfer- Kunst- Antiquitäten- und Handwerkermarkt (pottery, antique, art, and artisans' market) first weekend of April and October in the Fussgängerzone (pedestrian zone) in the town center. This market is part of the twice-a-year city festival. Organized by Alida Schleusener, Waldfriedstrasse 1 5000 Köln 60, telephone (0221) 71 34 14.

Spielzeugbörse (toy market) fourth Sunday of October in the Stadthalle. Organized by Klaus Graeber, Hohenstein 73, 5600 Wuppertal 2, telephone (0202) 55 05 90.

Remschied 5630

Flohmarkt (flea market) first Sunday of every month year round (and occasionally the third Sunday as well) in the Bahnhofsvorplatz (square in front of the railway station) about six kilometers east of the city center. Organized by Gabrielle Wallon, Postfach 39, 4005 Meerbusch 1, telephone (02105) 56 51.

Rendsburg 2370

Flohmarkt (flea market) first Sunday of October at the Holtex parking lot. Organized by Gerhard Bauer, Wallgraben 44, 2000 Hamburg 90, telephone (040) 77 46 24.

Reutlingen 7310

Antikmarkt (antique market) first weekend of October at the Kaiserpassage in the city center. Organized by Sacha Brennessel, Klopstockstrasse 89, 7410 Reutlingen, telephone (07121) 5 34 24.

Flohmarkt (flea market) third Sunday of October year round at the 1A-Discount parking lot. Organized by Agentur Hofmann & Stapf, Talstrasse 134, 7024 Filderstadt, telephone (0711) 70 36 27.

Rheda 4832

Trödelmarkt (junk market) second Sunday of October in the Garant-Markt in the Wiedenbrück district. Organized by A. M. V. V. Jörn Werber, Am Grossen Holz 9, 4817 Leopoldshöhe, telephone (05208) 14 23.

Rheine 4440

Trödelmarkt (junk market) second Saturday of every month at the Festplatz on Osnabrückerstrasse. Organized by Galerie G. Krenky, Heidestrasse 9a, 4900 Herford, telephone (05221) 5 67 41.

Rheinstetten 7512

(Please also see Karlsruhe.)

Antik- und Trödelmarkt (antique and junk market) second weekend of October at the Ufganhalle in the Forchheim district.

Organized by Hans W. Nippen, Im Ferning 4, 7505 Ettlingen, telephone (07243) 1 21 06.

Rheydt 4050

(Please see Mönchengladbach.)

Rinteln 3260

Antik- und Trödelmarkt (antique and junk market) second Sunday in October at the Extra-Parkplatz on Bahnhofstrasse. Organized by Novema Hannover, Hahnensteg 22, 3000 Hannover 91, telephone (0511) 41 74 02.

Rockenhausen 6760

Trödelmarkt (junk market) third Saturday of October in the town center. Organized by Horst Zehnpfennig, Pestalozzistrasse 54, 6504 Nierstein, telephone (06133) 5 85 11.

Rodgau 6054

(Please also see Offenbach.)

Antikmarkt (antique market) last Sunday of October in the Radsporthalle (bicycle racing hall) in the Jügesheim district. Organized by M. Kregel, Kirchhohl 36, 6200 Wiesbaden 41, telephone (06127) 49 06.

Rosbach vor der Höhe 6365

Trödelmarkt (junk market) every Saturday year round at the Möbel Einkaufzentrum (shopping center). Organized by Schmidt-Moebus, telephone (0639) 4 10 33.

Rosenheim 8200

Flohmarkt (flea market) second Saturday of every month year round at Küpferlingstrasse 62.

Organized by Karl Hetzel, at the same address, telephone (08031) 8 39 41.

Roth 8501

Antik- und Trödelmarkt (antique and junk market) first weekend of October at the Stadthalle. Organized by Messebüro Garon, Federmannweg 3, 7900 Ulm, telephone (0731) 1 37 03.

Rothenburg ob der Tauber 8803

Antikmarkt (antique market) first weekend of October at Schrannenplatz, just inside the city wall on the north side of town. Organized by Firma Weber, Semmelstrasse 42, 8700 Würzburg, telephone (0931) 1 37 03.

Rottach-Egern 8183

Antikmarkt (antique market) first weekend of November at the Gasthof Zur Post in the suburb of Egern. Organized by Max Koch, Jakob-Hagenbucher-Strasse 16, 8000 München 50, telephone (089) 29 53 06.

Rottweil 7210

Antikmarkt (antique market) first Sunday of October in the Stadthalle. Information from Südorga Langlotz GdBR, Höllturm-Passage 1, 7760 Radolfzell, telephone (07732) 31 52.

Trödelmarkt (junk market) fourth Saturday of October in the EZA-Markt. Organized by Agentur Floma, Industriestrasse 15, 7340 Geislingen, telephone (07331) 4 04 51.

Saarbrücken 6600

Trödelmarkt (junk market) second Saturday of every month year round at St. Johannaplatz in the Fussgängerzone (pedestrian zone) in the city center. Information from Stadtverwaltung, Marktamt, 6600 Saarbrücken, telephone (0681) 38 01 ext. 8 26.

Antikwoche (antique week) first Thursday through Sunday of October at the Saarmesse (Saar fairgrounds). Organized by H. P. Deutschmann, Rheinstrasse 76, 6200 Wiesbaden, telephone (0621) 37 52 75.

Ansichtkarten Tauschtreff (picture card exchange meeting) first Monday of every month at the Gasthof Fürst Ludwig. Organized by J. Güth, Türkenstrasse 7, 6600 Saarbrücken, telephone (0681) 3 18 19.

Spielzeug- und Modelleisenbahnmarkt (toy and model train market) second Sunday of November at the Saarlandhalle. Organized by Kirschner & Patarek GmbH, Ostwall 39, 4150 Krefeld 1, telephone (02841) 2 62 60.

Saarlouis 6630

Antik- und Flohmarkt (antique and flea market) last Sunday of October at the Parkhaus on the ring road. Organized by Inge Grossöhmig, Ostschachtstrasse 21, 6605 Friedrichsthal, telephone (06897) 8 63 63.

St. Augustin 5202

(Please also see Bad Godesberg and Bonn.)

Antik- und Trödelmarkt (antique and junk market) first weekend of October in the Gewerbehalle on Gutenbergstrasse in the Menden district. Organized by Hermann & Lampert, Hasselholzerweg 9, 5100 Aachen, telephone (0241) 7 20 21.

Antikmarkt (antique market) first weekend of every month year round in the Ratsstuben in the town center. Organized by Rolf à Brassard,

Rheinstrasse 4, 5434 Dernbach, telephone (02602) 7 08 39.

Antik- und Trödelmarkt (antique and junk market) first and third Sunday of every month. Location varies between the Kirmesplatz in the Furth district and the HUMA-Ladenpassage. Organized by Norbert Junge, Talbahnstrasse 4, 5190 Stolberg, telephone (02402) 2 30 07.

Salzkotten 4796

Antik- und Kunstmarkt (antique and art market) second weekend of October at the Stadthalle. Organized by A. M. V. V. Jörn Werber, Am Grossen Holz 9, 4817 Leopoldshöhe, telephone (05208) 14 23.

Sande 2945

Trödelmarkt (junk market) second Saturday of July in the town center. Organized by the Ordnungsamt, 2945 Sande, telephone (04422) 6 31.

Schleswig 2380

Flohmarket (flea market) third Sunday of October at the Schleimarkt. Information from E. Kohler, P. A. M. Veranstaltungen, Bornbrok 1-3, 2330 Eckernförde, telephone (04351) 29 80.

Schliengen 7846

Trödelmarkt (junk market) Easter Sunday and the last Sunday of September at the Festhalle und Vorplatz. Organized by Feyer, telephone (07635) 95 12.

Schloss Holte 4815

Antik- und Trödelmarkt (antique and junk market) first Sunday of October at the

Dixi-Parkplatz in the Stuckenbrock district. Organized by A. M. V. V. Jörn Werber, Am Grossen Holz 9, 4817 Leopoldshöhe, telephone (05208) 14 23.

Schongau 8920

Antiquitäten- und Sammlermarkt (antique and collectors' market) second weekend of October in the Pfarrheim district. Organized by Alexander Schröder, Salzstrasse 5, 8952 Marktoberdorf, telephone (08342) 52 72.

Schramberg 7230

Flohmarkt (flea market) third Saturday of October near the Depot- Markt. Organized by Marktorganisationzentrum Michaela März, Gerwingstrasse 1, 7742 St. Georgen, telephone (07724) 34 05.

Schwäbisch-Gmund 7070

Flohmarkt (flea market) first and third Saturday of October at the Schlecker-Gelände. Organized by Heinz A. Seegerer, Taubenberg 11, 8990 Lindau, telephone (08382) 68 58.

Trödelmarkt (junk market) second Friday of October and November at the Festplatz in the Schiesstal district. Organized by Agentur Zelinka, Gmündstrasse 18, 7070 Schwäbisch Gmünd, telephone (07171) 8 52 32.

Antikmarkt (antique market) fourth Sunday of October in the Stadtgartenhalle. Organized by K. D. Maier, Neuffenstrasse 13, 7031 Stenenbronn, telephone (07157) 29 61.

Antikmarkt (antique market) second Sunday of November at the Saalbau in the Stadtgarten. Organized by Antiquariat Peter Kiefer GmbH, Ebersteinstrasse 14, 7530 Pforzheim, telephone (07231) 1 72 72.

Schwäbisch Hall 7170

Trödelmarkt (junk market) second and fourth Sunday of October in the Gartenschauhalle and the Marktzentrum in the Steinbach district. Two organizers sponsor this market: you can receive information from K. D. Meier, Neuffenstrasse 13, 7031 Steinbronn, telephone (07157) 29 61, or from Agentur Zelinka, Gmündstrasse 18, 7070 Schwäbisch Gmünd, telephone (07171) 8 52 32.

Schwalmstadt 3578

Floh- und Antikmarkt (flea and antique market) first Saturday of November at the Hexenturm Breisach. Organized by Friedhelm Knoth, Stettinerstrasse 4, Ziegenhain-Schwalmstadt, telephone (06691) 63 06.

Flohmarkt (flea market) second weekend of November at the China-Park. Organized by Rode Messen, Schloss Sickendorf, 6420 Lauterbach 7, telephone (06641) 30 26.

Schweinfurt 8720

Antiquitätenmarkt (antique market) first weekend of October in the Dekanats-Zentrum. Organized by Firma Weber, Semmelstrasse 42, 8700 Würzburg, telephone (0931) 1 3703. Another antique market is held the same weekend in the Stadthalle, organized by Peter Fuchs, Bahnhofstrasse 5, 6940 Weinheim, telephone (06201) 1 22 32.

Trödelmarkt (junk market) third Sunday of October in the Plaza Selbsbedienung parking lot. Organized by Reinhard Preuss, Antoniusgasse 25, 6228 Eltville, telephone (06123) 7 46 11.

Schwerte 5840

Antiktage (antique fair) either the first or third weekend of October (varies year by year) in the Schloss Haus Ruhr. Organized by Alida Schleusener, Waldfriedstrasse 1, 5000 Köln 60, telephone (0221) 71 34 14.

Schwetzingen 6830

(Please also see Heidelberg.)

Antik- und Trödelmarkt (antique and junk market) third Sunday of October in the Schloss (castle). Organized by Margit Buzecki, Ausstellungsdienst, Stettfelderstrasse 7, 7526 Ubstadt-Wieher 3, telephone (07251) 6 33 94.

Seeheim 6104

Antikmarkt (antique market) first Sunday of October in the Sporthalle in the Jugenheim district. Organized by M. Kriegel, Kirchhohl 36, 6200 Wiesbaden 41, telephone (06127) 49 06.

Seesen 3370

Flohmarkt (flea market) second Sunday in October at the Alderplatz. Organized by Heinz A. Seegerer, Am Riess 8, Postfach 612, 8100 Garmisch-Partenkirchen, telephone (08821) 5 14 62.

Senden 7913

(Please also see Ottmarsbucholt.)

Flohmarkt (flea market) every Sunday from March through October at the Adler Gelände. Organized by Heinz A. Seegerer, Taubenberg 11, 8990 Lindau, telephone (08382) 68 58.

Siegburg 5200

Trödelmarkt (junk market) alternates the first and third and second and fourth Sunday year round of each month at the Massa Einkaufzentrum. Organized by Nikolaus Dollmann, Teichstrasse 16, 5000 Köln 30, telephone (0221) 53 17 44.

Siegen 5900

(Please also see Neunkirchen 5908.)

Antik- und Trödelmarkt (antique and junk market) first or second Saturday of the month from April through November at the Rathaus in the Geisweid district, about seven kilometers north on highway 62 from the Hauptbahnhof (main rail station). Organized by Dieter Endres, Sonnenhang 6, 5242 Kirchen, telephone (02741) 6 16 11.

Antikmarkt (antique market) third Sunday of February and second Sunday of October at the Bismarckhalle, located at the end of the bridge leading to the autobahn. Organized by Theodor Wessling, Kurhausstrasse 31a, 4690 Herne 2, telephone (02325) 4 30 31.

Antik- und Sammlermarkt (antique and collectors' market) second weekend of March and October in the CEE Einkaufzentrum in the Eiserfeld district, five kilometers south of the city center, and first Sunday of November in the Siegerlandhalle. Organized by Kogel & Lauber, Kornmarkt 10-12, 6900 Siegen, telephone (0271) 5 15 01.

Antikmarkt (antique market) fourth weekend of October at the Siegerlandhalle. Organized by Norbert Junge, Talbahnstrasse 4, 5190 Stolberg, telephone (02402) 2 30 07.

Trödelmarkt (junk market) third Sunday of October in the Einkaufzentrum Minimal in the Eisserfeld district. Organized by Kogel &

Lauber, Kornmarkt 10-12, 6900 Siegen, telephone (0271) 5 15 01.

Schallplattenbörse (record exchange) first Sunday in October at the Siegerlandhalle. Information from F. Rosenkrantz, Am Schieferweg 7, 5900 Siegen, telephone (0271) 33 11 79.

Kunstmarkt (art market) first weekend of November at the Siegerlandhalle. Organized by Kogel & Lauber, Kornmarkt 10-12, 6900 Siegen, telephone (0271) 5 15 01.

Sigmaringen 7480

Spielzeugmarkt (toy market) first weekend of November at the Stadthalle. Organized by Bruno Conrad, Falkenstrasse 21, 7965 Ostrach 8, telephone (07558) 10 10.

Sammlertreff: Militaria (collectors' meeting: military items) first Friday of November at the Gasthof Waldfrieden. Organized by Hohenzollerischer Münzverein 1969, H. Pfister, Postfach 543, 7480 Sigmaringen, telephone (07571) 5 16 61.

Simmern 6540

Antik- und Trödelmarkt (antique and junk market) first Sunday of October at the Globus Handelshof. Organized by Reinhard Preuss, Antoniusgasse 25, 6228 Eltville, telephone (06123) 7 46 11.

Sindelfingen 7032

Spielzeugmarkt (toy market) second Sunday of October at the Stadthalle. Organized by Dr. Rolf Theurer, Wunnensteinstrasse 23, 7144 Asperg, telephone (0741) 3 44 42.

Singen 7700

(Please also see Hilzingen.)

Antik- und Trödelmarkt (antique and junk market) the first Friday, Saturday, and Sunday of June in the Innenstadt. This market is part of the annual Hohentweilfest. Organized by Südorga Langlotz GdBR, Höllturm-Passage 1, 7760 Radolfzell, telephone (07732) 31 52.

Sinzig am Rhein 5485

Adventsmarkt (Advent market) the weekend before Christmas in the Innenstadt (inner town center). Organized by R. Grossmann, telephone (02237) 5 20 66.

Solingen 5650

Flohmarkt (flea market) second or third Sunday of every month at the Hauptbahnhof (main railway station) in the city center. (This otherwise rather undistinguished city in the Ruhr is the source of the famous Solingen knives). Organized by Gabrielle Wallon, Postfach 39, 4005 Meerbusch 1, telephone (02105) 56 51.

Kunsthandwerkermarkt (artisans' market) first week of November at the Schloss Burg. Organized by Stadt Solingen, Potsdamer Strasse 41 (Rathaus), 5650 Solingen, telephone (0212) 2 90 23 10.

Spielzeugbörse (toy exchange) second weekend of November in the Foyer Konzerthaus. Organized by Stadt Solingen, Potsdamer Strasse 41 (Rathaus), 5650 Solingen, telephone (0212) 2 90 23 10.

Speyer 6720

Antikmarkt (antique market) second Sunday of October in the Agidienhaus. Organized by

Antiquariat Peter Kiefer GmbH, Kirchstrasse 4, 7537 Remchingen-Wilferdingen, telephone (07231) 1 72 72.

Stadthagen 3060

Hobby- und Trödelmarkt (hobby and junk market) first Saturday of every month year round in the Festhalle. Special markets also take place the third weekend of March (Fruhjahrkrammarkt), third weekend of October (Herbstmarkt), and last weekend of November through December 20 (Weinachtsmarkt). Information from Stadt Stadthagen, Verwaltung der Festhalle, Bahnhofstrasse 17, 3060 Stadthagen, telephone (05721) 40 21.

Starnberg 8130

Antikmarkt (antique market) first weekend of October and November at the Undosa-Festsaal. Organized by Max Koch, Jakob-Hagenbucher-Strasse 16, 8000 München 50, telephone (089) 29 53 06.

Antikmarkt (antique market) third weekend of October at the TSV-Halle. Organized by Alexander Dohn, Linprunstrasse 57, 8000 München 2, telephone (089) 55 31 31.

Steinheim an der Murr 7141

Flohmarkt (flea market) first Sunday of October in the Top-Kopf Bau-Center. Organized by Agentur Floma, Industriestrasse 15, 7340 Geislingen, telephone (07331) 4 04 51.

Stolberg 5190

Trödelmarkt (junk market) second Sunday of October at the Einkaufzentrum on Mauerstrasse. Organized by Norbert Junge, Talbahnstrasse 4, 5190 Stolberg, telephone (02402) 2 30 07.

Straelen 4172

Antik- und Trödelmarkt (antique and junk market) third weekend of July in the Innenstadt. Organized by the Stadtverwaltung der Stadt, 4172 Straelen, telephone (02834) 70 20.

Straubing 8440

Flohmarkt (flea market) first Sunday of every month from April through October at the Arcobräukeller. Organized by D. K. Gerhard Stock, Am Hang 9, 8422 Riedenberg, telephone (09442) 22 49.

Stuttgart 7000

(Please also see Böblingen, Ditzingen, Gärtringen, Gerlingen, Korb, Ludwigsburg, and Walblinen.)

Flohmarkt (flea market) every Saturday year round at Karlsplatz. This market is one of the largest in Germany. Twice a year, in spring and fall (dates vary from year to year), the center of the old city becomes a tremendous market. Hundreds of vendors display porcelain, silver, furniture, art work, toys, dolls, and other interesting items. Organized by the Marktamt der Stadt, 7000 Stuttgart, telephone (0711) 2 16 50 07 and 2 16 50 59.

Antik- und Trödelmarkt (antique and junk market) second Sunday of every month at the Stadthalle in the western suburb of Korntal. Access is easiest by car: get off Autobahn E70-A81 at Stuttgart/Zuffenhausen, go south from Zuffenhausen to Korntal. Access by train to the Korntal station, then walk. (Service is very infrequent on Sunday.) Organized by Dieter Krauss, Pfarrweg 32, 7064 Remshalden, telephone (07181) 47 08.

Flohmarkt (flea market) first Sunday of October at the Kelterplatz in the Zuffenhausen district, about four kilometers north of the

Hauptbahnhof (main railway station). Organized by Agentur Walter GmbH, Postfach 1171, 7140 Ludwigsburg, telephone (07141) 2 76 01.

Ansichtkarten-Börse (picture and postcard exchange) second Saturday of June, September, and November at the Gustav-Siegle-Haus. Organized by Manfred Breitsprecher, Paulinenstrasse 44, 7000 Stuttgart, telephone (0711) 61 73 63 or 61 69 13.

Sammlertreff: Orden- und Militaria (collectors' meeting: medals and military items) third Friday of October at the Gaststätte Apostel. Organized by Helmut Dangelmaier, Postfach 300302, 7000 Stuttgart, telephone (0711) 85 85 74.

Puppenbörse (doll and puppet exchange) last Sunday of October and first Sunday of November (may vary from year to year) at the Hotel International in the Stuttgart-Möhringen district. Information from M. Wanke, Baarerstrasse 10, CH-6300 Zug, Switzerland, telephone country code 41 (42) 21 21 78, or the hotel at (0711) 7 20 21. Also, an additional doll and puppet market is held the first Sunday of November in the Kursaal in the Bad Cannstadt district. Organized by Dr. Rolf Theurer, Wunnensteinstrasse 23, 7144 Asperg, telephone (07141) 3 44 42.

Tönisvorst 4154

Trödelmarkt (junk market) fourth Sunday of October at the Massa-Einkaufzentrum. Organized by Norbert Junge, Obersteinstrasse 51, 5190 Stolberg, telephone (02402) 2 30 07.

Töstedt 2117

Trödelmarkt (junk market) first Saturday of October in the Innenstadt. Organized by Matthies, 2117 Tostedt, telephone (04182) 14 15.

Traunstein 8220

Antik- und Trödelmarkt (antique and junk market) first and third weekend of October in the Turnhalle. Information from Messebüro Garon, Federmannweg 3, 7900 Ulm, telephone (0731) 3 0574.

Trier 5500

Antik- und Trödelmarkt (antique and junk market) second Sunday of October in the Ration-Warenhaus in the Trier-Nord district. Organized by Reinhard Preuss, Antoniusgasse 25, 6228 Eltville, telephone (06123) 7 46 11.

Antik- und Sammlermarkt (antique and collectors' market) fourth weekend of October at the Europahalle. Organized by WEWO Antikmärkte, Rudi-Stefan-Allee 14, 6520 Worms, telephone (06241) 7 58 71.

Trochtelfingen-Hald 7416

Sammlertreff: Militaria (collectors' meeting: military items) first Friday of every month year round at the Gasthof Haidhof. Organized by Albert Latus, Im Reutele 25, 7400 Tübingen 5, telephone (07071) 7 15 65.

Troisdorf 5210

Trödelmarkt (junk market) second and fourth weekend of October in the Fussgängerzone in the town center. Organized by Junge & Schönenbrücher, Talbahnstrasse 4, 5190 Stolberg, telephone (02402) 8 27 67.

Antik- und Trödelmarkt (antique and junk market) second Sunday of November at the Massa parking garage. Organized by Nikolaus Dollmann, Teichstrasse 16, 5000 Köln 30, telephone (0221) 53 17 44.

Tübingen 7400

Trödelmarkt (junk market) first Saturday of October at the Festplatz and third Sunday of October at the Handelshof. Organized by Firma Syntis, Jakobsgasse 29, 7400 Tübingen, telephone (07071) 2 70 22.

Handwerkermarkt (artisans' market) second weekend of October at the Nonnenhaus. Organized by Firma Syntis, Jakobsgasse 29, 7400 Tübingen, telephone (07071) 2 70 22.

Ulm 7900

(Please also see Neu-Ulm and Senden.)

Trödelmarkt (junk market) first Sunday of every month at the Donaubastion. Organized by Agentur Zelinka, Gmündstrasse 18, 7070 Schwäbisch Gmünd, telephone (07171) 8 52 32.

International Kunst- und Antiquitätentage (international art and antique days) first weekend of October in the Donauhalle. Information from Organisation Märkte-Messen Mezger, Zeppelinstrasse 4, 7710 Donaueschingen, telephone (0771) 1 39 99.

Vallendar 5414

Flohmarkt (flea market) third weekend of October along the Rheinpromenade. Organized by Rolf à Brassard, Rheinstrasse 4, 5434 Dernbach, telephone (02602) 7 08 39.

Vechta 2848

Antikmarkt (antique market) first weekend of November in the Festsäle Waldhof. Organized by Franz Stefan, An der Mühle 32, 4052 Korsenbroich 4, telephone (02166) 8 35 09.

Veitshöchheim 8702

(Please also see Würzburg.)

Militaria- und Antikbörse (military item and antique exchange) first weekend of November at the Mainfrankensäle. Organized by Firma Weber, Semmelstrasse 42, 8700 Würzburg, telephone (0931) 1 37 03.

Verl 4837

(Please also see Gütersloh.)

Trödelmarkt (junk market) first Saturday of every month year round in the Ost-westfalenhalle in the Kaunitz district. Organized by Gemeindeverwaltung, 4837 Verl, telephone (05246) 30 41.

Viernheim 6806

(Please also see Heidelberg and Mannheim.)

Flohmarkt (flea market) third Sunday of October at the Toom-Markt. Organized by M. Lukas, Mönchhofstrasse 14a, 6806 Viernheim, telephone (0621) 72 15 03.

Viersen 4060

Trödelmarkt (junk market) third Sunday of October at the Festhallenvorplatz. Organized by Norbert Junge, Obersteinstrasse 51, 5190 Stolberg, telephone (02402) 2 30 07.

Villingen 7730

Flohmarkt (flea market) second Saturday of October in the Volksbankparkplatz. Organized by Marktorganisationzentrum Michaela März, Gerwingstrasse 1, 7742 St. Georgen, telephone (07724) 34 05.

Trödelmarkt (junk market) third Sunday of October in the Tonhalle. Organized by Klaus Scheppe, KS-Management, Fidel-Fischer Strasse 1, 7580 Bühl, telephone (0723) 48 95.

Walblinen 7050

(Please also see Stuttgart.)

Antik- und Trödelmarkt (antique and junk market) fourth Sunday of October at the Bürgerzentrum. Organized by H. & H. K. Fischer, Uhlandstrasse 18, 7255 Rutesheim, telephone (07152) 5 43 77.

Waldbröl 5220

Antik- und Trödelmarkt (antique and junk market) first or second weekend of October (varies year by year) in the Innenstadt (city center). Organized by Richard Altmann, Mediascher Gasse 13, 5276 Siel 3, telephone (02262) 18 66.

Waldkraiburg 8264

Antikmarkt (antique market) first weekend of October at the Zappesaal. Information from (08141) 1 85 81.

Waldshut 7890

Flohmarkt (flea market) fourth Saturday of October at the Familia Einkaufzentrum parking lot. Organized by Südorga Langlotz GdBR, Höllturm-Passage 1, 7750 Radolfzell, telephone (07732) 31 52.

Wangen im Allgau 7988

Antikmarkt (antique market) first weekend of November in the Stadthalle. Organized by

Messebüro Garon, Federmannweg 3, 7900 Ulm, telephone (0731) 3 05 74.

Wassenberg 5143

Trödelmarkt (junk market) first Sunday of October at the Kontra parking lot. Organized by Christel Diener, Erklerenzstrasse 71, 5138 Heinzburg-Dremmen, telephone (02452) 6 24 01.

Wasserburg am Inn 8090

Antikmarkt (antique market) first Saturday of October at the Halbinsel. Organized by Südorga Langlotz GdBR, Höllturm-Passage 1, 7760 Radolfzell, telephone (07732) 31 52.

Wegberg 5144

Trödelmarkt (junk market) first and fourth of October in the Stadtmitte (city center). Organized by R. Leines, Talstrasse 32, 4050 Mönchengladbach 3, telephone (02166) 60 25 10.

Weilburg 6290

Flohmarkt (flea market) third weekend of October or first weekend of November (varies year by year) in Kirmesplatz. Organized by Rolf à Brassard, Rheinstrasse 4, 5434 Dernbach, telephone (02602) 7 08 39.

Weil der Stadt 7252

Flohmarkt (flea market) second Sunday of October at the Festplatz. Organized by Peter Gailer, Eberhardstrasse 49, 7000 Stuttgart 1, telephone (0711) 24 43 80.

Weilerstadt 5354

Trödelmarkt (junk market) second Sunday of October at the Imbert parking lot. Organized by Junge & Schönenbrücher, Talbahnstrasse 4, 5190 Stolberg, telephone (02407) 8 27 67.

Weinsburg 7102

(Please also see Heilbronn.)

Antikmarkt (antique market) second Sunday of October in the Hildthalle. Organized by Agentur Floma, Industriestrasse 15, 7340 Geislingen, telephone (07331) 4 04 51. This hall is used for other antique and fle markets sporadically during the year.

Weiterstadt 6108

(Please also dee Darmstadt.)

Trödelmarkt (junk market) fourth Sunday of October and second and fourth Sundays of November at the Toom-Markt. Organized by Reinhard Preuss, Antoniusgasse 25, 6228 Eltville, telephone (06123) 7 46 11.

Welver 4777

Trödelmarkt (junk market) second Saturday of October in the Bördehalle. Organized by Antiquitäten Fritz, Am Markt 13, 4777 Welver, telephone (02384) 31 32.

Welzheim 7063

Antik- und Trödelmarkt (antique and junk market) second Sunday of October in the Justinus-Kerner-Halle. Information from H. & H. K. Fischer, Uhlandstrasse 18, 7255 Rutesheim, telephone (07152) 5 43 77.

Wermelskirchen 5632

Flohmarkt (flea market) third or fourth Sunday of October (varies from year to year) in the Güterbahnhof (freight rail station). Organized by Gabrielle Wallon, Postfach 39, 4005 Meerbusch 1, telephone (02105) 56 51.

Wesel 4230

Antik- und Trödelmarkt (antique and junk market) first or second Saturday or Sunday of every month in the Niederrheinhalle. (The exact day depends on when the hall isn't otherwise occupied.) Information from U. Hermann, Stauffenstrasse 20, 4600 Dortmund 1, telephone (0231) 10 23 10, or from Schneider und Partner GmbH & Co. KG, Hufstrasse 50 4100 Duisburg 11, telephone (0203) 3 90 86.

Flohmarkt (flea market) second Sunday of October in the Dudel-Passage. This market is part of the annual Drehorgefestival. Organized by Gabrielle Wallon, Postfach 39, 4005 Meerbusch 1, telephone (02105) 56 51.

Wetzlar 6330

Flohmarkt (flea market) second Saturday of every month year round on the Lahninsel (Lahn Island). In some months this market continues through Sunday. Organized by Rolf à Brassard, Rheinstrasse 4, 5434 Dernbach, telephone (02602) 7 08 39.

Wiesbaden 6200

Antik- und Trödelmarkt (antique and junk market) second Sunday of most months in the Grosso-Markt on Hasengartenstrasse. Organized by Reinhard Preuss, Antoniusgasse 25, 6228 Eltville, telephone (06120) 87 44. This organizer occasionally uses other sites in Wiesbaden.

Trödelmarkt (junk market) third Saturday of October at the Festplatz in the Naurod district. Organized by M. Kriegel, Kirchhohl 36, 6200 Wiesbaden 41, telephone (0627) 49 06.

Musik- und Schallplattenbörse (music and record exchange) first Sunday of November at Lehrstrasse 13. Organized by Kogel & Lauber, Kornmarkt 10-12, 6900 Siegen, telephone (0271) 5 15 01.

Wiesloch 6908

Antik- und Trödelmarkt (antique and junk market) first weekend of November at the Stadthalle. Organized by WEWO Antikmärkte, Rudi-Stefan-Allee 14, 6520 Worms, telephone (06241) telephone (06241) 7 58 71.

Winnenden 7057

Antik- und Trödelmarkt (antique and junk market) first and second Sunday of October in the Stadthalle. Organized by H. & H. K. Fischer, Uhlandstrasse 18, 7255 Rutesheim, telephone (07152) 5 43 77. Other organizers use this hall throughout the year for similar events.

Witten 5810

(Please also see Bochum and Dortmund.)

Antikmarkt (antique market) first Sunday of October at the Saalbau. Organized by Theodor Wessling, Kurhausstrasse 31a, 4690 Herne 2, telephone (02325) 4 30 31. Other organizers also use this location for markets throughout the year.

Wittingen 3120

Antikmarkt (antique market) second Sunday of October at the Stadthalle. Organized by Ch.

Schlinkmann, Im Sandmorgen 8, 3153
Lahstedt 3, telephone (05172) 22 65.

Wittmund 2944

Antikmarkt (antique market) second Sunday of
October in the Stadthalle. Organized by
Inter-Antik, Michael Becker, Mommsenstrasse
10, 4006 Eckrath, telephone (02104) 4 61 52.

Wörth am Rhein 6729

(Please also see Karlsruhe.)

Antik- und Trödelmarkt (antique and junk
market) second weekend of October at the
Bienwaldhalle. Organized by Margit Buzecki,
Ausstellungsdienst, Stettfelderstrasse 7, 7526
Ubstadt-Weiher 3, telephone (07251) 6 33 94.

Wolfsburg 3180

Trödelmarkt (junk market) first and second
Sunday of every month in the Stadthalle.
Organized by Ch. Schlinkmann, Im Sandmorgen
8, 3153 Lahstedt 3, telephone (05172) 22 65.

Worms 6520

Antik- und Trödelmarkt (antique and junk
market) second Saturday of every month at the
Nibelungen-Center. Organized by WEWO Antikmärkte, Rudi-Stefan-Allee 14, 6250 Worms,
telephone (06241) 7 58 71.

Floh- und Trödelmarkt (flea and junk market)
first Saturday of October at the Festplatz near
the Rheinbrücke (along the river.) Ample
parking is available. Organized by Erich Lösch,
Eisenbergerstrasse 10, 6520 Worms, telephone
(06241) 2 85 19.

Modellauto- Blech- und Spielzeugbörse (model car and tin soldier and toy exchange) first Sunday of November at the Jahnturnhalle. Organized by Erich Lösch, Eisenberger Strasse, 6520 Worms, telephone (06241) 8 87 19.

Wuppertal 5600

Flohmarkt (flea market) every Sunday year round in the Bayer-Parkplatz in the Elberfeld district. Organized by Gabrielle Wallon, Postfach 39, 4005 Meerbusch 1, telephone (02105) 56 51.

Antik- und Trödelmarkt (antique and junk market) first Sunday of October in the Schützenplatz and adjacent Schützenhalle in the Beyenburg district. Organized by R. Leines, Talstrasse 32, 4050 Mönchengladbach 3, telephone (02166) 60 25 10.

Schallplattenbörse (record exchange) third Sunday of October in the Stadthalle. Organized by Kogel & Lauber, Kornmarkt 10-12, 6900 Siegen, telephone (0271) 5 15 01.

Spielzeug- und Modelleisenbahnmarkt (toy and model railroad market) second Sunday of October at the Stadtsaal in the Vohwinkel district. Organized by Kirchner & Patarek GmbH, Ostwall 39, 4150 Krefeld 1, telephone (02841) 2 62 60.

Wurselen 5102

(Please also see Aachen.)

Trödelmarkt (junk market) third Saturday of October on Lindenplatz. Organized by Hermann & Lampert, Hasselholzerweg 9, 5100 Aachen, telephone (0241) 7 20 21.

Würzburg 8700

(Please also see Vietshöchheim.)

Antikmarkt (antique market) third weekend of October at the Frankenhalle. This is a major regional show. Organized by Firma Weber, Semmelstrasse 42, 8700 Würzburg, telephone (0931) 1 37 03.

Antikmarkt (antique market) first weekend of November at the Mainfrankensäle in the suburb of Vietshöchheim. Organized by Firma Weber, Semmelstrasse 42, 8700 Würzburg, telephone (0931) 1 37 03.

Zell am Harmersbach 7615

Trödelmarkt (junk market) fourth Sunday of October in the Ritter-von-Buss-Halle. This town is in the Black Forest region near Freiburg. Organized by Klaus Scheppe, KS-Management, Fidel Fischer Strasse 1, 7580 Bühl, telephone (07223) 48 95.

Zell 7321

(Near Esslingen.)

Spielzeugmarkt (toy market) fourth Sunday of October in the Veranstaltungshalle. Organized by Udo Schoffer, Friedensstrasse 12, 7300 Esslingen, telephone (0711) 31 50 86.

Zeltingen 5553

(Please also see Bernkastel-Kues.)

Antik- und Trödelmarkt (antique and junk market) first weekend of October on the Moselpromenade. Organized by Marktveranstaltungen Albert Becker, Händelsstrasse 46, 5660 Wittlich, telephone (06571) 6 99 50.

Zons 4047

(Please also see Düsseldorf.)

Antiquitätentage (antique days) first weekend of November at the Bürgerhaus. Organized by Brass-Villegas, Gladbacherstrasse 32, 4060 Viersen 1, telephone (02162) 3 18 18.

Zweibrücken 6660

(Please also see Pirmasens.)

Trödelmarkt (junk market) third Saturday of October at the Alexanderkirche. Organized by Stadtverwaltung, Ordnungsamt, Herzogstrasse 7, 6660 Zweibrücken, telephone (06332) 8 82 76.

Specialized Markets City by City

For details on the markets in this chapter, please see the preceding chapter, "Markets A to Z."

Antique Days

Baden-Baden

Antiktage (antique days) third weekend of October.

Bad Soden

Antiquitätentage (antique days) second weekend of October.

Bocholt

Antiquitätenmarkt (antique market) first Saturday of October.

Borken

Floh- und Antiquitätenmarkt (flea and antique market) first Sunday of every month.

Brüggen

Antiquitäten Fest (antiques fair) first weekend in October.

Celle

Kunst- und Antiquitätentage (art and antique fair) first weekend in October.

Dortmund

West-Antique (Westfalia antique show) second Thursday through following Sunday of November.

Düsseldorf

Antiquitäten Ausstellung (antique show) for 10 days in March.

Essen

Internationale Antiquitäten-Messe (international antiques fair) third week in November.

Frankfurt am Main

Antiquitätenwoche (antique week) usually the second and third weeks of October.

Giessen

Antiquitätentage (antique days) first weekend in October.

Goslar

Antiquitäten- und Kunsttage (antiques and art days) second weekend of October.

Gummersbach

Antiktage (antique days) first weekend in November.

Hannover

Antiktage (antique days) first weekend of November.

Köln

Antiquitätentage (antique days) second weekend of October.

Antiktag (antique day) second Sunday of October.

Leonburg

Antiktage (antique days) second weekend of October.

Ludwigshafen

Antiktage (antique days) third Friday, Saturday, and Sunday of October.

Mainz

Antiktage (antique days) first weekend of November.

Memmingen

Kunst- und Antiktage (art and antique days) first Sunday of November.

München

Antik- und Kunstwoche (antique and art week) mid October.

Kunst-und-Antiquitätenmesse (art and antiques fair) second half of October.

Neumünster

Antiquitätentag (antique day) last Sunday of October.

Paderborn

Antiktage (antique days) first Friday through following Sunday of October.

Saarbrücken

Antikwoche (antique week) first Thursday through Sunday of October.

Schongau

Antiquitäten- und Sammlermarkt (antique and collectors' market) second weekend of October.

Schwerte

Antiktage (antique fair) either the first or third weekend of October (varies year by year).

Ulm

International Kunst- und Antiquitätentage (international art and antique days) first weekend of October.

Zons

Antiquitätentage (antique days) first weekend of November.

Art Markets

Altenkirchen im Westerwald

Kunsthandwerkermarkt (art and artisans' market), the last Sunday of October and the first Sunday of November.

Castrup-Rauxel (Schwerin)

Antik- und Kunstmarkt (antique and artwork market) last weekend of October.

Celle

Kunst- und Antiquitätentage (art and antique fair) first weekend in October.

Gladbeck

Antik- und Kunstmarkt (antique and art market) first weekend of October.

Hagen

Kunstmarkt (art market), Musikbörse (music exchange), and other antique-related events the first Sunday of every month.

Hamm

Kunstmarkt (art market) second Sunday of October.

Hilzingen

Kunst- und Trödelmarkt (art and junk market) third Sunday and Monday of October.

Karlsruhe

Kunsthandwerkmarkt (art and handicrafts market) second weekend of October.

Kunst- und Antikmarkt (art and antique market) first weekend of November.

Kassel

Antik- und Kunst Woche (antique and art week) first weekend in October every year.

Konstanz

Kunst- und Trödelmarkt (art and junk market) second Saturday of October.

Lohmar

Kunst- und Töpfermarkt (art and pottery market) first weekend of October.

Memmingen

Kunst- und Antiktage (art and antique days) first Sunday of November.

Minden

Kunstmarkt (art market) first weekend of October.

München

Antik- und Kunstwoche (antique and art week) mid October.

Kunst- und- Antiquitätenmesse (art and antiques fair) second half of October.

Plankstadt

Kunsthandwerkermarkt (artisans' market) first Sunday of November.

Recklinghausen

Antik- und Kunstmarkt (antique and art market) first and fourth weekend in October.

Remagen

Töpfer- Kunst- Antiquitäten- und Hand- werk-ermarkt (pottery, antique, art, and artisans' market) first weekend of April and October.

Siegen

Kunstmarkt (art market) first weekend of November.

Solingen

Kunsthandwerkermarkt (artists' market) first week of November.

Artisans' Markets

Bad Kreutznach

Antik- und Handwerkmarkt (antique and handcrafts market) first Saturday in October.

Bielefeld

Antik- Trödel- und Handwerkermarkt (antique, junk, and artisans' market) last Sunday in June.

Dortmund

Handwerkermarkt (artisans' market) first Sunday of May.

Duisburg

Handwerkermarkt (handicraft workers' market) third Sunday in September.

Enniger-Ennigerloh

Antik- Trödel- und Handwerkermarkt (antique, junk, and artisans' market) second Wednesday in July.

Gelsenkirchen

Antik- Trödel- und Handwerkermarkt (antique, junk, and artisans market) first Friday and every weekend year round.

Gerolstein

Antik- Trödel- und Handwerkermarkt (antique, junk, and artisans' market) second weekend of June.

Karlsruhe

Kunsthandwerkmarkt (art and handicrafts market) second weekend of October.

Kaunitz-Verl

Handwerkermarkt (artisans' market) first Saturday at every month.

Langenberg

Handwerkermarkt (artisans' market) third Sunday of October.

Remagen

Töpfer- Kunst- Antiquitäten- und Handwerkermarkt (pottery, antique, art, and artisans' market) first weekend of April and October.

Tübingen

Handwerkermarkt (artisans' market) second weekend of October.

Coin and Medal Markets

Essen

Münzen- und Medallenbörse (coin and medals exchange) third Sunday.

Frankfurt am Main

Sammler- und Münzenbörse (collectors' and coin exchange) first Thursday of every month.

Karlsruhe

Münzbörse (coin exchange) one Sunday of October (sometimes first, other years third).

Linz am Rhein

Münzen- Briefmark- und Postkartenmarkt (coin, stamp, and postcard market) fourth weekend of January.

Mannheim

Münzbörse (coin exchange) first Sunday of October.

Nürnberg

Münzbörse (coin exchange) third Sunday of October.

Osnabrück

Münzbörse (coin exchange) first Sunday of October.

Pirmasens

Briefmarken- und Münzen- Sammlerbörse
(postage stamp and coin collectors' exchange)
fourth Sunday of the month.

Doll and Toy Markets

Bielefeld

Puppen- und Spielzeugmarkt (puppet and toy market) first Wednesday through Friday of October and November.

Düsseldorf

Puppen- und Spielzeugbörse (doll, puppet and toy exchange) third Saturday of every month.

Frankfurt am Main

Puppenbörse (puppet exchange) first Sunday in October.

Hamburg

Puppenbörse (doll and puppet exchange) first Sunday of November.

Hannover

Puppenbörse (doll and puppet exchange) first Sunday of October.

Heidelberg

Antik- und Puppenmarkt (antique doll and puppet market) second Sunday of November.

Antik- und Puppenmarkt (antique and puppet market) third Sunday in October.

Heilbronn

Eisenbahn- Spielzeug- und Puppenmarkt (railway, toy, and puppet market) first Sunday of October.

Karlsruhe

Eisenbahn- Puppen- und Spielzeugbörse
(railway, puppet, and toy exchange) first Sunday
of November.

Nürnberg

Puppenmarkt (doll and puppet market) first
Sunday of October.

Stuttgart

Puppenbörse (doll and puppet exchange) last
Sunday of October and first Sunday of November
(may vary from year to year).

Military Items Markets

Gunzenhausen

Tauschtreff der Militaria (military item meeting) first weekend of October.

Sigmaringen

Sammlertreff: Militaria (collectors' meeting: military items) first Friday of November.

Stuttgart

Sammlertreff: Orden- und Militaria (collectors' meeting: medals and military items) third Friday of October.

Trochtelfingen-Hald

Sammlertreff: Militaria (collectors' meeting: military items) first Friday of every month year round.

Veitshöchheim

Militaria- und Antikbörse (military item and antique exchange) first weekend of November.

Toy Markets

Bielefeld

Puppen- und Spielzeugmarkt (puppet and toy market) first Wednesday through Friday of October and November.

Celle

Spielzeugbörse (toy exchange) first Saturday of November.

Duisburg

Antikspielzeug- und Phonomarkt (antique toy and phonograph market) third Saturday of October.

Düsseldorf

Puppen- und Spielzeugbörse (doll, puppet, and toy exchange) third Saturday of every month.

Frankfurt am Main

Spielzeugmarkt (toy market) first Sunday of November.

Freiburg-im-Breisgau

Spielzeugmarkt (toy market) first Sunday of October.

Gelsenkirchen

Spielkartebörse (playing card exchange) last Sunday of October.

Hamburg

Modellbahn- und Spielzeugmarkt (model railroad and toy market) fourth Sunday in October.

Heilbronn

Eisenbahn- Spielzeug- und Puppenmarkt (railway, toy, and puppet market) first Sunday of October.

Karlsruhe

Spielzeugmarkt (toy market) last Sunday of October.

Eisenbahn- Puppen- und Spielzeugbörse (railway, puppet, and toy exchange) first Sunday of November.

Kiel

Spielzeugbörse (toy exchange) third Sunday of October.

Ladenburg

Spielzeugmarkt (toy market) second Sunday of October.

Leverkusen

Spielzeugmarkt (toy market) first Sunday of October.

Moers

Spielzeugmarkt (toy market) third Sunday of October.

Mülheim am Main

Altes Spielzeug Markt (old toy market) first Sunday of October.

Mülheim am Ruhr

Spielzeugmarkt (toy market) first Sunday of fall months.

Antik- und Spielzeugmarkt (antique and toy market) fourth Sunday of October.

Neuss

Modellspielzeugmarkt (model toy market) last Sunday of October.

Nürnberg

Spielzeug- und Sammlerbörse (toy and collectors' exchange) fourth Sunday of October.

Osnabrück

Modellspielzeugmarkt (model toy market) second Sunday of November.

Recklinghausen

Spielzeug- und Modelleisenbahnmarkt (toy and model railway market) second Sunday of November.

Remagen

Spielzeugbörse (toy market) fourth Sunday of October.

Saarbrücken

Spielzeug- und Modelleisenbahnmarkt (toy and model train market) second Sunday of November.

Sigmaringen

Spielzeugmarkt (toy market) first weekend of November.

Sindelfingen

Spielzeugmarkt (toy market) second Sunday of October.

Solingen

Spielzeugbörse (toy exchange) second weekend of November.

Wuppertal

Spielzeug- und Modelleisenbahnmarkt (toy and model railroad market) second Sunday of October.

Zell

Spielzeugmarkt (toy market) fourth Sunday of October.

Miscellaneous Markets and Fairs

Berlin

Foto, Hi-Fi, und Tecknik Markt (photography, hi-fi, and technical equipment market) first Sunday and fourth Thursday of every month.

Sammler- und Münzbörse (coin collector's exchange) third weekend of October

Bochum

Theater-Flohmarkt (flea market emphasizing theatrical items and props) third Saturday of every month.

Musikbörse (music and old record exchange and sale) middle of October.

Musik- und Plattenbörse (music and record exchange) first Sunday of November.

Bonn

Musikbörse (music exchange) second Sunday of October.

Bremerhaven

Musikmarkt (music market) second Sunday of October.

Dortmund

Comic-Tauschtag (comic day) second Sunday of October.

Sammlerbörse (collector's exchange) second Sunday of November.

Mineralenbörse (mineral exchange) last Sunday of October.

Duisburg

Antikspielzeug und Phonomarkt (antique toy and phonograph market) third Saturday of October.

Düsseldorf

Schallplatten und Musikbörse (record and music exchange) third Sunday of October.

Essen

Schallplatten- und Musikbörse (record and music exchange) first Sunday of October.

Frankfurt am Main

Sammler- und Münzenbörse (collectors' and coin exchange) first Thursday of every month.

Ansicht- und Postkartenmarkt (picture and postcard market) last weekend of October.

Frechen

St. Martinsmarkt (St. Martin's Market) October 10 and 11.

Freiburg-im-Breisgau

Photo-Börse (photo exchange) first Saturday of November.

Gelsenkirchen

Mineralenbörse (mineral and rock exchange) second weekend of November.

Gütersloh

Kinder Flohmarkt (children's flea market) first Saturday of every month.

Hagen

Kunstmarkt (art market), Musikbörse (music exchange), and other antique-related events the first Sunday of every month.

Hamburg

Modellbahn- und Spielzeugmarkt (model railroad and toy market) fourth Sunday in October.

Heilbronn

Eisenbahn- Spielzeug- und Puppenmarkt (railway, toy, and puppet market) first Sunday of October.

Herford

Brauereisouvenir-Tausch (brewery souvenir exchange) third Friday of October.

Karlsruhe

Eisenbahn- Puppen- und Spielzeugbörse (railway, puppet, and toy exchange) first Sunday of November.

Koblenz

Schallplatten- und Musikbörse (record and music exchange) third Sunday in October.

Langenfeld

Funk- Radio und Trödelmarkt (television, radio, and junk market) second Sunday of October.

Leverkusen

Sommerfest (summer festival) second weekend of June.

Volksfest (people's festival) flea market third weekend of June.

Weinachtsmarkt (Christmas market) from the first day of December to the third Sunday of December.

Seefest (lake festival) third weekend of July.

Linz am Rhein

Münzen- Briefmark- und Postkartenmarkt (coin, stamp, and postcard market) fourth weekend of January.

Lippstadt

Weinachtsmarkt (Christmas market) second weekend of November and third weekend of December.

Lohmar

Kunst- und Töpfermarkt (art and pottery market) first weekend of October.

München

Auer Dult (a festival of religious origin) three times a year for ten days. The Maidult takes place at the end of April and beginning of May, the Jacobidult takes place at the end of July and beginning of August, and the Kirchwiedult takes place at the end of October.

Filmbörse (film exchange) third Sunday of October.

Ansichtskartetausch (postcard exchange) second Monday of November.

Fotobörse (photography exchange) first weekends of February and October.

Ansichtskartenbörse (view and post card exchange) first Sunday of February, May, and October, and second Sunday of November.

Medallienbörse (medal and coin exchange) second weekend of October.

Tauschbörse-Briefmarken (postage stamp trading exchange) every other Saturday in October and November.

Münster

Schallplatten- und Musikbörse (record and music exchange) fourth Sunday of October.

Mutterstadt

Schmuckwoche (decoration week) first 10 days of October.

Nürnberg

Mineralen- und Fossilienbörse (rock and fossil exchange) second weekend of October.

Ansichtkarten- und Papierbörse (picture and paper exchange) second Sunday of October.

Paderborn

Schallplatten- und Musikbörse (record and music exchange) first and last Sunday of October.

Pirmasens

Briefmarken- und Münzen Sammlerbörse (postage stamp and coin collectors' exchange) fourth Sunday of the month.

Plettenberg

Maimarkt (May market) the first weekend of May, and Weinachtsmarkt (Christmas market) the first weekend of December.

Recklinghausen

Spielzeug- und Modelleisenbahnmarkt (toy and model railway market) second Sunday of November.

Remagen

Spielzeugbörse (toy market) fourth Sunday of October.

Saarbrücken

Ansichtkarten Tauschtreff (picture card exchange meeting) first Monday of every month.

Spielzeug- und Modelleisenbahnmarkt (toy and model train market) second Sunday of November.

Siegen

Schallplattenbörse (record exchange) first Sunday in October.

Sinzig am Rhein

Adventsmarkt (Advent market) the weekend before Christmas.

Solingen

Kunsthandwerkermarkt (artisan's market) first week of November.

Stuttgart

Ansichtkarten-Börse (picture and postcard exchange) second Saturday of June, September, and November.

Wiesbaden

Musik- und Schallplattenbörse (music and record exchange) first Sunday of November.

Worms

Modellauto- Blechspielzeugbörse (model car and tin soldier and toy exchange) first Sunday of November.

Wuppertal

Schallplattenbörse (record exchange) third Sunday of October.

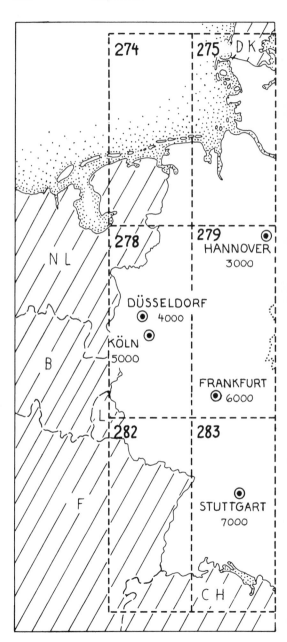

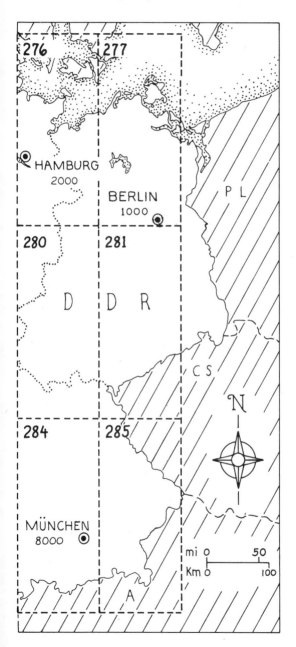

276 277

HAMBURG
2000

BERLIN
1000

P L

280 281

D D R

284 285

C S

N

MÜNCHEN
8000

mi 0   50
Km 0   100

A

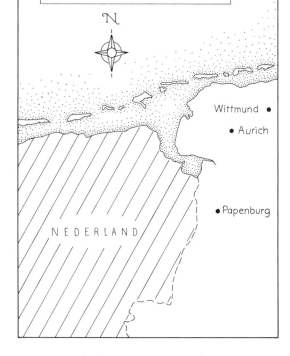

⊙ HAMBURG (KEY CITIES)

● OSNABRUCK (CITIES)

● Tübingen (TOWNS & VILLAGES)

Only cities, towns, & villages
with at least one market or
fair are shown.

mi 0   10   20   30
Km 0   20   40   60

N

Wittmund ●

● Aurich

● Papenburg

N E D E R L A N D

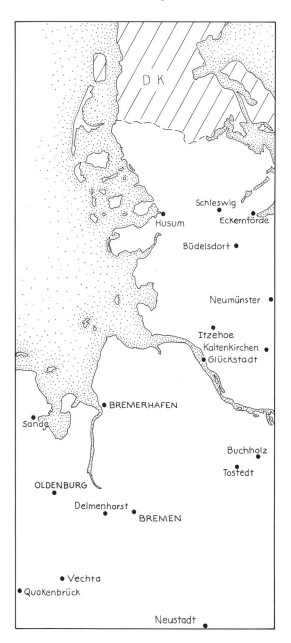

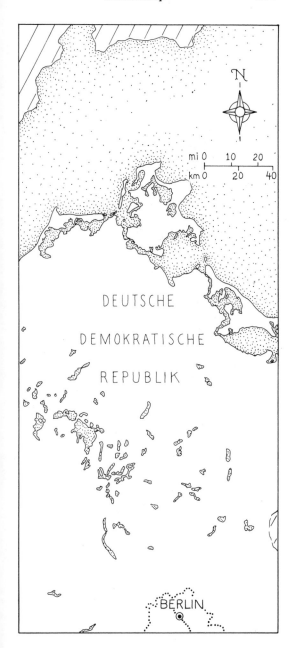

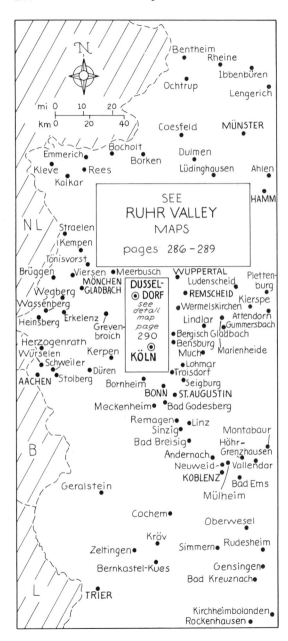

Bramsche
Belm
Bad Nenndorf
Langenhausen
Garbsen
HANNOVER
OSNABRÜCK
Minden
Lübbecke
Stadthagen
Barsinghausen
Lehrte
Hasbergen
Georgs-
marienhütte
Melle
Herford
Bad
Salzuflen
Rinteln
Altwarmbüchen
HILDESHEIM
Hamelin
Preussische
Oldendorf
BIELEFELD
Lemgo
Gütersloh
Ennigerloh
Holte
Verl
Schloss Holte
Holzminden
Beckum
Lippstadt
Bad Driburg
Welver
Salzkotten
Paderborn
Nörten-
Hardenberg
GÖTTINGEN
Meschede
Korbach
KASSEL
Lichtenfels
Melsungen
Bad Berleburg
Kreuztal
Schwamstadt
Siegen
Marburg
Neuenstein
Neunkirchen
Dillenburg
Herborn
Lauterbach
Giessen
Limburg
Wetzlar
Fulda
Weilburg
Kelkheim
Diez
Rosbach
Hofheim
Bad Homburg
Niederhausen
Eschborn
Gelnhausen
Hanau
WIESBADEN
FRANKFURT
OFFENBACH
Hochheim
Neu-Isenburg
Rodgau
MAINZ
Raunheim
Nieder-Olm
Weiterstadt
Aschaffenburg
Veitshöchheim
Ingelheim
DARMSTADT
WÜRZBURG
Alzey
Worms

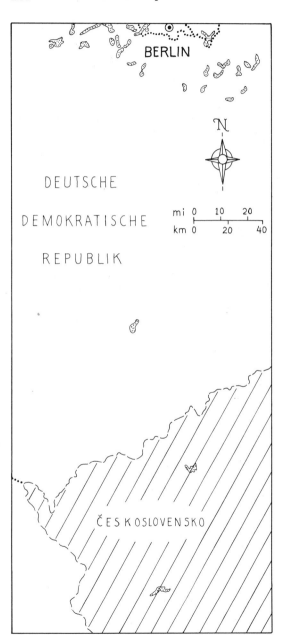

BERLIN

N

DEUTSCHE

DEMOKRATISCHE

REPUBLIK

mi 0   10   20
km 0   20   40

ČESKOSLOVENSKO

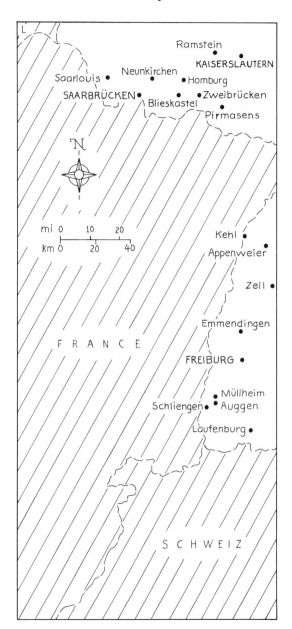

Eisenberg Frankenthal
Viernheim Mutterstadt
Bad MANNHEIM
Dürkheim LUDWIGSHAFEN
Diedesheim HEIDELBERG
Ladenburg Schwetzingen Mosbach
Neu- Hockenheim Künzelsau
stadt Speyer Wiesloch Bad Friedrichshall
Landau Germersheim Rappenau Neuenstadt
Graben Neckarsulm Weinsberg
HEILBRONN
Worth Beilstein Schwäbisch
KARLSRUHE Dutlach Hall
Forch- Besigheim Marbach Ascha-
heim Ettlingen Ludwigsburg Backnang Gschwend
Pforzheim Winnenden Welzheim
Gaggenau Leonberg Körb Schwäbisch
Gernsbach STUTTGART Korntal Gmünd
Baden- Esslingen
Baden Sindelfingen Ostfildern Göppingen
Böblingen Eislingen
Nürtingen Ebersbach
Metzingen
Tübingen
Reutlingen
Mössingen Blaubeuren
Trochtelfingen
Balingen Ehingen
Schramberg
Rottweil
Villingen Sigmaringen Biberach
Bad Dürrheim Fridingen

Singen Ravensburg
Radolfzell
Waldshut Bermatingen
Wangen

A

S C H W E I Z

FL

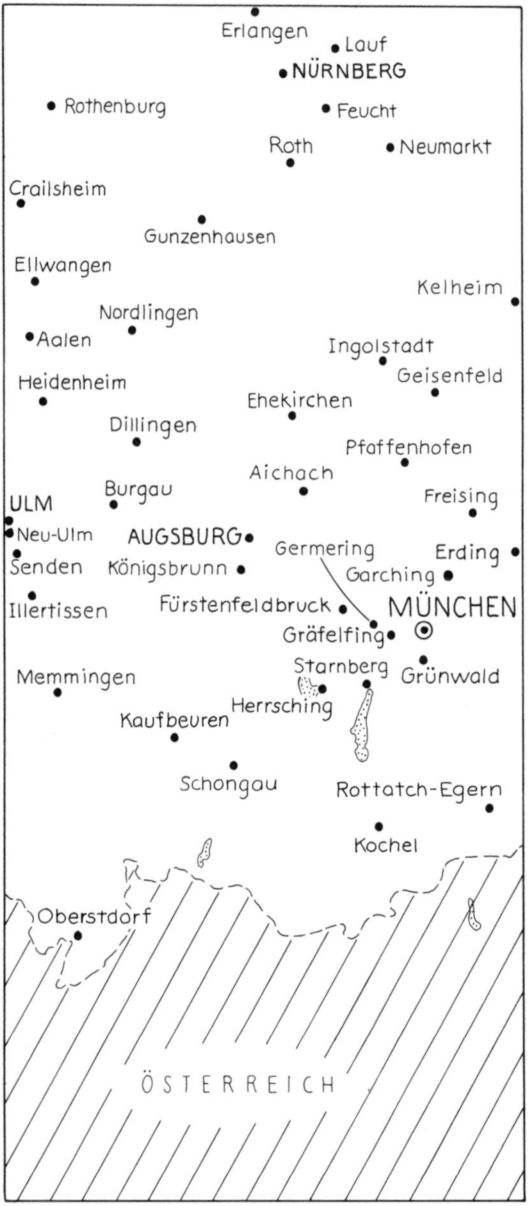
Erlangen
Lauf
NÜRNBERG
Rothenburg
Feucht
Roth
Neumarkt
Crailsheim
Gunzenhausen
Ellwangen
Kelheim
Nordlingen
Aalen
Ingolstadt
Heidenheim
Geisenfeld
Ehekirchen
Dillingen
Pfaffenhofen
Aichach
Burgau
ULM
Freising
Neu-Ulm
AUGSBURG
Germering
Erding
Senden
Königsbrunn
Garching
Illertissen
Fürstenfeldbruck
MÜNCHEN
Gräfelfing
Starnberg
Grünwald
Memmingen
Herrsching
Kaufbeuren
Schongau
Rottatch-Egern
Kochel
Oberstdorf
ÖSTERREICH

N

mi 0   10   20
km 0   20   40

ČESKOSLOVENSKO

• REGENSBURG

• Straubing
• Deggendorf

Passau

• Dingolfing

• Landshut

• Waldkraiburg

• Wasserburg

Laufen

Traunstein

• Rosenheim

Oberaudorf

ÖSTERREICH

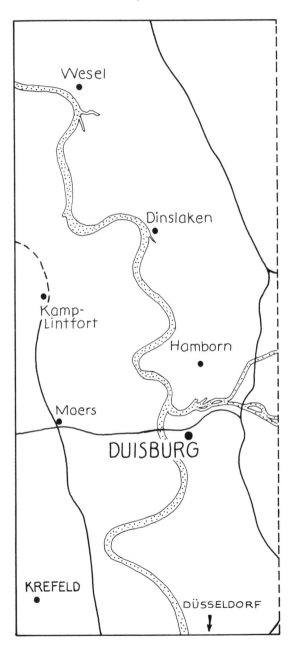

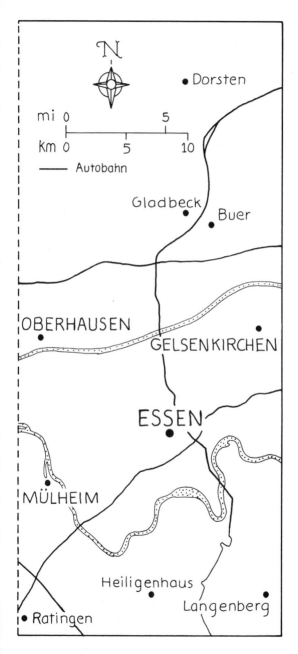

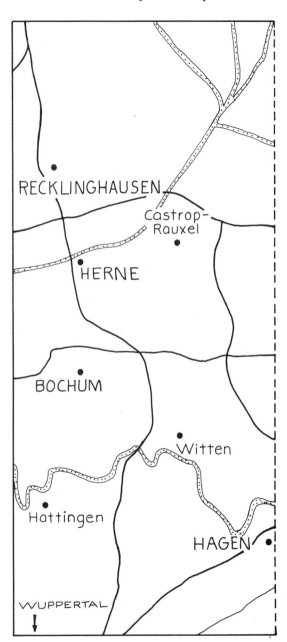

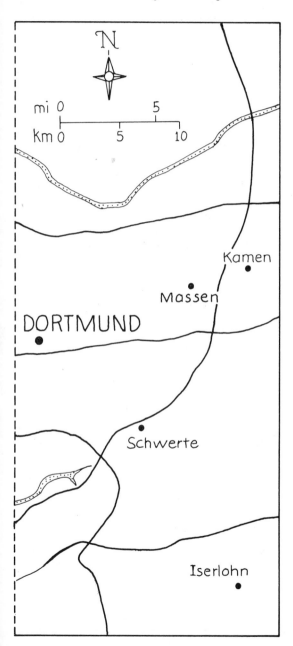

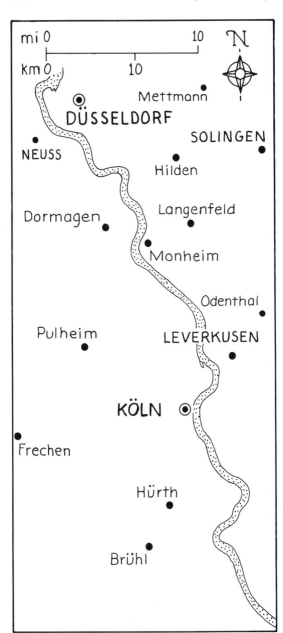

List of Maps

Index

Will You Help?

Time passes, events change. Almost as soon as this book went to the printer, things changed: some shows moved location, others were cancelled, others increased in size or scope, others gained a focus on a particular type of item. Some flea markets may move because of urban renewal or other reasons.

Won't you please let us know? If you do, we'll be able to improve future editions of this book. Then, future readers can benefit from your findings.

Either tear out this page, or feel free to use other sheets of paper.

Sincerely, Travel Keys.

What did you find different?

What problems did you find?

Are there any tricks you know to avoid this problem?

What markets or fairs moved time or place?

What was your greatest success and most wonderful find?

Thank you very much!

Please send your comments to:

Travel Keys
P.O. Box 160691
Sacramento, Calif. 95816 U.S.A.

Order Blank

We'll ship your order postpaid as soon as we receive it and a check, money order, or credit card information.

Title   Total

Manston's Travel Key Guides

Manston's Flea Markets of Britain $9.95   _____

Manston's Flea Markets of France $9.95   _____

Manston's Flea Markets of Germany $9.95   _____

Manston's Travel Key Europe $9.95   _____

Collins Phrase Books

French Phrase Book $4.95   _____

German Phrase Book $4.95   _____

Greek Phrase Book $4.95   _____

Italian Phrase Book $4.95   _____

Spanish Phrase Book $4.95   _____

Californians please add sales tax: _____
Postage and Handling included   0. 00
Overseas Airmail: Add $8.20 per book   _____
Total: $

Payment by check:
Please make checks and money orders payable to *Travel Keys.*
If your check is not drawn on a U.S. bank, please send in your currency and add equivalent of $4.00 to cover costs of exchange.
Please do not send checks drawn on a foreign bank (except from Canada) in U.S. dollars.

(Over, please for credit cards orders and mailing address for orders)

Credit card orders:

We accept VISA and MasterCard, as well as Access and Carte Bleu. Credit card orders may be placed by telephone as well as by mail.

You may call (916) 452-5200 24 hours a day for credit card orders.

For all credit card orders, we need:

Credit Card number:

Expiration Date:

4-Digit Bank # (M/C only):

Signature:

Date:

Send order to:

Name:

Address:

City, State or Province:

Zip or postal code:

Your daytime telephone number:

About the Author:

Peter B. Manston, travel and food writer, has been roaming through Europe for years, searching for antique fairs and street markets, collectors' meets and auctions for almost as long. He's collected centuries-old silver, glass, crystal, and wood carvings.

His fascination with antiques and collectables and the hunt for them are clearly evident in the details of the markets, fairs, and auctions described: not only how large each one is, but what types of items predominate, how to find them, and more.

He has organized the material to make it easy to use this book, and hopes you'll find as many delightful and valuable items as he has.

Good Luck and Happy Hunting!